RADIO HEAD

UP AND DOWN THE DIAL
OF BRITISH RADIO

JOHN OSBORNE

POCKET
BOOKS

LONDON • SYDNEY • NEW YORK • TORONTO

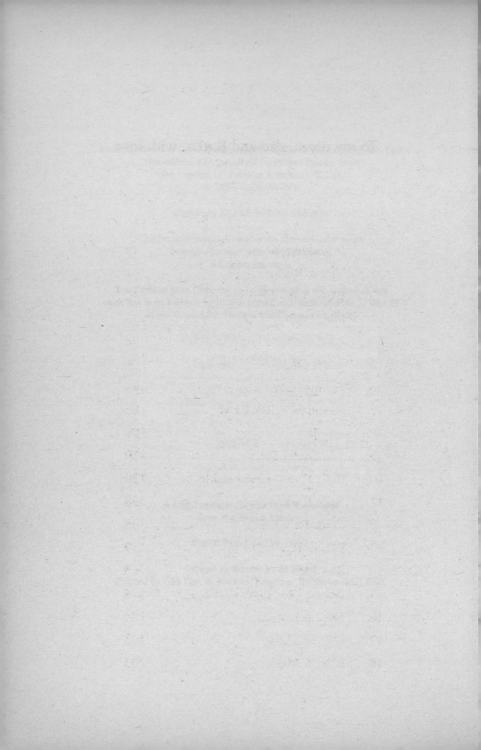

CONTENTS

	Introduction	vii
1.	Virgin Radio	1
2.	BBC Asian Network	15
3.	John Peel	31
4.	BBC Radio 2	38
5.	talkSPORT	56
6.	Tommy Boyd	74
7.	Resonance 104.4 FM	85
8.	The Jazz	100
9.	The *Radio Times*	110
10.	BBC Radio Humberside	120
11.	BBC Radio 4	130
12.	Mark Radcliffe	148
13.	Future Radio (1)	159
14.	Kiss FM	165
15.	Classic FM, BBC Radio 3	174
16.	*Just a Minute*	184
17.	Capital FM	193
18.	BBC 6 Music	203

19.	*Test Match Special*	218
20.	Radio Broadland	226
21.	BBC Radio 1	238
22.	Online Radio	256
23.	BBC Radio Five Live	263
24.	BBC 7	271
25.	Future Radio (2)	280
	Acknowledgements	287

INTRODUCTION

I grew up in the eighties, the age of colour television and Nintendo, but it was radio that appealed to me in a way that MTV and Super Mario never could. When I was about nine years old my mum introduced me to the Radio 4 comedy *Just a Minute* and I loved it so much that I would record it on tape and listen to episodes over and over again. Eventually I started twisting the dial, hopping between stations, hoping to find voices that matched my mood, and as I gradually discovered new programmes my radio became much more than an inanimate object in the corner of my room.

Radio is an integral part of our everyday lives. We make appointments with our favourite programmes and become attached to the familiar, reassuring voices of the presenters we tune in to every day. Radio binds communities together, is an invaluable source of entertainment for the elderly, the visually impaired, for those who live alone, for commuters, long-distance drivers, places of work. Radio affects everyone. It allows people to vent frustration, communicate unrequited love, engage in political debate, hear new music. It makes people laugh, happy, informs them of events, developing situations, stories that they would not otherwise hear. It has an immediacy, whether it is Chamberlain stating that war on Germany is declared or Danny Baker announcing the death of Kurt Cobain on Radio 1.

Over the years, radio has continued to evolve, from the BBC Home Service in the 1930s through to pirate radio and the birth of Radios 1, 2, 3 and 4. With the Internet it is expanding more than ever, and the developing digital technology means there is a continual demand. At its best, radio can be a more enjoyable and accessible medium than any other. It can mark people's lives; I remember being fourteen and hearing John Peel play a Smiths song. It was 'How Soon is Now' and if my life has ever had an epiphany, that must be the moment. I was captivated by Morrissey's voice and lyrics, both containing a beauty I had never realized existed, and I stopped doing my homework, transfixed, before the chorus had even started. The Smiths had split up ten years previously, but to me in my bedroom, that moment was as exciting as if I was hearing the song on its release in 1984. Since that night I have developed a thirst to hear new bands, new music that will thrill me in the same way. I listened to Peel's show every night that I possibly could; it was a very special part of growing up, a way of escaping the stress of exams and teenage life. I remember hearing Steve Lamacq play 'Girls and Boys' by Blur on his Radio 1 evening show, and the next day I rushed out to buy that week's *NME* to read about all the new bands he had played, and listened to Radio 1 every night to hear the song again. When I spent a year in Germany teaching English as part of my degree, I heard a Hamburg-based DJ called Paul Baskerville play 'What a Waster' and 'Time for Heroes' by the Libertines. There have been many times I've been excited on hearing new music, but those particularly stand out as spine-tingling moments, and it's what makes listening so special, moments that stay with you for ever. And it's not just music; I remember the time Terry Wogan read out a letter from a woman who had sent her grandchildren Christmas cards and written inside 'Buy your own presents' and not until weeks later discovered the gift vouchers she had forgotten to enclose.

There was the time I heard a woman tell a story on Tommy Boyd's late-night Sunday show on talkSPORT. She had been sat opposite a skinhead on a train, and after reading some of her book she peeled open the red wrapper of the Kit Kat she had bought at the station, snapped off a finger of chocolate and ate it. She put the remaining Kit Kat back on the table but the skinhead reached over, snapped the second finger off and ate it. The lady was stunned and angrily broke the third piece, putting it in her mouth. Straight away the skinhead took the remaining finger and swallowed it whole, glaring at her. Later that morning when getting something out of her handbag she found the Kit Kat she had bought that morning, still untouched.

I decided to do something with my love of radio. Despite being a regular listener since those early days of enjoying *Just a Minute*, I had barely scratched radio's surface. Scrolling through the presets of my digital radio I realized how much radio there was that I had never heard, and would have no reason to listen to. So I started to tune in to a different station every day and wrote about what I heard. I listened from the moment I woke up, listened while I was at work and carried on until I went to bed. I had a job doing data entry and so was able to listen at my desk to the sounds of the radio stations of the UK rather than office conversations. I discovered stations I never knew existed, listened to shows I had never heard before, from Dynamite MC on Kiss FM to *Woman's Hour* on Radio 4. I decided to try to learn about radio and speak to people I had grown up listening to, as well as those who worked in key roles in the radio industry. Some of those I ended up spending time with included Mark Radcliffe, Stuart Maconie and the editor of the *Radio Times*, to find out their thoughts about radio in the twenty-first century, what makes radio so exciting, and to learn about something I feel so close to, yet know so little about.

1

VIRGIN RADIO

'I am contemplating horticulture.'

(email to *The Geoff Show*)

It's 7.30 a.m. and I listen to Christian O'Connell as the nation butters its toast, straightens its hair. The theme of today's show is marriage: the listener who tells Christian the best story of their wedding wins two first-class tickets to New York to attend the premiere of the film *27 Dresses*. Sandra is on air; I brush my teeth, tie my tie.

'I was nineteen and looking after my sister's house while she was away,' she tells O'Connell, 'and there was a knock at the door. A man was stood there with a baby boy in his arms. He asked for my sister and when I told him she'd gone on holiday he looked really disappointed and turned away. I had never seen a man who looked so sad, so I called him back, asked if he was okay. He turned round, said he needed someone to talk to, so I invited him in. He told me his girlfriend had just left him for another man and she had told him that no court in the world would give custody to him ahead of the baby's mother.

'He had seen a lawyer,' Sandra continues, 'who told him the only way of getting custody of his son would be if he was married. He told me he didn't know many women, certainly not any who would agree to marry him. And without even thinking about it I said: "You could ask me."'

'He looked at me, then went down on one knee and said: "Will you marry me?"'

'You have to be joking!' O'Connell says, aghast. I am standing by the front door, keys in my hand. I have to leave for work but I can't, I want to hear more of Sandra's story.

'And six days later we were married.'

'But surely you didn't love each other?' Christian asks.

'We discussed that, but agreed to worry about it later, the baby had to come first. And this was twenty-five years ago.'

'What an incredible story!' O'Connell says, a trill of excitement in his voice for the first time this morning. 'I want the movie rights! I want to get Tom Hanks and Meg Ryan involved!'

I take out my new portable radio and headphones, bought especially so I can carry on listening as I go to and from work. I don't want to miss out on a single minute. As I walk, O'Connell reads out texts and emails that are already flooding in to the show. People say that Sandra has restored their faith in humanity, that, like me, they are late for work because they didn't feel able to stop listening.

'There's already been two calls from tabloid newspapers asking for Sandra's story,' O'Connell tells his increasingly gushing listeners as I get into work at 9.15.

'Sorry I'm late,' I say to Alan Medlicott, who looks up from the folder his head is buried in and nods. Alan Medlicott is my boss, a tubby man with bright-red cheeks. He sits opposite me, next to Craig the new boy, who has a cherubic face, the side-parting of a bank manager. Craig's eighteen years old and has a pension plan, a briefcase and a nodding Gromit toy perched on his computer. Alan Medlicott likes him because he's very good with spreadsheets and offers to do overtime. We work in the corner of the room furthest from the main entrance, so to arrive late involves a walk of shame across the open-plan office. You can sense everyone looking up from their desks, smirking as you shuffle to your seat to start your day, bleary-eyed, yawning.

Last night I was in the pub with my friend Mark, telling him I was going to listen to a different radio station every day, and he asked if I had ever listened to Christian O'Connell.

'He's brilliant,' Mark told me, 'easily the best person on radio.' Ever the diligent friend, I tuned in to Virgin when my alarm woke me this morning, but didn't like it. O'Connell, the self-styled 'daddy of morning radio', seemed to have an abrupt presenting style bordering on the aggressive, not just to listeners who call in, but towards his producer, Brian, whom he treats like the kid at school who can't afford Nike trainers. O'Connell was involved in a high-profile transfer to Virgin from London station XFM and is considered to be one of the most exciting DJs around, mainly by Mark.

'Are you coming out with us tonight, Brian?'

'I can't. My cat's got to have its teeth removed.'

3

'What! That's a ridiculous excuse. You just don't want to come. I can smell a load of bull shhh . . .'

'No, honestly, I would come out, but I've got to take it to the vet's.'

'Bull shhh . . .'

A vet emails the show to say that the symptoms Brian describes sound like severe gingivitis, and the only way to stop the cat's intense pain is to go to a vet to have its teeth removed as soon as possible.

O'Connell chews over the situation now he has had an expert's opinion. 'Bull shh . . .' he repeats, sniggering.

Sandra is back on air again before the end of the show.

'Obviously you won the competition,' O'Connell tells her. 'You can tell your husband you're taking him to New York. No one else stood a chance! Is there anything you'd like to say to your new fans?'

'Well, just to let them know that life is for living, you have to take risks if you want to be happy. Just do what you want to do.'

'You're quite right, maybe that's the way we should all approach life. Brian, you're fired.'

O'Connell tells us that due to such demand, the conversation with Sandra will be replayed later on this morning. I really want to hear it again, I hadn't been paying attention at the beginning of her story because I assumed that the call would be as uneventful as the others I had heard.

It feels good to listen to the radio at my desk. I've been in the same job for six months and have already run out of conversation with Alan Medlicott and Craig. My work is a lethal cocktail of data entry and filing, listening to Virgin could be a welcome addition to my otherwise repetitive daily routine. Sandra's theory that 'you should do what you want to do' is an axiom far removed from my own life and the words stick in my head like a radio jingle. I cling to the safety net provided by the world of temping, where risks are minimal, in my case non-existent. Before I found this job I worked for a company three doors away, where I inputted slightly different data in a slightly different font and sat opposite people with slightly different faces. At first I thought of this kind of work as a stopgap, a way of earning some money while I developed the grand plan of what I was going to do with my life. But nothing ever materialized, and brittle temp jobs have become my career, with no end date, no chance to climb the corporate ladder. Occasionally there are perks, like finding a pen, or checking my emails without getting caught. Which is why listening to the radio at my desk appeals to me, it's a rebellion against Alan Medlicott, against the people with designated parking spaces who drive past me as I walk in the rain to and from work. Admittedly it's a tame rebellion, it's not exactly overthrowing the Cuban government or mods fighting rockers on Brighton beach, but these days I welcome anything that makes my day go by more quickly.

It's 10 a.m. and Russ Williams is on air. Russ has been part of the Virgin team since the station launched in 1993, when he presented *The Breakfast Show*. The first hour of his programme is devoted to classic songs from the eighties, and although it's always good to hear songs by Kate Bush, Duran Duran, the Stone Roses, Russ seems uninterested. When he names the songs he's just played – 'Hounds of Love', 'Wild Boys', 'Fools Gold' it sounds like he's reading a shopping list. Potatoes, semi-skimmed milk, dishwasher tablets. If I wanted to hear those songs I could just get myself an iPod.

'Okay,' Russ says, 'guess which song I'm about to play. It was a big hit in the seventies but not number 1 until the eighties. If you can guess what it is, text in.'

Why would anyone text in?

Who?

Why?

The answer, he reveals after the eleven o'clock news, is . . . drum roll . . . dramatic pause, tension, tension . . . 'Imagine' by John Lennon.

'Well done to everyone who got it right,' Russ tells us.

For the rest of the show, Russ isn't restricted to the eighties. In fact at one stage he plays a song from as recently as seven years ago. Virgin brands itself as a rock station, if a song's got an indulgent guitar solo, it's on the playlist. At one o'clock Russ is finished and my lunch break starts. I switch off my computer and take out the sandwiches I made last night. Today it's cheese and onion. Yesterday was cheese with no onion. I am living life on the edge. As I dine I listen to *Afternoon Tea* with Neil Francis. He plays ROCK music: Muse, Red Hot Chili Peppers, Aerosmith, then replays this morning's conversation between Sandra and Christian O'Connell.

'It's a lovely story,' he says at its heart-warming conclusion. 'But do you think Sandra's telling the truth?'

I had briefly dabbled with the fact that the story might not be true, that she could have made it up, that Sandra is a massive fibber, but decided that it doesn't really matter. It made entertaining radio and was something for people to listen to while they were eating their breakfast, time that would have otherwise been spent staring out of the window. There is a chance that Sandra is a fantasist, that she isn't even called Sandra, but I believe her. I think she's nice and that every word she said was true. Maybe that means I'm gullible, but I'm glad I heard her on the radio this morning, and I'm glad that she's going to New York with her real-life husband who definitely exists. But even if it's all lies then that's fine with me too, her story works as a parable, that if you take risks there is no limit to what you can achieve.

As I don't have a very good memory, I open up a blank Word document and start typing up Sandra's story. If I don't have a record of it, when I try to regale my friends with her anecdote one evening it will come out as 'There was a girl called Sandra, she was . . . somewhere . . . for some reason, and a guy came to her house and said . . . something . . . anyway, they're happily married now.' Typing this up has the added benefit that to anyone who looks across at me, it looks like I'm doing work. No one is going to look up and suspect I'm not inputting data, that I'm actually typing up an anecdote I heard on Virgin Radio.

'Today's mystery iPod belongs to Lee Sharp!' Neil Francis reveals. 'He's got a very eclectic music collection,' he says of the former Manchester United footballer and the next two tracks, the Foo Fighters and U2, are exclusively from his iPod. Conveniently, the two songs also fit perfectly into the type of music Virgin plays all day, every day. I go to the kitchen to make myself a cup of tea. Standing by the kettle is Kate, the only person at work I know well enough to talk to.

'Hi, John,' she says, warmly. It's nice to hear a voice which isn't coming through my headphones, so I take the earpieces out, let them dangle over my shoulder. I give Kate my mug and she pours tea from her pot. As we drink, I tell her Sandra's story.

'Do you think it's true?' I ask, still bitter at Neil Francis and his naysaying.

'It has to be,' Kate tells me, beaming a smile. I rinse out my cup, put it on the draining board.

'I think so too,' I say, my faith restored as I put my headphones back on.

At four o'clock I sit at my desk waiting for the clock to turn. I go to the toilet so I don't have to go in my own time. Since the Sandra story there has been little more than adverts and songs: Amy Winehouse, the Hoosiers, Snow Patrol. This isn't what radio was made for. It's a long way from families huddled around the wireless listening to Chamberlain declaring war. Nick Jackson presents the *Drivetime* show. He plays Oasis and the Pretenders and just as I think about turning my radio off to get ready to go home, there's a trailer for *The Geoff Show* tonight at ten.

'I was in Las Vegas with my brother recently,' Geoff says, his voice refreshingly cheery. 'He's not a rich man, my brother, in fact he owes various credit companies considerable sums of cash. We were on the plane on the way back and he had his head in his hands.

'"What's the matter?" I asked.

'"I'm calculating my debts, I think I've lost three grand."

'I felt really bad for him,' Geoff continues, 'so the next day I phoned to check he was okay. When he answered he seemed really chipper.

'"I didn't expect you to be in a good mood?"

'"Well you know how I thought I'd lost three grand? I've realized it was only two and a half. So I've been out this afternoon and bought myself an iPod and a digital camera!"'

I laugh out loud at my desk. Alan Medlicott and Craig look up and I have to disguise my glee as a cough. Eventually it is 5.30 and I am out of the door like a Japanese bullet train. I carry on listening as I walk home.

Nick Jackson announces a competition in conjunction with Renault Vans; the winner will receive a gadget to attach DAB digital radio to their car stereo. Gary is on air trying to win.

'There are five types of vehicles not allowed in the outside lane of a motorway. Gary, if you can name one you will win.' Jackson is so excited he sounds as if he'll burst.

Gary ums reluctantly as the tension builds. 'Pulling a trailer?'

'CONGRATULATIONS! You're a WINNER!'

I decide I may as well carry on listening to Virgin for the rest of the evening, there's nothing on TV and I've no plans to go out tonight, so I listen to Ben Jones on my settee. He's on air from seven o'clock until Geoff starts at ten. He plays 'Just Looking' by the Stereophonics 'who are appearing at Australia's V Festival'. There is more airplay for Scouting for Girls, and then 'North Country Boy' by the Charlatans.

'If you want to win tickets to watch the Charlatans at an exclusive gig, including a champagne reception and a meal at the Hard Rock Café, phone in now!' Jones urges. After a song by the Hoosiers, Mike, a policeman, is on the line trying to win.

'Are you a Charlatans fan, Mike?'

'I love the Charlatans,' Mike replies, sounding far too confident. As I make myself a cup of tea I hope he fails.

'Okay, here's your first question. Tim Burgess is the lead singer of which band?' Jones asks.

'Don't know.'

'The Charlatans,' Jones tells him.

'Oh,' says an embarrassed policeman.

'Eric Clapton stole the wife of which member of the Beatles?'

'Erm, pass.'

'Who sang the songs "It's My Life" and "Bad Medicine"?'

'Erm, pass.'

'Is that a tail I can see swinging between your legs?' Ben Jones asks after a few more questions incorrectly answered. 'We'll add up the scores, but I'm afraid it won't take very long.'

After a record by the Fray, Mike is back on air.

'That was unlucky,' Jones tells the policeman.

'Well, I've calmed down a bit. I'd be able to answer them now, I panicked earlier.'

'Okay. I'll give you a chance to redeem yourself. Who sang the songs "Bad Medicine" and "It's My Life"?'

'Don't know.'

'Okay,' Ben Jones says, letting him off the hook. 'You have one of the lowest scores since we started running this competition. But we're going to give you the prize anyway. You're going to watch the Charlatans!'

This is a mockery! I like the Charlatans. And I like free champagne. Why can't I have the tickets? This guy deserves nothing. I put sausages in the oven, listen to ROCK music as I wait for them to brown.

'I met a guy today I've not seen for seven or eight years,' Geoff says after a track by Run–D.M.C. 'He told me he was in a pub with his mate and after a while they went looking for somewhere else to drink. They chose a pub at random, went inside and my mate saw someone he recognized sitting at the bar. Then someone else came up to him and said: 'Glad you could make it.' A few minutes later he realized the pub was full of people he recognized: he'd accidentally turned up at his school reunion.'

Geoff lets out a chuckle at the end of his story. He is a refreshing and engaging raconteur and immediately the most likeable person on Virgin. Since Christian O'Connell's show this morning the output has been very similar, it has been difficult to differentiate between the presenters or to get excited by any of the songs they've played. Geoff plays songs that can't fail: the Beatles, David Bowie, the Arctic Monkeys. But most of all it is Geoff who makes the show entertaining, he manages to be funny without being arrogant, which is rare on radio.

'Something slightly embarrassing happened to me today,' he tells Annabel, who works on the show with him. She came to Virgin on work experience in 2001 and has stayed there ever since. 'I was in a coffee shop waiting to meet a friend. There were only two comfy chairs so I sat on one, saved the other. But then an Islamic woman came and asked me if the chair was free, so I said yes. I knew it wasn't, but I didn't want to appear Islamophobic. I thought she'd have had a hard time since September 11th. I've been smiling at Muslims ever since,' Geoff says, laughing merrily, like Frank Bruno being tickled by Brian Blessed.

'Why didn't you tell her you were waiting for a friend?' Annabel asks.

'They might not have turned up. Or been late. And she would have looked at the empty seat and been really disappointed in me. I have a crippling social anxiety. I don't understand how things work. Maybe I should become agoraphobic. I would do much less damage if I never left the house.'

Annabel reads a story emailed in response to a subject mentioned earlier: 'Things people do at work they're not supposed to'.

'Twenty years ago I was a porter at the World Trade Center. All the offices were empty in the evenings. At the time I used to manage bands, so I would pick an office and pretend it was my own. It had a view overlooking Manhattan, I pretended I was a mogul. Then I was caught one night with all my papers spread out in front of me, talking on the phone, my feet on the desk, and was sacked.'

'That was before electronic fobs,' Geoff says, chuckling. 'Fobs have ruined night shifts.'

'Drunk versus Stoned' is a competition at midnight. I listen in the kitchen while drinking a cup of tea and making tomorrow's sandwiches.

'Are you drunk? Are you stoned?' Geoff asks. 'Do you want to come on air, face your adversary in a battle of wits? We're not glamorizing drinking or smoking the herb. Just offering people a route out by letting them win . . . a radio. So if you are drunk or stoned, phone in. Not if you are both,' Geoff says, sternly. 'You'll be no use to us.'

Ali is the first contestant, a nurse in London.

'Drunk Ali, do you understand that long-term drinking can result in permanent brain damage, serious mental disorders, a weakening of the heart and liver disease, including the potentially fatal cirrhosis?'

'Yes.'

'Okay. Your time starts now. Which Australian actress has just announced she is pregnant with her third child?'

'Kylie Minogue?'

'No.'

'Not a vintage round,' Geoff tells her after her sixty seconds. He plays 'Ruby' by the Kaiser Chiefs and the next contestant is Stoned Alex, playing online poker.

'Are you aware that cannabis can cause a variety of mental health problems, from anxiety to paranoia, as well as causing actual psychotic states?'

'Yeah.'

'Okay, your sixty seconds start now. How much is a second-class stamp?'

'No idea.'

They both end up with five points, resulting in a tie-break. The first person with the right answer wins.

'In which country would you find Gothenburg?'

'Norway?'

'No.'

'Romania.'

'No.'

'Denmark.'

'No.'

'Sweden?'

'Drunk Ali wins!'

By the time the show ends, I am in bed, my ears spinning after a full day of listening to Virgin. Geoff plays 'The Saturday Boy' by Billy Bragg, because he went to watch his gig last night and had been to meet him backstage.

'All hell will break loose tomorrow because I haven't stuck to the playlist. But I'll not worry about that just now, let's just enjoy the rest of the show. We started really well tonight and then petered out,' he says to Annabel with refreshing honesty. The show ends with 'I am', where listeners email to sum up their day in one sentence. Annabel reads them out, Geoff laughs heartily in the background:

– I am glad I phoned in sick today, it's been brilliant.

– I am eating pizza in the bath.

– I am learning French to impress a boy.

– I am feeling sick after walking in on my parents having sex.

– I am contemplating horticulture.

2

BBC ASIAN NETWORK

'There are an increasing number of Asian women who cannot cook.'
'I know. I married one.'

(Nihal)

The booming laugh of Geoff means I wake with a smile on my face and the desire to listen to another station for the day. My face covered in shaving cream, I switch on the radio in my kitchen as the country snaps, crackles and pops.

'The most likely person to bump into a parked car is aged between twenty-five and thirty-four, female, driving a small blue hatchback, and will be in a supermarket car park on a Saturday afternoon,' says the female presenter, who sounds like she fits firmly into the demographic she describes. 'If you bumped into a parked car and made a dent would you leave a note?' she asks.

'Of course,' her colleague in the studio replies.

'Liar!' she laughs. 'Do you think men are better drivers than women?'

'I'm not saying anything,' he replies, perhaps wisely, and the next song comes on, by Avril Lavigne. I am listening to the BBC Asian Network. It is not a station I have ever heard before and am intrigued. When I first decided to try out kinds of radio I wouldn't otherwise listen to, this was the station I thought of first, something I wouldn't normally tune in to, which is why it's exciting to give myself the opportunity.

After two records the presenter, Sonia Deol, talks about the increasing problem of faith healers advertising in the Asian press. It has been a recent phenomenon with adverts full of unlikely boasts; promises such as 'a hundred per cent guaranteed success' and 'results every time'. Sonia interviews the head of Trading Standards. He explains that the faith healers get away with it because victims rarely complain.

'In the last two years there have only been a dozen complaints. People are either too embarrassed to report anyone to the authorities, or are superstitious that if they complain then the matter which the faith healer has been dealing with will never be resolved.'

The problems faith healers have been solving vary from the hysterical to the profoundly sad: from 'Please make my boyfriend be nicer to me' to 'I am struggling to cope without my late wife'. The faith healers thrive because people who seek them tend to be in a vulnerable state.

'It is against the code of practice,' the man from Trading Standards continues, 'but these people can easily change their name and telephone number. Also, it is hard to prove that somebody isn't a faith healer, they can counter any allegation by maintaining that they believe they possess this special power.

The only way they can be stopped is to have several people testifying who have all been victims of similar scams, and then it can be proved there is a pattern. One woman paid a so-called healer £15,000 and pretended to her family that the money she was raising was for an operation she needed to save her life.

'Text or write in if you know of any similar incidents,' Sonia encourages her listeners, and tells us about a story from the news: nine years ago a girl was murdered in India. Sonia speaks to the brother of the victim on the phone. He tells her it was an honour killing; his sister wanted a divorce and so her husband and mother-in-law murdered her, throwing her body into the River Ravi. Today is the end verdict and it is the lead news story on the Asian Network. The brother, Jigdeesh, had campaigned tirelessly over the last nine years and if not for him the case would never have been heard. Jigdeesh is critical of the role of the police and government in both Britain and India, saying he feels there was a lack of understanding of Punjabi family culture, and that his sister's case had been neglected too easily.

'Keira in London has emailed to say women are better drivers than men,' Sonia tells us. 'Ravi says his girlfriend is a danger on the road. Several of you have told us about friends and relatives personally affected by bogus faith healers. I'll pass all your information to Trading Standards,' she says and plays a new track by Asian artist Jannat.

The show plays a mixture of new Asian music, traditional Bollywood songs and more recognizable mainstream pop songs: Jay Z, Britney Spears, Beyoncé. The show closes with an item called Undercover Lover: a girl in year eleven fancies a boy in her class, they are both Muslim but she is too scared to talk to him. They make eye contact with each other all the time.

'I know he listens to this show,' the anonymous letter says. 'I wish we could talk instead of just looking at each other.'

I feel slightly pathetic that at the age of twenty-five I am in no better position than a year-eleven girl. My current lovelife extends to thinking that Poppy, a girl in accounts, is quite pretty, but I've never even spoken to her.

Nine a.m. brings Nihal on air. I say hello to Alan Medlicott and Craig. They wave, both of them on the phone. Neither of them hangs up and says to me 'What are you doing here?' Neither of them says 'Why do you keep turning up, day after day?' So I take my coat off and get on with my work. Nihal is one of Asian music's most important voices and is the lone name on today's schedule that I recognize, if only because I saw him on *Never Mind the Buzzcocks* once. I assume his passion is primarily new music, but this show is his day job and he clearly relishes tackling important issues. Today the main subject is whether honour killings are a genuine problem in the Asian community. He refers to the case featured on Sonia's show: the divorce that Surjit Athwal's mother-in-law would let happen 'over her dead body'. Nihal gives us more information about the case: the family forged letters claiming to be from police in London saying that Surjit Athwal was living in India with her new lover. Family honour had been so important and divorce was such a disgrace that today they are facing trial for murder. Nihal seems genuinely moved and appalled by the story and urges his listeners to call in if they have been affected by similar cases.

'I was beaten by my father for insulting my family honour,' Sira tells Nihal.

'Why?'

'I was fifteen years old and refused to marry the man my father intended to be my husband. Eventually I ran away from home and went into hiding.'

Nihal seems immediately concerned for her.

'I'm fine now,' she continues, 'and I love my dad. I do not blame him. He was under so much pressure from the extended family.'

'Family honour was more important to your dad than your happiness?' Nihal asks. Her agreement is barely audible.

Nihal asks Sira to stay on the line as other callers comment on her situation.

Abdullah tries to find justification in the actions of Sira's father. 'You should have spoken to your father about the subject. He was angry because he found out from other people you were not marrying the man he had chosen for you.'

'You can't justify the fact that he beat her up, can you, Abdullah?' Nihal asks, slightly taken aback. 'You are a father, you have a baby girl. How are you going to bring her up to be a strong independent woman?'

'I will make her respect me.'

'Surely you earn respect?'

'Sira was not giving her father respect.'

'I always respected my father,' Sira tells Abdullah, defiantly. 'I still do. Leaving my family at the age of fifteen made them respect me rather than disown me. We would not be as strong as we are now if I had stayed.'

A girl calls in whose sister was killed by her brother. She had wanted to get out of an arranged marriage because she was in love with a man, who despite being of the same religion, was not who her parents had intended her to marry. Their brother is now serving fourteen years behind bars.

'Have you been to visit him in prison?' Nihal asks.

'I went to see him for the first time last week. He was sentenced nine years ago.'

'And how does he feel?'

'He regrets doing it. Being in prison has given him a larger picture of life than he ever had living at home. It means he is not surrounded by the views of his family any more. He realizes he was wrong to try to restore family honour in the way he did.'

The discussion is uninterrupted for an hour. There are no trails for other shows, no adverts, and, most surprisingly given Nihal's reputation with Asian music, he plays no songs. A girl tells him that her father is making her study at university so that as a bride she is 'more sellable' and says she is genuinely concerned about the next generation of Asian kids.

The most disturbing story is Sofia's. She tells Nihal she was married in secret at the age of fifteen, and she finally realized it was over a year later.

'If my dad finds me, he will kill me,' she says, her words sending a chill from my headphones, making my fingers temporarily numb to type at the keyboard. 'I don't see my family any more. I live with a new boyfriend.'

'Are you in hiding, Sofia?'

'Yes.'

'Because of the religious beliefs of your father?'

'Not religious beliefs,' she answers. 'Social beliefs. It is the pressure of my father's family.'

'What will happen if your father finds you?'

'He will kill me,' Sofia repeats. At the end of the conversation Nihal wishes her the best and says he hopes they will follow the story up.

I was not sure what the Asian Network would be like today, but as soon as Nihal's programme began I was glued, captivated by a subject I know nothing about. There are two and half million British Asians in the UK, the vast majority of whom are under the age of thirty-five. This is the Asian Network's core audience, but it also appeals to older British Asians, as well as non-Asians. The station's objective now that it broadcasts on a national scale is the same as when it existed locally in Leicester – to maintain the special close relationship with its audience that local radio manages to achieve. For people in the same situation as those in touch with Nihal about honour killings this morning, this must be revelatory radio. The problems in my life extend to not being able to find my stapler. Sometimes it's easy to forget about people like Sira and Sofia while you are at work, swinging backwards on your chair, thinking about Poppy in accounts and what you're going to have for your tea.

When the issue of honour killings is finished, Nihal shows he is as comfortable dealing with less delicate topics, and just as skilfully. He tells us he is wearing blue socks with crossbows on them. They are his favourites. He talks to three teenagers in the studio about current Asian youth issues.

'The role of Asian women is changing,' one girl tells Nihal. 'Some Asian women can't even cook nowadays.'

'I know!' Nihal says. 'I married one.'

Another girl tells him she hates the 'sexualizing' of females.

'I hate it when men open the door for me,' she says. 'Or when they offer to pay for meals.'

'You hate that!' Nihal asks, amazed. 'If I ever walk through a door and see you I'll make sure it slams in your face,' he says, laughing. He talks to a man publishing a book of football poetry.

'Who do you support?' Nihal asks.

'Liverpool.'

'What is it about Asians supporting Liverpool?' he asks with mock fury. When they finish arguing about whether Tottenham are better than Liverpool they address the question of why so few Asians are professional footballers. The poet blames sport's vagaries, that the limited chance of success means Asian parents are reluctant to allow their children to take up football as a career. Nihal suggests it could have something to do with fasting for Ramadan and mentions the former Tottenham player Noureddine Naybet, who fasted for the duration of the festival despite it affecting his performance during an important part of the season.

At twelve is *The Wrap*, Asian Network's news bulletin. It includes a breaking story from the court, and the news that Bachan Athwal and her son Sukhdave, the mother and son involved in the honour killing case, have been sentenced. The son will serve twenty-seven years, his mother twenty. Clips are played from the interviews Nihal and Sonia conducted with key people involved in the case. It is odd to feel so attached to the news, to hear it unravel as the day has gone on. I listen while on my lunch break. For the first time this week it isn't raining so I eat my sandwiches outside as I walk to Comet. I go there at least once a week, it's the only shop within walking distance from the industrial estate. There are always other men in suits wandering the aisles, looking at big tellies and laptops, wondering what they are doing with their lives. These men are my brethren. In the car park there is a man who sells burgers, I eat there every pay day. In temp jobs it is important to set yourself attainable goals, give yourself rewards. Walking through the industrial estate is a very grey experience. There seems to be a constant gust of wind; cars sweep through puddles, spraying people too close to the kerb. I am cleverer than that. I have walked these streets before, I know where to stand so the splash won't reach me.

Back in the office I open up the Word document I started while listening to Virgin and read through Sandra's story, smiling that I wrote 'do what you want to do' in 48-point bold, underlined. I try to recall *The Geoff Show*, and start to type up a new entry; write about his friend turning up at the school reunion by accident and his brother buying a digital camera and iPod because in his eyes he had gained £500. I type up about the average car-park pranger being aged between twenty-five and thirty-four, and realize that listening to radio at work is the best thing I have done for months. I look forward to trying different stations, typing all the interesting things I hear as I go from frequency to frequency.

'Welcome along,' says Nikki Bedi cheerily as she starts her

show at half-past twelve. 'I hope you've been watching *Celebrity Come Dine with Me*. I was going to boycott the celebrity edition because I knew it wouldn't be as good, but no . . . still watched it. I love MC Harvey!'

I like Nikki, her voice carries the excitement of a toddler on Christmas morning. She describes herself as Anglo-Indian, her father being Indian, her mother English. When she runs through stories in the papers and mentions Britney's bitter custody battle she launches into a word-perfect version of 'If I bake this bitter butter it will make my batter bitter but a bit of better butter, that would make my batter better.' She doesn't even stumble. Hearing Nikki's voice overexcites me. I decide to send her an email, wondering what it would be like to hear her say my name.

Hi Nikki.

Can you play me a song? Any song.

From John, sat in an office in Norwich.

x

I put more thought into whether or not I should end the message with x than I have done for any task I've been given at work. At one stage I was contemplating xxxx.

Bedi talks about the DVD of *The Darjeeling Limited* with reviewer Sam Jones.

'I hope you like this, Sam. I love it. Tell us what it's about, in case anyone listening hasn't seen it.'

'It's a Wes Anderson film, three brothers go to India on a spiritual quest, starring Owen Wilson, Adrien Brody and Jason Schwartzman.'

'I have never seen such a beautiful man in the flesh as Adrien Brody. He is magical. Even boys think so. What did you think about the film?'

'Everything about it is good. Eight and a half out of ten.'

Nikki interviews Shahrukh Husain, a novelist who is preparing a talk and thesis on the reasons Asian novelists have been so successful in Britain recently. Kiran Desai has won the Booker Prize and Indra Sinha and Mohsin Hamid have also been nominated for the award since.

'I love Mohsin Hamid!' Nikki squeals. 'That book is amaaaazing!' I decide Nikki is the most charming lady on radio. She plays Justin Timberlake and just before the news says: 'That was for John, sitting at his desk in Norwich. Ha ha. Doesn't sound much fun, John.'

I didn't expect to have my email read out, certainly not so soon, I only sent it half an hour ago. It makes me feel quite strange, and I feel that everyone is looking at me. It was probably more exciting than it should have been. And it was so simple, you forget that people who request songs are actual, real-life people getting on with their lives. Nikki Bedi saying my name: that really shouldn't be the highlight of my day, yet it's the highlight of my week.

Nikki interviews a photographer, Daboo Ratnani. He tells her models should stand in front of the mirror for eight to ten hours a day.

'You've got to find your angles,' Nikki says. In between records Nikki asks Daboo questions about photography. 'Is there such a thing as an original thought any more? I'm not sure; I think everything is a version of a version of a version.'

25

Daboo agrees with her. 'Is colour important?' she asks. 'I don't think colour has added anything to any photograph ever.' Again, Daboo agrees with her. It is hard to find anything disagreeable about Nikki Bedi.

'A few months ago I put an advert in a London magazine stating "Asian male celebrity seeks companion for premieres and showbiz parties",' Adil Ray says at the start of his 3 to 7 show. He plays a selection of the voicemail messages he received in response.

'I'm an old auntie type in her forties who dresses in purple.'

'I believe my friends say I am stunning.'

'I have beautiful white teeth.'

Adil phones the callers back; a half-Chinese, half-Portuguese legal assistant seems very keen to be involved.

'I don't want a companion who is going to be starstruck if they meet celebrities,' Ray tells her. 'Would you handle it okay if you came face to face with . . . say Ronnie Corbett?'

'Oh yeah, I'd be fine,' she says, her voice portraying no excitement.

'When you say you are spontaneous, what do you mean?' he asks, barely able to conceal the giggling in the studio.

'I mean I do things without planning them. I make spontaneous decisions.'

'Well that's what spontaneous means . . . is there an example of something spontaneous you have done?'

'Gone on holiday.'

'You say you are witty. Can you give an example of that?'

'Not right now.'

'What are your measurements?'

'Erm. 34. Erm. 24. Erm . . . 36.'

'Let's hear that bit again,' Adil Ray says back in the studio, spooling back the message. 'I'm sure she's lying about her measurements. Too many hesitations.'

'I think she's telling the truth,' another of his posse in the studio says.

'34, 24, 36. Does that mean she has a big arse?'

'I don't know,' Adil's colleague says.

'It is the ideal figure for a woman,' a girl in the studio says. It sounds like he has an entire entourage in there with him. 'She must be making it up.'

'We need to find out,' Adil declares. 'Maybe we should invite her to the University of Hertfordshire when we go there on our uni tour next month. She can be our special guest.'

At 5.30 I leave work and Alan Medlicott waves, saying, 'See you tomorrow.' I smile and say the same to him. Every day I am not sacked is a mystery and a blessing. I carry on listening on my way home on my portable DAB radio. One of the consolations if I ever get mugged is that it looks just like an iPod, so if anyone steals it they'll be disappointed because instead of having hundreds of pounds of brand-new equipment they will just have a radio, albeit one with a really good signal. Back at my flat I go through today's post. I write 'Return to Sender' on most of the envelopes and put the rest in the bin. Switching on the radio in my living room I encounter a brand-new listening experience – Gagan Grewal.

Grewal switches from English to Punjabi and back again

sometimes several times within the same sentence. At first it is a bizarre concept but it quickly becomes accessible, the novelty of hearing two languages simultaneously adds flavour to the show. He plays new tracks by Asian artists and also interviews a Pakistani band who don't just release singles and albums but also record Bollywood soundtracks.

Even the news alternates between languages, the half-past eight bulletin is in English, at nine o'clock Punjabi, although English words manage to sneak in, passport photo, high school, identification parade.

The theme of today's show is nostalgia.

'What would you like bringing back from your childhood?' Grewal asks.

'*Knight Rider*,' a man phones in to say.

'*Thundercats*.'

'*Family Fortunes*.'

When I was at university I always felt out of my depth when students became nostalgic about TV shows. My memory isn't good enough to remember simple things like where I put my mobile phone or house keys, never mind a particular scene in an early episode of *Transformers*. I always knew it was time to go home from the pub as soon as anyone mentioned *Bagpuss*.

'I'd bring back Secret chocolate bars,' a girl tells Gagan.

'What are they?'

'They had flakes of chocolate on top,' she says.

'How come I don't remember them?' he asks, frustrated. 'My dad owned a sweet shop. We had every chocolate bar ever made on our shelves. I'm confused.'

*

'F F Friction. F F Friction,' says the trailer at the beginning of the next show.

At 10 p.m. we are told: 'This is Bobby Friction bringing you phat Punjabi vibes.' F F Friction has no time for nostalgia, he is too busy getting excited about new Asian music. The popularity of the music Bobby Friction champions can be shown by the weekly music show he co-presents with Nihal on Radio 1. When it first began it had the graveyard slot of 3 a.m. at the weekend. Soon it was promoted to a primetime slot, being aired simultaneously on the Asian Network and Radio 1, attracting a brand-new audience.

Friction is as strong a brand name as any other in the UK music scene today. He opens every show with a bhangra tune, which he says 'ticks every box for the whole international audience'. Ninety per cent of his playlist is what he calls 'bedroom stuff' – MP3s emailed from the laptops of emerging artists. 'There are no closed minds here. You don't need a label or to be a recognized name. Just MP3 your stuff to friction@bbc.co.uk or post your CD to our studio and if it's good I'll play it on the show. Good radio is simple radio.' He plays two more tracks, segued with the trademark F F Friction soundbite.

'It's so exciting playing tracks by people who have never been played before,' Friction says. 'This is why I love this show. On the phone we have Mikka, a Punjabi rapper in New York. Hey, Mikka.'

'Hey, Friction.'

'How did you get into music?'

'I was born, my dad gave me a guitar and now I'm here.'

'And was it a conscious decision to rap in Punjabi?'

'I just thought it sounded pretty good. Punjabi is an evolving language, it's exciting.'

'And what do you rap about?'

'Chilling.'

'And is there a shared community out in New York who are MCing in English? Do you all mix socially?'

'We are all brothers and sisters.'

The last song of the show is by Imran Khan, a 22-year-old Dutch hip hopper.

'This makes me want to take my clothes off and run around,' says Friction and I decide to do the same, but minutes later realize that when the show ends the Asian Network merges with Radio Five Live for the night, and I would feel awkward with no clothes on, swinging my T-shirt around my head listening to a phone-in about the congestion charge.

3

JOHN PEEL

*'That's the end of the show, it's time for me to walk Bernard
the dog.'*

It's midday on a Saturday and a lady at the bar orders her
second White Russian of the day. But I have not come here
today to examine the drinking habits of middle-class Norwich.
I am meeting Bearsuit to talk to them about the importance
of John Peel.

Bearsuit are a six-piece shambolic indie band. The fact that
they cannot be summarized in a simple sentence is perhaps why
they were so loved by Peel. Bearsuit epitomize the type of band
Peel championed. The DJ was credited as the man who pioneered
the careers of Pink Floyd, David Bowie, the Smiths but to his core
listeners, like me, he was always more synonymous with bands like
Bearsuit: shouty, loud, chaotic, passionate, and hailing from his
adopted home of East Anglia. Peel had a canny ability to cham-
pion bands that other radio presenters wouldn't go near. Bearsuit
were never going to appear on *Top of the Pops*, grace the front

cover of *NME* or headline Glastonbury, but then that was never what music was meant to be about.

One of my favourite parts of Peel's Radio 1 show was the Festive Fifty, where listeners voted for their favourite tracks of the year. I would be annoyed if I was invited to the pub on Christmas Eve to 'socialize' when I could be sitting in my room waiting to hear which position Gorky's Zygotic Mynci appeared at. Past winners of the Festive Fifty include Led Zeppelin, Nirvana and Pulp, and Bearsuit featured in the Top Five for four consecutive years, most notably in 2004, the year of Peel's death, when they were aptly beaten only by Peel's all-time favourite band, the Fall.

When I first started to listen to John Peel I kept a notebook on my desk which I filled with doodles, games of noughts and crosses with myself. I would write initials of girls I fancied and names of bands that Peel played that I liked. Looking at that book now, one of the bands written in bold felt tip is BEAR-SUIT. I also appeared to adore JW. JW's actual name has disappeared into sixth-form ether long since, along with my knowledge of trigonometry and the ability to conjugate German verbs, yet most of the bands on that list have stayed with me, their albums still in my CD rack, their tapes still in an old shoebox.

In April 2002 I won 150 records from John Peel's own collection in a Radio 1 competition. Every year the Peel show was nominated for a prestigious Sony Award, for which they were required to submit a brief description of the programme to the panel of judges. Peel was bored with doing this as he rarely won, and so suggested that if a listener wanted to submit a short synopsis of the show then he would send over a couple of boxes of records from his shed for their efforts. Without thinking much of it I wrote on a page ripped from my notebook: *Records you want to hear played by a man who wants you to hear them.*

A month later I got a phone call from Peel's producer, Louise, who congratulated me and said a van would deliver the prize to my house in Norwich in a few weeks.

After Peel's death listening to the records became incredibly poignant. I was living in Vienna when Peel died, I got the news by text message. When Radio 1 devoted an entire night of their schedule to his memory later that week, my dad, who by his own admission would describe the music Peel played as 'a racket', sat by the radio in our living room recording the whole show, perched on his armchair so that he could change the tape over every forty-five minutes. He did this for six hours, until 2 a.m., and did not miss a beat, knowing how important it was to me. When he gave me the tapes the next time I was home my eyes filled with water. The words 'the term genius is bandied about too easily' are bandied about too easily. But Peel was a genius, I realized that during the many nights I was listening to his show when I should have been asleep or doing coursework.

I decided to try to meet Lisa, Bearsuit's lead singer, to find out what it was like having John Peel as a fan. I had the idea in a pub in Norwich, shortly after my friend Yanny said 'Look, there's Lisa from Bearsuit' and tapped her on the shoulder. Judging by the glass of red wine in each of Lisa's hands and the Captain Morgan inside both me and Yanny, I decided that this wasn't the best time to engage her about the intricacies of the music business, the importance of airplay and whether she'd ever touched Peel's beard. I told Lisa I was a big Bearsuit fan but more importantly a huge fan of Peel, and asked if we could meet up one afternoon. She drunkenly agreed, told me to 'MySpace' her and me and Yanny went back to the bar for more rum.

Sobered up the next day, I was slightly unsure whether to send her a message or not, fearing embarrassment or rejection. To my surprise though, she replied almost straight away, suggesting a pub and a time and saying she would bring the rest of Bearsuit with her. I thought about doodling Lisa's initials in my notebook.

I go through to the beer garden with Jan, Lisa and Iain from Bearsuit. I know from Lisa's message that they played a gig in London last night, and all three look tired and like they would rather be in bed than talking to me. I wonder whether telling them the Sandra story would be a good way to break the silence when Lisa tells me about the gig.

'It was shambolic,' she says, running her hand through her jet-black hair and sipping white wine. 'I got drunk and fell into the drum kit.' Iain shakes his head with mock shame. 'So how come you wanted to meet us here?' Lisa asks.

'To ask you about John Peel,' I tell them. I feel awkward, and realize I should have prepared a list of questions. 'So, how important was he to Bearsuit?' I ask. The question is met with nervous giggles and members of Bearsuit pointing at each other.

'This always happens,' Iain tells me, adjusting his glasses. I decide to ask a less vague question.

'What was the first Bearsuit song John Peel played?'

'"Hovercar",' Jan says. 'I was listening that night without realizing it was going to be played. It was so exciting!' Jan is the utility player of Bearsuit, she can play up front or go in goal, her duties include flute, recorder, guitar, backing vocals and hand-claps.

'I was just excited that I saw our name on teletext,' Lisa adds.

'He declared on air straight away that he would give us a session. It was as simple as that,' Jan says, her voice trilling with excitement at the memory of experiencing something that so many bands longed for. *Peel Sessions* were the ultimate accolade for any aspiring musician.

'The version of "Hovercar" he played was just a demo recorded in Iain's bedroom by him and Lisa. It was rough and ready but Peel played it anyway, and he then played everything we ever sent him afterwards.'

Of the three, the blonde-haired Jan is the biggest Peel fan. She tells me she used to record every single show and make compilation tapes from them.

'I was very anal,' she says. 'I was obsessed. It has been hard to listen to those tapes since he died.'

'I used to make tapes too,' Iain, who shares lead vocals with Lisa, says. 'I would put together a drum and bass tape, an indie tape, a reggae tape. The stupid thing is I would cut out his introduction to the songs, I didn't realize at the time that hearing him talking was the most interesting thing.'

'How did Peel's death affect your airplay?' I ask.

'It really suffered,' says Jan. 'We release a new single in a couple of weeks, but it's only been played twice. Huw Stephens played it on his late-night Radio 1 show and John Kennedy played it on his XFM show, but there is no momentum.'

'John Kennedy said he really likes us!' Lisa adds, excitedly.

'He played us on his British Forces Broadcasting show. We've gone out to the troops!'

'We did an XFM session for him. It still hasn't gone out though,' Iain says, shaking his head. 'It's not the way that Peel worked.'

'The first time we met John Peel,' Lisa says, taking the reins of the conversation away from Iain once more, 'he asked whether we were bringing out an album. We told him things were starting to become a bit complicated with our record label, and he told us that he wanted to hear a Bearsuit album so much that he would pay for it to be made, if necessary resurrecting Dandelion, the old record label he used to run in the sixties.'

'Maybe we should have taken him up on that offer,' Jan muses, thinking of how things could have been.

'Is there anyone on radio now who would play a demo by a band who don't have a record label, in the same way that Peel did with Bearsuit?' I ask.

'Huw Stephens possibly would do. But he's only on Radio 1 once a week and his show's on in the middle of the night. He plays a lot of lo-fi but never next to a bluegrass song, or something from the 1920s.'

'Even though it's what we want,' Iain says, speaking as a fan rather than a singer in a band. 'Peel was an anomaly. No one is going to get close to the way he put a show together.'

'Radio 1 say they support new music,' Jan says, putting down her wine, 'but it is always the same six mainstream bands, bands who have a lot of PR behind them. Tom Ravenscroft is absolutely fantastic,' she continues. (Ravenscroft, the youngest son of John Peel, presents *SlashMusic*, a show on the now obsolete

Channel 4 Radio, available online.) 'I play his show at work and people say: "What the fuck is this!"'

And this is the reason that I loved Peel. I had always failed to grasp the exact words to articulate why I was a Peel fan, but Jan expressed it more succinctly than I have ever been able to. The reason I listened to Peel was for that moment when my house-mate, sister or whoever happened to be in my house would poke their head round my bedroom door and say: 'What the fuck is this?' Unless it was my dad. He'd just say: 'What's this?' He's polite like that.

4

BBC RADIO 2

'I'm listening in the shed. My wife's at Pilates so I'm fixing my bicycle.'

(email to Radcliffe and Maconie)

My alarm beeps, I lie in bed listening to *Wake Up to Wogan* and throughout the country duvets are being thrown to the floor, people are wrapped in towels waiting for the bathroom to be free. I like Terry Wogan, I'm not sure I trust people who don't. He brings a refreshing sense of cynicism to breakfast radio.

I'm not the age of Wogan's average listener; I am far too young and virile to be part of Radio 2's target audience, at least that is what I like to tell myself. I shower, get dressed and Lynn Bowles reads the traffic news as I use the ball of my fist to iron out the creases in my one remaining clean shirt.

The M42 is slow southbound.

There's a breakdown on Junction 7 of the M6.

Engineering work has overrun on the M25.

'I know!' Wogan says, bitterly. 'I was stuck in it! How can the busiest commuter road in Europe have engineering work on a Monday morning?' he asks, his indignation genuine, delivered with characteristic contempt of the foibles of everyday Britain shared by his millions of listeners.

'I don't like it when you're rattled,' Bowles tells him. She is providing a vital service for the country's motorists, her information means people know whether it is necessary to leave the house half an hour earlier, map out alternative routes, fill a flask with tea. The traffic news is a prosaic form of Radio 4's *Shipping Forecast*. There is no mention of South Utsire, Portland, Bay of Biscay. Instead there are motorway tailbacks, overturned lorries, temporary traffic lights. It does not paint the same poetic picture as a man on a fishing boat wearing a cagoule, his boat rocking against the waves, the horizon in his binoculars.

'I don't know whether your other listeners watched *Who Wants to be a Millionaire?* last night,' Wogan reads from an email. 'There was a young chap in the chair, fresh-faced and enthusiastic. He was struggling with the question of whether 'primavera' referred to autumn or spring. Eventually he got the answer right. I thought Oh bless him and said to my wife "I hope his mum's watching." When he finally took the money we found out he was a headmaster. I retired for the night feeling rather ancient.'

A radio station works when a presenter's voice, tone, ideology fuse with those of the listener. Wogan's listeners are a community, people who wear slippers and tut while reading the newspaper. Wogan affectionately refers to this group as TOGs: Terry's Old Geezers or Gals, who are described as people who have to ask questions like 'What did I come upstairs for?' These people aren't simply listeners to the show, they regularly contribute with letters and emails, anecdotes and jokes. They have a TOGs website, 'an online home for the bewildered' where they interact on discussion boards. They even get together, meet each other, dinner events in aid of Children in Need are regularly organized, hosted by Wogan and other regulars on the show, such as newsreaders John Marsh and Alan Dedicoat, who share the same self-deprecating, gentle, warm humour. The show is very calming; as you listen you are reminded that life is not as complicated and hectic as it can sometimes seem, that you can find the time to sit by the fire, put your feet up and eat bacon sandwiches. In fact, that is where Terry Wogan's show belongs, on the rug by the fire, or perhaps sitting up in bed, dipping soldiers into boiled eggs. But certainly not standing at the traffic lights, wearing a shirt and tie, with Asda to the left, a Ford garage on the right, standing next to a woman with a dog that keeps showing its teeth.

The choice of music is a gentle mix, predominantly pop ballads, from Leona Lewis to Stevie Wonder, drowned out by a burst of the Kaiser Chiefs. It is nine o'clock. I say hello to Alan Medlicott and Craig and switch on my computer. Craig is tying up his shoelaces, Alan Medlicott is cutting a banana into slices. *Pause for Thought* comes from Reverend Stephen Oliver, the Bishop of Stepney.

'I get this kind of thing all the time,' Reverend Oliver says, speaking about the alleged attack by Culture Minister Margaret Hodge against *The Last Night of the Proms*, claiming it is 'culturally narrow'. 'Cancel Christmas, atheists feel excluded! Banish Easter, some faiths might be offended! Before you know it there will be no national identity and no cultural richness. Politically correct thought police will condemn us to a grey, boring social landscape.'

At 9.30 Wogan hands over to Ken Bruce, who I have listened to before, but never for long. Whereas Wogan breezes through his show and always makes it very listenable, Bruce tends to resort to trotting out clichés and playing songs that made Genesis seem like the future of music.

'Are you eating a steak and kidney pie?' Lynn Bowles asks him, interrupting her own travel report.

'There's not much kidney,' he complains, and proceeds to read out the ingredients, the calorific content. This isn't golden radio. To be fair to Bruce, I'm not in a very good mood this morning; my shirt collar feels too tight against my neck, and I slept badly; I had a dream about men in balaclavas breaking into my flat. Now I'm tired and all I have to look forward to is my cheese and onion sandwich in three hours. My mood is summed up by the choice of the next record – Chris Rea. Ideally a radio presenter would be able to wake me from my slumber, inject enthusiasm, kickstart my morning, but as soon as Ken Bruce starts reading out jokes I want to rest my head against my keyboard, not to be woken until it's pay day.

'I was in a shoe shop, someone paid with a forged fifty-pound note.'

'Counterfeit?'

'Yes, she had two.'

And:

'Can I have some bacon please,' I asked the butcher.

'Leanback.'

'And I fell over.'

Pop Master is Ken Bruce's daily music quiz, the format barely changing in at least one hundred years. 'I like all music apart from reggae and country,' says Lynne from Cornwall, today's first contestant.

Question one is to name one member of Bucks Fizz. She names all four, a tactical show of intent. Her score of twenty-six is a good one. Next is Nick Dent of Northumberland. He doesn't beat twenty-six, Lynne wins, but misses out on the star prize, a digital radio, because she cannot name three Alison Moyet songs in ten seconds.

The show ends with James Blunt. I finger the cheese and onion sandwiches in my bag, but decide against eating them now. I don't want my day to peak too soon. Alan Medlicott reaches across to my side of the desk, giving me a pile of papers that need putting in order, stapling, filing. He opens and closes his drawers and gives me an 'I don't know where my stapler's gone' shrug.

'Have you got a stapler?' I ask Craig, but he shakes his head. I look around in desperation. Life shouldn't be this complicated. I think back to Virgin Radio, and how Sandra's life was turned round simply because a man with a baby appeared on her doorstep and decide to be proactive. I will borrow a stapler from Poppy.

Poppy is two years younger than me. I know this, her date of birth is on the intranet. She drives a Toyota Yaris and sometimes wears bright-red tights. I have never spoken to her but know from overhearing conversations that she dropped out of her first year at university and loves *Big Brother*. I walk over to her desk. I don't have a baby in my arms or a heartbreakingly sad story to tell her, but I've tucked my shirt in especially and am proud of myself for having a shave this morning. The world is mine for the taking. I walk to Poppy's desk. She looks up, her eyes sapphire blue, and smiles.

'Hi,' I say.

'Hi,' she replies, her voice gentle, the sound a cloud makes when it touches another.

'Could I . . . borrow your stapler? I've lost mine.'

She reaches over and hands hers to me.

'Thanks,' I say, swinging it like a pistol.

'That's okay,' she says, her lips cherry red, perfect teeth, blonde hair tied in a bobble. I walk back to my desk. That was it; my first attempt at speaking to Poppy. Next time I will rehearse. One day we will go out together. One day we will build our dream house, discuss catchment areas.

Jeremy Vine presents his current affairs programme after the midday news. This was once the terrain of Jimmy Young, who was relieved of his duties at the BBC at the age of eighty-one, and on his last show told listeners live on air that he didn't want to leave. Vine was a worthy replacement; a distinguished, affable and politically astute broadcaster, but most importantly he likes Morrissey, which is all I ask for in a radio presenter.

Vine has Tim Philips on the phone, the campaign manager for Animal Welfare International, discussing the disturbing video of a US marine throwing a puppy off a cliff.

'It shows a frightening level of desensitization,' he tells Vine. 'It is, to put it simply, brutality and cowardice.'

'But surely it's not as bad as the abuse of prisoners at Abu Ghraib is it?'

'Well, I think it is. This dog was tortured and killed. Quite rightly there has been a huge outrage about it. We have to start protecting the weakest in our society before we can protect everyone else.'

'Isn't it a concern that we manage to blank out over 600,000 civilian deaths in Iraq since 2003, but are all up in arms about a puppy?' Vine asks, using the interrogation skills he picked up as a presenter on BBC 2's *Newsnight*.

'I don't think that's the case. I don't think it's one or the other. You devalue your listeners' compassion if you say they care about the puppy but not about the people who have died. The dog is simply emblematic and symptomatic of a much larger concern.'

Vine advises people not to watch the video, it is only seventeen seconds long but horrific, an image he has been unable to shake. People who phone in react passionately.

'If I had my way he'd face a firing squad.'

'I'm worried about the psychological health of the marine. We don't know what he's been through, he may have seen his friends die.'

'The puppy was probably wagging its tail.'

This is when the traffic reporter, Sally Boazman, is effective. She chats to Vine, brings a lighter tone, a warmth, a distraction from the bleak images it is sometimes necessary to discuss. After more reports about the M25, and then the news headlines, the subject is parents who are beaten by their children. This is a show that does not shy away from difficult issues, and the image is unpleasant to register. Vine is humbled by an email sent in as soon as the subject is mentioned, a mother scared of her teenage son because he is so violent.

'My son Mark has been really bad for a couple of days. He didn't go to school yesterday, he said it was my fault because I didn't wake him. He continually insults me, says I am pathetic, stupid, fat and arrogant. He breaks my things, he breaks his own things, he says that no one will remember me when I die. He tells me I am going to die, he wants me to die. He tells me he wants to find me hanging upside down with my throat cut.' This is a son to his mother, Vine reprises. 'I'm finding it very hard to live with Mark. My only way is to disappear, walk out, give up. There is no cure, no help, no respite. I am without hope.'

A mother in Suffolk is on the phone.

'My son is twelve and has been increasingly worse ever since he was five: more aggressive, violent towards me, breaking all of his toys. His toy box has always been just a box of bits. My son said I am going to die, that he wants me to die, that no one will remember me.'

'The exact same words as the previous caller used?'

'That's why I phoned. It was so eerie, it could have been my son speaking.'

'That level of imagery is inexplicable.'

'Totally. Totally. I just don't know why. We feed him a good diet of fresh food, we don't give him ready meals. He goes to a small school so there is enough attention to go around all the pupils. We're a very normal village family, he's not spoiled, I can't understand any of it.'

'Thank you,' Jeremy tells her. 'Linda is also on the line, are you hearing echoes in these stories?'

'Yes, particularly the level of verbal abuse.'

'And have you experienced hatred from your son for a long time?'

'Yes, from the age of three he's tried to whack me. Recently he was very annoyed with his father about something and I got a punch in the face.'

'Did your husband step in?'

'Not on that occasion. It was the first time he had seen any violence between us and he was so shocked. They were rushing to go to school when it happened and my husband phoned later that morning to say he was so sorry.'

'You must feel you want to live somewhere else?'

'Mmm.'

'But you can't, you're his mother.'

'Absolutely.'

I am at the filing cabinets for *Steve Wright in the Afternoon*, armed with my stack of papers, a staple kerchunked into each corner. I've always quite liked Steve Wright; it feels like a guilty pleasure, but sometimes if I am on my own I will make sure that the door is locked, the curtains are drawn, I will switch off my phone and listen.

His *Breakfast Show* on Radio 1 was one of the first radio programmes I remember hearing, I would listen while getting ready for school. He popularized the American 'zoo' format, filling his studio with a posse to clap and whoop on demand. As Wright has become one of radio's elder statesmen he has dispensed with such chaos, instead using two co-hosts, Tim Smith and Janey Lee Grace, themselves presenters in their own right, who bring a touch more Radio 2 maturity to proceedings. After glossing over the day's news and last night's TV, Wright begins Factoids, where the three presenters wow each other with trivial, often spurious facts:

- Pigeons can remember 12,000 images at a time.
- The higher your IQ the more you dream.
- Twenty per cent of men have never used a screwdriver.

I have spent hours at these filing cabinets over the last six months and am sure that no one would be any the wiser if I just took the stack of company reports Alan Medlicott puts on my desk and hurled them into a skip. I take a pen and in the margins of the report at the top of the pile I write down *20 per cent of men have never used a screwdriver*. I file it in its rightful place, hoping that one day it will be discovered and someone will say 'hmm'. On the next report I write down: *The largest speaking part of any Shakespeare play is Hamlet*.

And soon more and more company reports are factoided:

- The average adult falls asleep seven minutes after putting the light out.
- Plumbers eat more salads than any other profession.
- There has only ever been one person born on the Tube. It was at the Elephant and Castle, and the baby was christened Thelma Ursula Beatrice Eleanor, her initials spelling 'tube'.

Suddenly filing is fun. Steve Wright is playing Golden Oldies, a section of his show where a listener chooses their selection of old records, and Alistair Burns of Loch Lomond has done a fine job, selecting David Bowie, New Order and 'Love Shack' by the B-52s. I get overexcited during 'Love Shack' and wish the volume on the radio in my pocket could be turned even higher. It's a good job no one walks into the filing room as the song plays, they would find me with a whistle in my mouth, glosticks in each hand, riding an overturned filing cabinet like a surfboard. You don't realize the beauty of some songs until you are alone in a room, bored, with headphones on. I'm not in a bad mood any more. In fact if Ken Bruce had played 'Love Shack' at 9.30 this morning I'm sure I would now be declaring him the greatest living DJ. But he didn't. He played Chris Rea and Paolo Nutini.

The first of Steve Wright's celebrity guests is Steven Berkoff. The actor is in the studio to promote his new book *My Life in Food*.

'I developed a passion for ethnic food,' he tells Wright. 'The kind of meal that will stay with you for a long time. Actors eat out twenty times a week. Food is important. You are away from your family, and as a result have an emotional reaction to what you eat. I always identify chicken soup with my mother. Even if I'm in Miami I'll still go round restaurants looking for soup the way she made it, a dumpling in the bowl. And when I can't find it, it upsets me.'

Wright plays 'Time for Heroes' by the Libertines and for once I look at my watch hoping that it isn't time to go home just yet. The next celebrity guest is Ian Anderson, lead singer of Jethro Tull, shattering a long-held belief of mine that the singer was a bloke called Jethro Tull. You don't think of people called Ian fronting prog rock bands. It is the band's fortieth anniversary, and Anderson is on the show to promote a special tour and their re-released album, but it is fish that he is most enthusiastic to discuss, as he has owned several salmon farms.

Next on air is one of the most controversial figures in the history of radio. It's not Simon Mayo, it's Chris Evans. It was a brave move by then-controller Lesley Douglas to bring Evans back from radio wilderness in 2005. Radio 2 traditionalists thought it was a risky move, too bold a gamble for a station that still cherishes *The Organist Entertains* and *Big Band Special*. Douglas had already established a reputation for enlisting the services of people whose backgrounds are predominantly in television, such as Jonathan Ross and Mark Lamarr. Evans's arrival provoked over a thousand people to complain, but those who remember him in his Radio 1 *Breakfast Show* pomp knew it was a risk well worth taking. Since his comeback, Evans has never fully recreated the notoriety that made him a household name, which involved buying Virgin Radio and subsequently being sacked by the station, but in the first two years of his second chance at the BBC he won two prestigious Sony Gold Awards for Radio Personality of the Year.

'I love Thursdays,' Evans says at the start of the show. 'It reminds me of collecting my brown envelope of money when I worked in a warehouse.'

Woman's Minute is a feature where female listeners are given a minute on air. Today the question Evans poses is 'What is the next treat you are going to give yourself?'

'I'm going to have Botox,' Tracy tells him.

'I'm going to Venice on Tuesday,' says Debbie Thompson.

'I'm about to have a Bounty and a cup of tea,' says Julie, who is in a hire car because someone bumped into the back of her Toyota last week.

It is 5.30, I say goodbye to Alan Medlicott and Craig, but before I put my coat on walk over to Poppy.

'Thanks,' I say, returning the stapler. She smiles, puts it in its right place on her meticulously organized desk. I walk away and think of Poppy as I walk home.

Rebecca Pike, the show's business correspondent, conducts a daily interview with somebody involved in a topical business story. The feature is sometimes serious, sometimes more relaxed, the tone that Radio 2 has adopted for their whole schedule. Today she speaks to Graham Kerr, a spokesman for Energywatch, about reports that poorer customers in the UK are being charged more for gas and electricity because they are on a pre-paid meter. The interview is never more than conversational, with Kerr promising that the poorest will be looked after and are not being exploited. Next, Evans issues Pike her daily challenge, submitted by a listener, which she has to solve before her next bulletin in an hour.

'Is it true that curry has overtaken fish and chips as the nation's favourite takeaway?'

Pike promises that when she returns in an hour she will tell us the answer. While she is Googling, Evans plays the Hoosiers and the Cure, after which Nigel Barden, the show's food and drink expert, makes his weekly appearance in the studio to talk about peas.

'I love mushy peas!' Evans yelps. 'How were they invented?'

'Completely by accident. They weren't intended to be eaten

like that, it was just the easiest way of preserving them. I'm going to teach you how to make pea fritters.'

'Do you want to try some, Sally?' Evans asks his travel reporter. Talking about traffic jams is clearly hungry work and she devours a fritter, declaring it to be incredible. After giving out the recipe, Evans plays 'There's a Guy Works Down the Chip Shop Swears He's Elvis' by Kirsty MacColl, and then Rebecca Pike is back with her answer about curry.

'The latest research I have found shows that fish and chips are still the nation's favourite takeaway, followed by a meal down the local pub. Chinese restaurants come third, followed by pizza places, leaving curry houses in fifth place.'

I am hungry, I have not eaten since my sandwich earlier this afternoon, so put on my headphones and walk to the chip shop, where I listen to the end of Evans's show, and the start of another radio legend, Bob Harris.

I say yes to salt and vinegar as Harris plays 'Gunslinger' by John Fogarty and am back at my flat dolloping tomato ketchup when he plays the Gougers. Despite what their name implies, the Gougers aren't a punk band, they are Country and Western, with a female singer who sounds like she's married to a man in a cowboy hat. I imagine her tending the bar in a saloon. The regulars know to look, but not touch.

'You'll recognize this immediately,' Harris says before the next song. And I do, but feel ashamed. It's a country version of the Dire Straits song 'Walk of Life'. I recognize it because I have a couple of friends who are Dire Straits fans. 'Try it,' they said to me one night, offering me the Greatest Hits as though it was white powder wrapped in cellophane. I shook my head. I was not going to cave in to peer pressure, did not want to experience the Dire Straits side effects: nausea, apathy, the burning sensation when you go to the toilet.

Harris plays more songs by people with deep voices singing about getting drunk, empty dreams and Tennessee. He ends the show with an Alison Krauss duet with Robert Plant and then a Willie Nelson song, 'I'm Alive'.

'The lyrics are beautiful,' Harris says, alluding to his own struggle with cancer over the last eighteen months. He only recently recovered and was able to present shows again.

After Fran Godfrey reads the news it is time for Radcliffe and Maconie, who start their show with 'Waking Up' by Elastica and suddenly I feel sixteen again.

'They were a great-looking band,' Mark Radcliffe says, who presented a late-night Radio 1 show in the mid-nineties when I was first getting into music and bands like Elastica. 'We'll play that for Clare Stone, who sent us a box of cakes which we ate while attending what is laughably called our "Planning Meeting".'

After the new single by Gnarls Barkley, Radcliffe reads an email.

'The wife is watching Crufts so I've escaped to the shed.'

'Have you heard that William Hill has suspended all betting on one of the events?' Stuart Maconie asks. 'There has been a flurry of bets for one particular discipline, which can only suggest they are worried about some kind of superdog.'

'I've never been in a betting shop in my life.'

'Not even for a free pen?'

'No, I go to Argos for that.'

'Don't you find the catalogues take up so much room you always end up jostling with the people either side of you?'

'No,' Radcliffe tells his co-host. 'I take my security with me. It's like Michael Jackson in Hamleys when I go to Argos. I'm out of there with a new alarm clock while Northwich is still asleep.'

'Ian's texted in,' Maconie says, after '20th Century Boy' by T.Rex. 'Is it plain or self-raising to make Yorkshire puddings?'

'Oh no! We've had this before. I can't remember.'

'I'm in my shed too,' emails Gary. 'My wife's at Pilates so I'm fixing my bicycle.'

'I hope that's not a euphemism.'

Radcliffe and Maconie's guest is Noddy Holder, former lead singer of Slade, also known as the show's regular television reviewer. The programme he is discussing tonight is *The Hard Sell* on BBC 4, which presents a history of advertising.

'I'm familiar with the world of advertising because I've been involved in TV campaigns for various brands,' Holder tells the co-hosts.

'I'm glad you've got something to supplement the meagre "Merry Christmas Everybody" royalties,' Radcliffe tells him.

'Advertising holds a mirror up to society,' Holder tells us. 'In 1955 it was considered perfectly normal for Stanley Matthews to advertise cigarettes. The Stella Artois slogan "reassuringly expensive" summed up the eighties. And in all beer adverts, there are always three men in a bar. It's one of advertising's firm rules: a man by himself is thought to be lonely, two are considered homosexual, but three men in a pub are probably just mates having a good time.'

Radcliffe and Maconie's show mixes new and old music. They play the new single by new band the Draytones, followed by 'The Immigrant Song' by Led Zeppelin. Holder introduces a Show and Tell, a feature where a guest is asked to bring in a record and tell a story about it.

'When Slade first went to the US we were supported by Aerosmith. It was before they were big, and they were likeable lads striving to make it. Then their album *Toys in the Attic* became huge and they got into drugs. Soon they were one of the biggest bands in America and they asked us to do some shows with them. During one gig we had finished but the organizer was at the side of the stage frantically gesturing for one more song. And we finished it and he did the same, and this carried on for half an hour. Aerosmith refused to go on for an hour and a half, and we later found out it was because they had asked in advance for white towels in the dressing room, but been given yellow. The promoter had to search Kansas City late on a Sunday night to find forty fluffy white towels, that he eventually had to buy from a hotel. By the time the band were on stage the great atmosphere we had created had been killed and the gig was ruined. We were from Wolverhampton and couldn't understand it; you work so hard for five or six years, losing money, living in squalor, and as soon as you have success you behave so strangely.'

Noddy chooses to play the Aerosmith song 'Dude (Looks Like a Lady)'.

'Tell that story you just told us!' Holder tells Maconie.

'Well, I heard about a gig they did in Boston. It was their hometown and they hadn't played there for two years, but when they turned up they showed their manager the setlist and it was exactly the same as the last time they performed, all the songs were in the same order.

'"It looks like you haven't got any new material," he argued with them.

'"We haven't," they replied.

'"Well at least change the order around a bit so people don't notice."

'So they started with the song they normally closed on, "Walk This Way". And when they finished it, they said: "Thank you Boston, goodnight!" When their manager came to get them backstage they said to him "That was a great gig" only to be told they'd only performed one song.'

When the show finishes I switch off my radio, dig out Elastica's first album and reminisce about my teenage years, when Elastica, Blur and Pulp were on Mark and Lard's Radio 1 show. It was the first time I felt I had an identity, that Britpop was really exciting and I was part of it. I press play on my CD player and nudge the volume round to full blast. After a morning of Ken Bruce and data entry, I've deserved it, and go to bed thinking about which station I will listen to next.

5

TalkSPORT

'Crime prevention is a cover-up, a way to survey society.
There is a force that wants to see what we're up to.'

(email to late-night talkSPORT)

Today I choose to listen to talkSPORT, a station I have tuned in to regularly for years, and look forward to listening today. I'm growing increasingly absorbed with radio; I like to ask my friends about their favourite shows, re-evaluate my feelings about them by whether they prefer Chris Moyles to Terry Wogan. I'm fascinated by people's choice of station; I can't get into a taxi without considering the life of the driver based on what they are listening to. Someone's choice of station says as much about them as the car they drive, how long they grow their sideburns or the names they give their children.

I wake at 7.30 and brush my teeth as Alan Brazil and Ronnie Irani, the hosts of the talkSPORT *Sports Breakfast*, wonder whether Arsenal will miss their influential midfielder Mathieu Flamini if he signs for AC Milan, as has been rumoured in the morning papers. This is the niche that talkSPORT have carved for themselves: football, football, football, an obligatory mention of rugby or snooker, then football, football.

'Kevin Keegan has said that the Premiership is in danger of becoming the most boring league in the world,' Brazil, the Ipswich footballer turned *Breakfast Show* presenter, reads from this morning's tabloids. 'Text in to tell us what you think. Also, let us know what else you think is predictable,' requests the sociable Scotsman.

'You turning up a minute before we go on air,' former England cricketer Irani tells him.

After adverts for cars, computer games and Sky TV, the travel reporter Jerina Adams tells us about an accident on the A1 at Gateshead and queues on the M4. Ronnie Irani wonders whether people still play French cricket, and decides that Arsenal will definitely miss Flamini. Texts come in about Kevin Keegan's comments.

'The Premiership is boring. The Spanish league is the best in the world.'

'The Premiership is amazing. Keegan is just jealous he'll never win it.'

'Even the French league is better than the Premiership.'

I carry on listening to people talking about footie as I walk to work. Leaving the house at the same time every morning means I become familiar with the daily routines of strangers. I see the same people in the same places. I know if I am early or late because I can judge by people around me. At 8.35 I should see a man walking an Alsatian. At 8.45 I always pass four school-boys, three of them with their hands in their pockets, the fourth straddling a bicycle. At 8.50 a lady in a red coat waits at the pedestrian crossing. Every day is the same. I say hello to Alan Medlicott. He looks worried about something, perhaps he's an Arsenal fan and is worried about Flamini joining AC Milan. Tommo, the station's horse-racing correspondent, brings us today's tips. I text my friend Mark. *If you pass the bookie's can you put £10 on for me on Megapick. It's a dead cert.*

I've always wanted to use that expression.

Gaunty is on at ten. It's not me calling him Gaunty, it's his listeners, his fans, those who contact the show, but most worryingly of all, himself.

'That's right, Gaunty's buying a place in Cyprus,' he tells us, responding to an email saying *I see the fat pig has been on holiday again.* 'I've been over there for a week, it's the second time I've visited and it's wonderful, there's no crime and people don't walk down the street drunk. It's so much better than Broken England.' After a trailer for Alan Brazil's *Sports Breakfast*, Steve in Zurich is on the line.

'Gaunty, we moved to Zurich to give our children a better upbringing away from the gun crime of London. The kids here are all well behaved, they have respect for each other and it's because the Swiss have compulsory military service. When you are eighteen you go in for sixteen weeks, and go back for four more weeks every two years until your thirty-fourth birthday. It ensures discipline in kids while they're growing up, and it's something the UK needs to embrace.'

'I agree,' Gaunt tells him. 'It would give kids in this country a sense of purpose, and is a way of repairing Broken Britain. Mario in Barnet is on the phone. Mario, you've called to talk to me about Cyprus. Surely Mario's an Italian name?'

'I'm Greek Cypriot.'

'You have got a beautiful country, my son. Gaunty's investing, it's a beautiful place. What's the military service like over there?'

'I had to do compulsory service, even though I have a British passport,' Mario replies, sombrely. 'I was taken away from my wife and children for six months.'

'You did something for your country though, son. That's something to be proud of.'

Jerina brings more travel news, there's an overturned caravan on the M25, the accident at the A1 at Gateshead has been sorted out towards the northbound interchange, there are signalling problems at Hemel Hempstead.

'We've got Damien Green on the phone, the shadow minister for Immigration. Damien,' Gaunt says, addressing his guest with a new-found politeness, 'Britain is bursting at its seams, what are you going to do about it?'

'Well, we're trying to control levels of migration at the moment. It's important we have not just the right kind of people in our country but the right number of people.'

'I was at Heathrow yesterday,' Gaunty tells him, 'and there was such a long queue going through customs but I thought to myself, Be patient, Gaunty, if you want to keep the illegals out, this is just immigration officers doing their job. The bottom line though must be "Is Britain full?"'

'No, not full, but access needs to be controlled.'

'Thanks for speaking to us,' Gaunt says to him. 'I'm different to Damien Green, though,' he declares when his guest has been disposed of. 'I say Britain is full and it has been full for years. Only extremely highly skilled people should be allowed into our green and pleasant land. People who are unskilled, get lost! Go away! We don't need you. Britain . . . is . . . full.'

I really don't want to listen to the rest of Gaunt. I've listened to talkSPORT often enough to realize that the presenters adopt deliberately antagonizing tones in order to provoke their listeners to text and call in, enraged that the presenter has the audacity to express such views, whether it's about Arsenal selling Flamini or Gaunt's notion of 'Broken Britain'. I know that disagreeing with someone is healthy and a necessary part of our everyday lives. For example, my favourite team is Liverpool while my friend Paddy supports Aston Villa, but despite this we manage to get on. My favourite in Girls Aloud is the blonde one while my friend Gommy thinks they should all be shot. We all have different opinions. But it's good to have views that differ from other people's, to listen to radio that is outside of your comfort zone. Jon Gaunt is too much though, he's riling me – I can sense my blood pressure increase, my knuckles whiten, my face redden. I am falling for his plan; this is how he wants me to feel. The fact that he's so confrontational is annoying. The fact that I disagree with practically every single thing he says infuriates me. But what I hate more than anything is his claim that he is a 'mouthpiece for Britain', that he is saying what everyone else is thinking. He's not saying what I'm thinking, if he was it would make boring radio, just repeating *I hate Jon Gaunt, I hate Jon Gaunt*.

'We've got Simon in Leicester on the phone to talk about Broken Britain. What have you got to say, Si?'

'I've been a victim of car crime twice. Both times the police have just dealt with it over the phone, there's been nobody sent out to take fingerprints or to see the damage. Also, I had an incident on New Year's Eve – a guy down the road had a party and when some people were leaving they stole from my property, a Christmas wreath from my front door. And I phoned the police to explain what had happened and all they could say was "What do you want us to do? It's New Year's Eve." I pay to service that police force and that's the response I get!'

After the midday news and more adverts for cars, computer games and Sky TV, 'Gaunty' is back on air with something else on his mind.

'I was on the plane from Cyprus yesterday,' he tells us, once again boasting of his travels, 'and this woman sat near me was tanked up, out of her trolley, being abusive to the air stewardess. So they stopped giving her alcohol. But here's the thing: she had a little girl. A little girl! She should have been arrested. The pilot should have radioed ahead and the police should have met this drunk at the runway. The worst thing though was that she had car keys in her hand. If you are that bird and are listening now, you are an unfit mother! A disgrace! What do you think about that, Moose?' he asks Ian Abrahams, the morning's sports reader.

'Well I don't really understand why people need to drink on a plane at all.'

'Of course you should be able to!' Gaunt shouts at him. 'Just because people like this woman abuse it, we shouldn't all be punished! Shut up with your pathetic opinions! Don't divert the argument, we're not talking about whether alcohol should be banned on planes, we're talking about this woman and whether she should have been arrested! Go to Cuba, Moose. You're a fascist. A fascist!'

'Planes are dangerous though,' he says, and seems slightly surprised at having to defend his view so vigorously. 'If there's an emergency you need to have your wits about you. When you're on the beach or in your hotel you can drink as much as you want, enjoy yourself then. But planes can be dangerous, if someone is out of control it puts the other passengers in danger. I manage to fly without drinking.'

'Shut up, Moose. You don't ever drink anyway. Get out, you stinking hypocrite. Who agrees with me? The woman should be arrested, the pilot should have reported her. It worries me, it really does.'

Mark in Preston calls. 'So there was a woman drunk on an aeroplane who was going to drive home?' he clarifies.

'That's right.'

'So when she was driving home she could have had a smash, her little girl could have been injured?'

'That's right.'

'So why didn't you do anything about it? Surely if you've seen this going on it's your responsibility to report it to the police?'

'I've just told you! The captain of the plane, who happened to be a woman, it's her responsibility. The clue is in the title. She is the captain. I was the passenger. The airline have a duty of care. The police should have been there to meet her. Why you're trying to twist this round to make me look guilty is beyond me!

She is neglecting her daughter. Harry in Glasgow is on the phone. Hello, Harry.'

'I agree with the last guy.'

'Well, you're a prat as well,' Gaunt says, his anger punctuated with the sound of the phone line going dead. 'What is it with you lot?' he asks, bewildered. 'It's not my fault if she was drunk. It's not my responsibility. The captain should have done something, not me. If you don't like me, phone up and say I hate your guts and you're fat. Why bother to pretend you're trying to make a point? You're missing the important part of the argument. Jason is in Wimbledon. Jason, these people are morons!'

'I know, Gaunty,' he says with a derisory snort. 'With this sort of philosophy you'd be too scared to have a drink in the pub, they'll be taking the car keys off every bloke that's had a drink! Come on, people, wake up! It's the captain's job to report something like that!' Jason says, sticking up valiantly for the Cyprus-loving presenter.

'Thanks, Jason,' Gaunty says. 'If there's anyone who works for an airline who wants to back me up, a captain, or a stewardess, or one of those extremely heterosexual male air stewards, please call up. I really felt for that little angel stuck on the plane with her drunk mum.'

At one o'clock I listen to Hawksbee and Jacobs outside, desperate for fresh air, still slightly on edge after hearing Gaunty's show. I pace up and down the car park like an expectant father. Peering through the window, I see Poppy eating salad from a Tupperware box. I want to tell her not to worry, I will protect her from Jon Gaunt. She will be safe with me. I will let nothing bad happen to her. It's all over now, Hawksbee and Jacobs will help me through the afternoon. I like listening to them; Alan Brazil's *Breakfast Show* talks about the Premiership and says how good Ronaldo is, whereas the amiable Hawksbee and Jacobs celebrate the minutiae of the football world.

'I don't understand why goalkeepers leave a towel in the back of the goal,' Andy Jacobs ponders. 'Surely it's giving the opposing striker something to aim for. If he turns and looks up and all he can see is a flash of white, that's where he's going to shoot.'

'Maybe he should give it to someone on the front row to hold during the match,' Paul Hawksbee suggests. 'A friendly away fan.'

'There's a story in the *Sun* today about Crawley Town, that their season tickets have gone up to £500 because when they sent out letters to supporters reminding them to renew their tickets, they forgot to put stamps on the envelopes and were dealt with a big bill from the Post Office.'

'That sounds a lot, £500.'

'My Chelsea season ticket is £800 and I get to see Joe Cole, Lampard, Ballack. That sounds ridiculous.'

'Chris Davies is here, author of the book *Behind the Back Pages*, the travels of a sports reporter. You must have seen hundreds of games?'

'Thousands, I would imagine. I've seen two hundred Ireland games alone.'

'And what have been the biggest changes since you started out?' Jacobs asks.

'Obviously computers and mobile phones make things much easier. But the main difference is the way teams interact with the press nowadays. It's all changed. You wouldn't get Fabio Capello announcing the England team at a press conference reading from a packet of fags, like Jack Charlton did when he was manager of Ireland. And when the press say to him "You've only named ten players" reply with "Well you all know who the goalkeeper is." Journalists used to regularly go out after the game with players and managers, we had a very good relationship, but that was before this media spotlight, a time when football was much lower profile. It could never happen now. If anything happened while we were with the players we would keep it secret. Sports journalists still would do, but the news side of the media wants stories, gossip, scandal.'

'Isn't there a story about you being pickpocketed in Colombia?' Hawksbee asks.

'There is, my money was safe, I kept that hidden in my sock, and I had my hands in my pockets the whole time. But you've got to hand it to the fella, as soon as I took a hand out to adjust my sunglasses he was in there, swiped the contents of my pocket and had run away before I could react. All he took was my long-term car park ticket for Heathrow. But I'd have rather he took all my money. If you've ever tried to get your car out of Heathrow without a ticket you'll know how much hassle it is.'

'So are you asked by kids how they can get into sports reporting?'

'Yeah, quite often. I just tell them they've got to start with local papers, work their way up. It's important to have your own style and to work hard. If you are talented, the chances are you will be spotted, but be prepared to start at the bottom.'

Chris Davies seems to be addressing me personally now, telling me he has achieved so much just by working hard, that this is how he's been able to have a career doing something he loves. There is no divine right that has put him there; just as Chris Evans had to work in a warehouse before he got a job in radio, Stuart Maconie worked in an Oldham cotton mill. They all had to start at the bottom, get their fingernails dirty. The only difference between these people and me is that they set their goals and achieved them, making their life more interesting, more fulfilled. It's only recently, as I've ensconced myself in the world of radio that it's dawned on me that radio is something I have always wanted to be involved with, yet never done anything about. When I was at university I really wanted to be part of the student radio station, but was never proactive enough to find out how to become part of it. I imagine it would only have taken one email, to turn up at one meeting and speak to the right person, but I never found the motivation and looking back I regret it. I'm sure there are a lot of people like me, who have had aspirations they never fulfilled. I look around the open-plan office and wonder how many dreams have been left out in the car park, I think about the ambitions saved as Word documents that cannot be opened because the password has been forgotten. Nobody dreams of working in an industrial estate in Norwich.

After adverts for cars, computer games and Sky TV, Hawksbee and Jacobs refer back to the story about Crawley Town.

'We've got the chairman on the phone asking to speak to us. Victor Marley, hello.'

'Hello, Paul, hello, Andy, I listen to your show all the time, it's good to talk to you.'

'Glad to hear it. What have we done to upset you?'

'It's not you, it's this story that someone's got hold of and put in the paper. We do have season tickets available at £500, but they are in the executive lounge, with a match day host, a two-course meal, glass of wine, coffee and tea at half-time, TVs to check other scores throughout the match.'

'The full corporate experience then?'

'That's right. And for our best season ticket in the ground it's £275 a season, which works out at around £10 a game.'

'So the papers have twisted it slightly. What happened with these stamps?'

'It is true that some were sent out wrongly. We ran out of regular envelopes and used slightly larger ones, without realizing we hadn't put more postage on. As soon as we were aware of our mistake we went straight down to the Post Office to explain. It affected around twenty-five people, and we've let them know that if they come to us with a receipt from the Post Office we'll refund the money they had to pay.'

'It's frustrating the way papers twist things,' Jacobs says once they have said goodbye to Marley. 'They take such extreme examples, sensationalize the story, and a couple of mugs like us fall for it.'

During the news, Macca, the sports reader, tells us that Tommo's prediction was right, and Megapick won. I text Mark. *Megapick won! I told you it was a cert. Can I have my money please?*

I decide not to reveal who my tipster is. Sometimes it is better to be mysterious. It can be my and Tommo's secret.

'Today we're going to be talking about England's chances of ever winning a World Cup,' Adrian Durham says, on air at four o'clock presenting *Football First*. 'The FA have told Fabio Capello that if he gets to the semi-final of the World Cup, and the semi-final of the European Championships in 2012, then it will be considered a success. I think it's a disgrace, the FA are giving him licence to fail. We should be winning trophies.'

'I think we'd do well to reach a semi-final,' his co-host Mickey Quinn tells him. 'England are a second-rate footballing nation and don't look like winning anything.'

'I take personal exception to that,' Durham snaps. 'Are you being serious? We are a world-class side, we have world-class players.'

'Who have never achieved anything.'

'Lampard, Rooney, Gerrard.'

'Who didn't even manage to qualify for Euro 2008!'

Durham and Quinn kick around sporty jingoism for another hour, people phone up and words come out but no one seems to be actually saying anything. They need something to get their teeth into, a big match to review or reflect on. I sit at my desk thinking how none of this actually matters. Talking about whether there are too many overseas footballers in the Premiership and whether or not Arsenal will miss Flamini is ultimately pointless, nothing is resolved. I say goodbye to Alan Medlicott and Craig and listen to talkSPORT as I walk home.

'Have you seen the papers today, Quinny?' Durham asks. 'There's pictures of British girls on holiday abroad, drunk, passed out in streets and on the floors of bars. I'd like to know what is wrong with British women. You go on holiday to Sweden and France and see all these beautiful women, they look much better, are much classier. Text in to let us know what's wrong with British women.'

After getting overexcited about England's chances of winning trophies in future World Cups, Durham reads out texts.

'The problem with British women is they don't like football,' Andy in Reading rather predictably suggests.

'The problem though,' Durham argues, 'is that a lot of women pretend that they do like football nowadays. It's that pseudo intellectual . . . stuff.'

'Aren't we going down the MCP route?' Quinn asks. 'Male chauvinist pigs?'

'Well . . . whatever. Another text here says "What's wrong with women? Michelle Marsh, Keeley, Lucy Pinder. That's what's wrong with women."'

'What's wrong with them?' Quinny asks. 'I like Michelle Marsh.'

'Matt has texted in to say he hates women with tattoos. Quite right. Tattoos are disgusting. There is something deeply psychologically wrong with you if you have a tattoo.'

'Lindsay who answers the phones is covered in them,' Quinn says. 'The Illustrated Woman.'

'Do you know who else has got a tattoo? Robin.'

'Robin who reads the news? Where's she got hers?'

'Well, where do you think she's got hers? She's the most predictable girl; she fancies Jon Bon Jovi, she likes eating chocolate, she watches rubbish TV. What else is predictable about Robin? Her tattoo is just above her bottom. Gail in Brighton is on the phone. What would you like to say?'

'Well, I just heard your conversation about women not liking football and I think it's disgraceful. I'm desperate to go to the FA Cup Final but it's my husband who won't let me.'

'What's wrong with British women, Gail?' Quinn asks.

'Nothing! What are you moaning about?'

More texts come in to the show. Some men like football. Some women like football. Some men don't like football. And so it goes on.

'What are you going to talk about in your show?' Durham asks Jim Proudfoot who presents the show that follows.

'The same as you, really,' Proudfoot replies.

It's not a ringing endorsement for the next three hours of talkSPORT, and I sit listening to people talking about the Premiership, the England team, the Premiership, Kevin Keegan, the Premiership and Ronnie O'Sullivan.

Ten o'clock on a weekday night at talkSPORT used to be home to James Whale, who was at the station from 1995 to 2008, and when he left following the London mayoral elections he left a void for a lot of his listeners. When a radio presenter suddenly departs it is like splitting up with a loved one, you have gradually accumulated bits and pieces of their daily routine, their friends and family become recurring characters in your own life. You know their likes and dislikes, political leanings, you make a nightly appointment with them, they keep you company until you go to sleep. And then one day you switch your radio on and they aren't there any more, it's the voice of someone else instead. It's like a character being written out of your favourite soap. It's *The Archers* stopping overnight, with no final episode, no chance to say goodbye.

On air tonight is Max Rushden, fresh from BBC Radio Cambridgeshire.

'Today we're talking about plastic bags,' he says, his voice young, vibrant, contrasting starkly with the curmudgeonly Whale. Marks and Spencer have started charging five pence for their plastic bags. Is that a good thing? Does it annoy you? Phone and tell us what you think. I'd be interested to know how many plastic bags you have in your house. Also, and this is Ash's idea, tell us how old you are and what you're doing.'

'It's a kind of radio census,' adds Ash, the laid-back producer.

'Sylvia in Selby is on the phone,' Rushden says after adverts for cars, Sky TV and computer games. 'Hello, Sylvia.'

'Hello, Max. When I was young there was no such thing as carrier bags. Your mum had a shopping bag and you put everything in there. We never needed plastic bags. The polythene is such a horrible sight, when I'm driving in the countryside I hate seeing bits of bags tied up in the branches of the trees.'

'Thanks, Sylvia. Alan is on the phone. How many bags have you got in your house, Alan?'

'I've just counted them up. Seventy-nine.'

'We might do a spot check,' Ash says when Rushden encourages more people to count their bags, 'so don't think about making numbers up just to win.'

People text in to take part in the census.

– Simon in Rotherham, 41, having a beer.
– Neil in Birmingham, 36, driving a petrol tanker.
– Ben in Ipswich, 21, on the toilet.
– Matt, Oldham, 37, weighing myself naked on the bathroom scales.

Leon in Redditch is on the phone: 'I work in a factory making plastic bags. You can put additives in the bag so it will dissolve, it will turn to powder. That would solve the problem of recycling. Black bags are recycled carrier bags. That's why they smell.'

Jim calls in. 'I'd like to talk about the disaster that is New Labour. Did you hear what Hazel Blears said today?'

'We're not really talking about politics today, Jim. When we are I'll be happy to talk to you.'

'I only called you because it's much easier to get through to air than when Gaunty's on.'

'I know Gaunty well. I'll tell him you'd like to speak to him.'

'How dare he!' says Ash with mock petulance. 'We have millions more listeners than Jon Gaunt.'

'Police today revealed that only 3 per cent of crimes are solved by using CCTV footage,' Max continues after the news. 'Call in with your views on CCTV, and also keep counting those carrier bags.'

Ken calls in. 'We are headed towards a Big Brother society. These CCTV cameras worry me. Crime prevention is a cover-up, they are a way to survey society. There is a force that wants to see what we're up to. According to the Bible, there is a man who will appear as the Antichrist. He is going to further expand and develop this surveillance society. This will affect the economic climate of the whole planet. In my opinion, these are the early stages of something that's coming in the future. He will command the people of every nation to put a mark on their forehead. If people do not have this mark then they will not be able to participate in any economic activity anywhere in the world. Not even buying food. There are very difficult times ahead.'

'Thanks, Ken. I'm not entirely sure what you're talking about. Next we have Vicky in Croydon.'

'Well, for once I agree with Ken,' she says. 'Big Brother is coming. Middle of May, can't wait!'

More people take part in the survey:

- Pete, 35, winning the league with Fulham on Championship Manager.
- Bob, 30, surfing the net on the bench in his garden.
- Mary in Ireland feeding her donkey, Murphy, with ginger biscuits.
- John, 28, in Bristol, lying in bed next to his sleeping fiancée.

Pauline calls in. 'I've got a hundred and thirty-two plastic bags.'

'Have you just counted them now?' Max asks.

'Yes. I really enjoyed doing it as well,' Pauline says, which makes Max laugh. I make tomorrow's sandwiches and go to bed, listen to the rest of the show with my light off, wondering whether or not Flamini is irreplaceable, how much I won at the bookies on Megapick. I try not to think of Jon Gaunt, I don't want to have nightmares, so I close my eyes and think about Pauline, sat on her kitchen floor, counting carrier bags, a smile on her face.

6

TOMMY BOYD

'Two years in Fleet Street, two years as a stand-up comedian, two years as a dolphin trainer.'

One of my radio heroes is Tommy Boyd, and as soon as I decided to speak to people connected with radio his name was the first on my list. I think he's the most engaging, passionate presenter involved with talk radio and I'm really excited to speak to him. He used to present *The Human Zoo*, a Sunday night show on talkSPORT in which the phone operators and studio staff were given the night off and listeners who called in would go straight to air to speak to Tommy without being screened. This resulted in the most bizarre collection of phone calls; people would call in who were lonely, drunk, unhappy. There were poets, singers, people who had stories to tell, abuse to dish out, issues to raise. I was fascinated by the mix, the sublime to the ridiculous and back again, often within the same phone call. Tommy would give advice, critique their music and comedy or just hurl abuse back if he felt it was required. He was equally at ease whether he was talking to a caller about religious extremists or his favourite cheese.

The most frequent type of calls were from people that could best be described as 'nutters'. A lot of people would wait on hold, often for over an hour just to shout 'cock' on live radio. Some people would call in and say 'Timmy Mallett', referring to Boyd's co-presenter on *Wackaday*, the eighties children's TV programme. The callers thought they were genuinely winding Boyd up.

I didn't listen to the show for the nutters. It wasn't taxi drivers' opinions on capital punishment, pastiches of Motown hits, or people claiming they were the Messiah who had me listening week after week. For me the show was special because occasionally someone would engage Tommy in conversation, ask his advice, tell him about their day, share a snapshot of their life. Tommy Boyd made beauty out of the mundane; a Morrissey of the airwaves, he would make people realize that being grumpy on a Sunday is a perfectly normal human emotion, that the whole country feels the same, that they are not alone.

When the show was on air I was in my first year at university and being up on a Sunday night was not a problem as I didn't have to be out of bed again until Tuesday, and even then it didn't really matter if I slept through. But I understood the sentiment and was very aware that for a minority, Tommy Boyd was making a difference to their lives, people treasured the time he was on air. He bettered them, he advised, he encouraged, he tutored.

Emailing radio stations had become part of my daily routine at work and it was exciting to hear Nikki Bedi say my name on Asian Network. Since listening to Christian O'Connell on

Virgin I spent a lot of time thinking about radio, managed to find the old recordings of *Just a Minute* from when I was little, and also a stack of tapes from *The Human Zoo*. Boyd had long left talkSPORT and I wondered what he was doing now, and hoped he was still involved with radio. I found an email address for him at his new station, Southern Counties, and so emailed, telling him I was a big fan. At first there was no response, but one day I got to work, checked my computer and found he had replied. I asked if I could speak to him and he suggested I call him the next day. I prepared some questions but was fairly sure I wouldn't need them; I had heard Tommy often enough to know that he would have plenty to say, I felt prompting him would be unnecessary.

'Thanks for speaking to me, Tommy,' I say when his producer connects me to the studio.

'No problem.'

'I loved *The Human Zoo* and wondered if you could tell me some more about it.'

'Our idea was just to open things up and let listeners do what they want to do, really,' Tommy says, his speech patterns identical to when he is on air, articulate, thoughtful, pausing when necessary to pinpoint the exact word to express himself in the most succinct way possible. 'I did it late on a Sunday night, which is an anarchic time anyway, you're pissed off, you've got school or work in the morning. I like the format of Sunday night radio, you have a licence to do things. I think there's quite enough radio where people have calls screened and their point groomed and massaged by operators and then they have to wait twenty minutes before they get put through to a presenter who talks to them under a dull veil of enthusiasm. We just let people come through to air.'

'Are there any stand-out callers from *The Human Zoo*?'

'Yeah,' Tommy says instantly. It's clearly a question he's been asked at dinner parties and by fans many times before. 'This guy phoned up one night and said, "I want to complain about this programme, it's awful." And I realized that he didn't know he'd come straight through to air. He thought he was talking to a switchboard operator or the producer. So I said, "Yeah it's rubbish, isn't it, mate?"

'"Well, what are you going to do about it?"

'"There's not much we can do, it's laid out to be this way."

'"Well I've been driving along and I can't believe it! It's one rubbish call after another."

'So I played him along for about twenty minutes and eventually I said, "Let me get this straight. You're complaining about the format of the programme, and yet you don't understand the format. You're complaining about something . . . and you don't understand it; the programme involves calls going to air unscreened."

'"So I'm on air?"

'"Yeah, you've been on air for about twenty minutes."

'"Well, that's another example of how appalling you are."

'"Well, don't you realize how appalling *you* are, complaining about something without understanding it? Surely you should know what something is before you have a whinge about it? You're probably just in a bad mood because you've got to go to work tonight."

'"How do you know I've got to go to work tonight?"

'"Who else is driving on a motorway on their own at 11.40 at night? What do you do?"

'"I'm an airline pilot."

'"And you don't want to go to work, do you mate?"

'"I love my job."

'"No. You're a liar. You don't want to go to work. You'd rather have a bottle of wine and shag the missus. I understand human nature. There is something or someone who is upsetting you in life at the moment. You're arsey. You're used to getting your way. You phoned in just now because you felt the need to be superior to someone. I think you need to go away and have a good hard look at how you are with people. I don't like you and I don't think many people do like you."

'Anyway,' Tommy continues to me, 'the call went on like that for thirty-five minutes. I enjoyed it and the listeners enjoyed it because he was an example of someone in a bad mood because he didn't want to go to work and so decided to take it out on me. I enjoyed that. I tried to encourage him to shed his baggage but he wasn't interested. Those who listen and understand what it is I am doing tend to get something out of it. We've had a few poignant calls from people who are lonely.'

'That's the thing I enjoyed about the show,' I tell him. 'It had very tender moments.'

'We could sometimes go for ten or fifteen calls and just get garbage. It's like panning for gold I suppose. You get a lot of mud and then a bit of gold dust. The important thing for you to realize is *The Human Zoo* wasn't as good as people remember it.' He pauses, allowing me to digest the point. 'It's the Elvis Presley syndrome. If Elvis hadn't died he'd have been a laughing-stock.

Same with Marilyn Monroe. You kill off an idea like that and in the passing years afterwards people say "Oh yeah I loved *The Human Zoo*." It was all right. It was basically dangerous. Nobody ever said "fuck". Apart from me, once. I was so relaxed I forgot I was on air.'

'I read somewhere that you're the most sacked person on British radio. Is that the case?'

'Only because people haven't been sacked enough. I'd sack between 80 and 90 per cent of people involved in radio today if I was in charge. I've been sacked twice by Kelvin MacKenzie, which I am immensely proud of, because you should judge a man by his enemies. And if he wants to be an enemy of mine, which I think he does, then I'm very happy about that. I've had lots of different jobs. I don't like to stay in one place for too long, you get a bit woolly. Not that Wogan for example has, he's as fresh as a daisy every day. I generally don't renew contracts. A mate of mine said to me that I must be the most sacked man in broadcasting and the next thing I knew it was on the Internet. I've had twenty-seven jobs. I tend to be somewhere for a year or two.'

'How long have you been in your current job?'

'Well . . .' Tommy says, with a reticent laugh, 'not wanting to get my producer worried but getting on for two years.'

'Is that one of your longer jobs?'

'Yeah. Two years in Fleet Street, two years as a stand-up comedian, two years as a dolphin trainer. Then I was on *Magpie* for three years, which was a children's TV show, then three years on *What's Happening?*, which was a quiz show on telly. Some of the jobs overlap because you can do TV and radio at the same time.'

'So who are your radio heroes?'

'William Joyce,' he tells me with clarity. 'He's not really a hero . . . because he was a Nazi. But I don't think they should have hanged him because they didn't like his show.'

'Is that what happened?'

'Yeah. They hanged him because they didn't like his fucking radio show. Excuse my language. He broadcast from Berlin during the Second World War, in English, spouting Nazi propaganda. It was politically incorrect but they captured him and hanged him for treason. I wouldn't say he was a hero but he sticks out in my mind. The key thing here is that when he was on, in England during the Second World War, it was the most popular show on the radio. Can you explain that?'

I hesitate while establishing whether the question is rhetorical or not.

'Kenny Everett was good,' he says, suggesting the former, 'I liked him a lot. The most inventive person since Kenny Everett has been Chris Evans. Wogan of course is on a different playing field to the rest of us.'

'Is there anyone that you listen to regularly?'

'I often listen to French radio. When you work in radio, listening to radio is like being at work. You can be in the bath or making a slice of toast and you think to yourself "What's he going on about now?" or "He could have done that better." So I listen to French radio, which I can pick up because I live on the coast, but it means I'm not at work because I don't understand French. So it's sometimes quite soothing to have it on. Also they don't seem to have a playlist on their radio stations so you can hear Edith Piaf, Johnny Hallyday, Franz Ferdinand, Hoagy

Carmichael and then its just two French geezers yakking to each other. Also, I can pick up hospital radio from a mast and the other day I heard the most charming forty-five-minute interview with Richard Branson's mother, which was only meant to be broadcast to the hospital, but I picked it up, and you wouldn't have got that anywhere else because everyone on radio thinks that if it goes on for more than three or four minutes people get bored. Which is bollocks of course. But when you start to say that there are other ways of doing it someone will say "Well this is the way it's always been done."'

'One of the best things I've heard on the radio,' I say, remembering something I heard a few years ago, 'was on the Ian Collins talkSPORT show. All the phone lines went down and he had no records to play so it was just two men in a studio talking to each other for three hours. It would never have been done under other circumstances.'

'I had a similar situation myself,' Boyd says. 'It was at Southern Counties about ten years ago when everything went down and I didn't have anyone else there. So I just talked for four hours. There was a big thing about it in a Brighton newspaper, this guy was driving home at half-past ten and when he got to his driveway he couldn't get out of his car and stayed listening until midnight. And he wrote an article about it, but local papers don't support local radio stations. So he picked on the fact that I said "bugger" while on air. I'd said something like "We're nearly finished now which is a good job because I'm completely buggered." So he faked a story about complaints. Nobody had complained. But he rang me up to get a quote about it. And he said it was the most unmissable radio he had ever heard. I asked him why, and he said because it was unconventional. And you can't hear that anywhere else. It's always people saying let's introduce our gardening correspondent, if you have any gardening questions then phone in. Hilda is with us and she'd like to talk about hydrangeas. And do you know what, John – that's bollocks. It's shit. Shit!'

Tommy is really raising his voice, his passion makes my speakerphone wobble. 'And we all think that. Everybody does. Not just me, not just radical presenters; all presenters in radio, all producers, all researchers, they all think the same. Everyone thinks that radio is mostly shit. And we all sit around and joke about it. "What a load of shit we're putting out." Isn't that awful?'

'It is.'

'I mean there are a few good things going on,' Tommy says, his voice calm again. 'Jonathan Ross is funny on a Saturday lunchtime. Wogan makes me laugh. I don't listen to Radio 1. Radio 3 is okay sometimes. Nice little tunes you've never heard before. Radio 4's funny. I can't listen to any of the commercial stations.'

'You mentioned local papers not supporting local radio. Do you think local radio is in decline?'

'I think they need to start thinking very seriously about the threat the Internet poses. There are stations that transmit using radio waves from masts they spend thousands on, and they're doing it under the rigid control of Ofcom. So the guys on there can say "fuck". They can be as controversial as they like. Whether that's right or wrong is neither here nor there. Most people would like to hear what that sounds like and would find it much more virile than what already exists.'

'So is the Internet something you use a lot? You do podcasts, don't you?'

'I work for a station called Play Radio. I do a show on a Sunday night. It's the future. We don't screen anybody. You can sit there with your PC screen and have not only the sound coming out of it but all the various chatrooms with people talking about what they're listening to, so you build communities that come together. You can also go to the page that shows streamed moving TV pictures of what's going on in the studio. Not terribly interesting but better than the stills you get on most radio web pages, which refresh themselves every fifteen minutes. It's quite interesting to watch what the presenters are getting up to while they are reacting to the callers. It's the future and radio will struggle to compete once Internet broadcasting gets going. Everyone knows that but nobody knows what to do about it.'

'So what's the future for you?'

'I like to be unconventional. A bit radical. But at the same time to be as professional as possible. I'd like to get involved with a radio station and really shake it up, get involved with management. I'm very interested in the Internet. I also like football so I'd like to manage a football team. Maybe Brighton and Hove Albion.'

Talking to Tommy was something I thought I would never do. I once tried to call in to *The Human Zoo*, at around midnight, when he was talking about which football managers would make good ice skaters. Glenn Hoddle would, Arsène Wenger wouldn't, he decided, quite rightly. Bobby Robson wouldn't even be able to lace his skates. I wanted to phone in to suggest Ruud Gullit, but after a few minutes on hold realized that I probably wouldn't be able to get through. It is odd to speak to somebody on speaker-phone that you have only previously heard on the radio. I kept forgetting that Tommy was just talking to me and not to a whole audience, that at times my participation was required in the conversation. But then that was always Tommy Boyd's style, whether he was on talkSPORT and speaking to the nation or on Southern Counties Radio speaking to . . . well, Brighton, you always felt that he could be talking just to you, someone who had answers to your questions, that he was someone passionate about making a difference, rather than just being that bloke that used to work with Timmy Mallett on *Wackaday*.

7

RESONANCE 104.4 FM

'An oasis of subversion within a desert of corporate ass-
rimming; a place to hear tomorrow's new music today.'

(*NME*, about Resonance FM)

'Most modern Iranian music is substandard,' the lady on the radio says, 'but the next record is some exciting Afro-Persian jazz hip hop.'

I'm listening to Resonance FM, an arts-based London community station and the programme is *Six Pillars to Persia*. It is 1.30 in the afternoon, I am eating sandwiches at my desk and looking forward to the rest of the day, supplementing my data entry with something much more arty.

'From rebel artists and exiled writers to social entrepreneurs,' host Fari Bradley continues, 'we preview a picture of the hotch-potch that is the Iranian diaspora in the arts now.' She plays London-based Black Blooms and then the latest song by Pouya Mahmoodi, the Iranian guitarist.

The other night I was in the pub talking about radio. Most of my sentences nowadays begin with 'I was listening to Stuart Maconie', or 'Did anyone hear Geoff last night?' Some people seem to be too busy in their lives to listen to Geoff, although gratifyingly a couple of my friends have started to listen to him, and also some people I know have started tuning in to Nihal. There is nothing more enjoyable than introducing your friends to something they like, something they wouldn't have heard if it hadn't been for you. As I told my friends who are interested in music and radio about my conversations with Tommy Boyd and Bearsuit, the subject turned to other stations I should try out, and a few people around the table turned out to be unified in their love of Resonance FM. Immediately I knew it had to be one of the stations I listened to; no one was able to describe Resonance to me, they just shook their heads, smiled, told me to give it a listen, promised it would be worthwhile. The station's transmitter is at London Bridge, but only reaches as far as Zone 6, so its online presence is vital to those further afield, industrial estates all over the country. After the self-proclaimed hotchpotch of *Six Pillars to Persia* is *Creature Curios* – presenter Bridget Nicholls interviews Sir Patrick Bateson, Professor of Ethology at Cambridge University and the President of the Zoological Society of London.

'What made you want to study animals?' the youthful Nicholls asks her guest, an elderly man whose regal presence seems to be making his interviewer slightly nervous.

'There is a family member from generations ago who studied genetics; in fact it was he who gave it its name. And as I grew up I would hear stories about him, the family were so proud of this ancestor and his achievements. As a boy I would go off by myself in the afternoons studying woodland near my house. I became a birdwatcher. I told a teacher I wanted to do this for ever, and he suggested that if I did a PhD then I would indeed be able to do this for the rest of my life. So from an early age I was already geared to do a PhD. I became very interested in how animals and plants develop and that they react differently depending on their environment. I was intrigued, for example, that some creatures prickle if they are exposed to predators. That fascinated me, the way that organisms develop to evolve.'

'What about something like manners in humans?' Bridget asks. 'Are manners innate? In *Oliver Twist*, for example, it is suggested that Oliver's manners are passed down from his mother.'

'That's a good point. It's not the case, though, manners develop much later in life. They are influenced by surroundings.'

'And are they a sign of intelligence?' Nicholls asks.

'Not at all!' Sir Patrick replies with a chuckle. 'There are plenty of intelligent people who have no manners at all.'

His thoughts are somewhat surprisingly interrupted by the host, who takes the opportunity to put on a Country and Western song called 'Manners'.

'One of my recent studies was on how the immune system affects behaviour,' Professor Bateson continues after the song. 'That if you are stressed, if you have lost your job or are going through a divorce then you are much more likely to get cancer. The human body gets cancers all the time but they are flushed out. Our body is exquisitely tuned, it has the ability to tell the difference between real tissue and invading bacteria. In periods of stress, the immune system is suppressed. People do not realize the extent to which your stress levels are connected with the likelihood of getting cancer, but that is the case. A lot of creationists are of the opinion that nature, the way that bodies and organisms work, is something that could only have been made by a creator as it requires such intelligence, that it is too precise to have just happened. But Darwin felt he could disprove this theory. He lost his faith and as a result claimed that the argument could be turned upside down – that there are so many horrors in the natural world which a divine creator would never have initiated. It is important to remember that the meaning of life is a non-scientific question, understanding life is not the same as understanding evolution.'

'So tell me about studies of animal behaviour you have been involved with.'

'Well, in central Moscow feral dogs get on trains, change trains, go to the market, eat fresh food, then come home.'

'That's amazing! Do they not get booted out by ticket inspectors?' she asks with a genuine thirst for information.

'No.'

'How do they know where to go?'

'There's actually a man who works on the Metro who is doing research into it. A theory is that one or more of the dogs may have been a pet at one time and travelled the routes with its owner, and therefore know innately where to go.'

'That's fascinating, Sir Patrick. Unfortunately, we've run out of time,' Nicholls tells her guest. 'And we've barely touched most of the subjects I wanted to talk to you about. We'll have to invite you back soon to continue our conversation.' Despite the lack of time she still plays a Country and Western song called 'The Monkey'.

Wendy Jones is in conversation with Will Ashon, whose new book *The Heritage* has recently been released.

'What's it about?' Jones asks. 'I couldn't follow it!'

'It's a 33-year-old woman telling the story of a friendship she had when she was fifteen that went off the rails,' Ashon explains.

'It's not as normal as that though. Would you say it's a future dystopia?'

'Well kind of, although I wouldn't say it's sci-fi,' the affable Ashon replies. 'It's just a slightly altered version of the real world, perhaps ten years in the future. It's like the amp on Spinal Tap that is turned up to eleven, it's just slightly tweaked from reality.'

'Can you explain your DNA idea to us?'

'I'm not from a science background, and it isn't intended to be scientific, but I had been reading in the papers about increasing uses of DNA. I heard people on the radio saying things like "We're sleepwalking into a surveillance society" yet these people are happy to have a Tesco Club Card if it means that they get special offers, even though your shopping habits are being broken down to work out the products you buy, how regularly you go to the supermarket and on which days. I found something on the Net where if you send this company a swab they'll tell you about your racial heritage. People make a big deal about this kind of thing but ultimately it shouldn't affect you. If I discover that my great-grandfather was black, for example, then that doesn't affect who I am or the way I behave just because someone has handed me a printout.'

'In your book you suggest a criminal gene. A baby is injected with this crime gene.'

'It's a mythical gene though. It ties in with the Blairite tough on crime, tough on the causes of crime. I'm not being coherent here, am I!'

'I'm enjoying it.'

'Excellent. Interestingly incoherent.'

'So what about genetics? Do they provide answers?'

'Well, that is what people want to believe, that it can provide clarity in certain situations. But there are people who are much more knowledgeable about DNA than I am who will tell you that it can't provide a final answer.'

'Lyrically, the book soars towards the end. Can you read some of it for us?' the presenter asks.

'I've never read any of it out loud before. I'm not sure if I can, five of the six characters are female, it makes me feel slightly strange.'

'If you don't want to you don't have to.'

'Well . . .'

'I've folded the page over for you,' she tells him, sweetly.

'Oh, you've selected which bit? Okay then.' Ashon's voice tenses as he reads an extract which includes fucks and shits.

'I love the speed and energy of your writing,' Jones, a kindly woman, tells him with motherly praise when he puts the book down. 'The rhythm of the language is incredible, I love the way the characters speak to each other.'

'I think teenagers' accents have changed in the last ten years. The way people used to speak once depended on the region they came from, but now the way kids speak is a combination of the language their parents use and where they have grown up, as well as cultural influences, idiosyncrasies brought over from America that have been absorbed through music and TV.'

'You actually run a hip hop label. Tell me about that.'

'It's called Big Dada. I wrote my first book on my palm pilot on the Tube going to and from work. Although it sounds very exciting to run a hip hop label it's essentially an admin job, chasing up stock, completing paperwork, making calls.'

'Do you think writers have a secondary creativity?'

'Well, most writers need to have a second job, I'm not sure if it's anything to do with creativity.'

'That's right, T.S. Eliot worked in a bank, didn't he? We've just had an email in, by the way, complaining about the swearing from the extract you read.'

'I did wonder about that!' Ashon says, laughing. 'You made me do it!'

'I know. I don't think of it as swearing if it's in a book though.'

'Really?' he asks, slightly incredulous at a lack of awareness that you imagine wouldn't be tolerated on more mainstream stations.

I go to the kitchen to get myself a drink but as soon as I walk through the doorway I stop and instinctively think about turning back, vaulting back to my seat. Poppy is stood with her back to the wall, her arms folded, her eyes pink and blotchy.

'Are you okay?' I ask, rising to the challenge. She nods, dabbing her eyes with the corner of a threadbare tissue. I don't know why she's crying. Maybe she's had bad news. Maybe she's having relationship troubles. Maybe she just trapped her little finger in the cutlery drawer. I decide not to ask, it's not really any of my business. Instead I pull down on the roll of kitchen towel, tear off a piece like I've beheaded a dragon and hand it to her. I look at the kettle in the corner, clicked to on but the plug out of its socket. She smiles as I correct her mistake.

'Do you want tea?' I ask, reaching down two mugs.

'Yes please.'

I know how she takes her tea. Milk, one sugar. This is information I shouldn't know.

'Do you want milk and sugar?'

'Yes please. Milk, one sugar.'

As the kettle purrs I battle with words in my head, try to for-
mulate a sentence, hoping that it comes out at least vaguely
coherently. I stand there next to her not saying anything, it's like
we're playing hide and seek and I'm counting to one hundred. I
am clutching for straws, do not know what to say.

'I heard a story on the radio the other day,' I tell her, and
she turns, seems interested as I tell her the story Sandra told
Christian O'Connell . . . 'Six days later they were married,'
I conclude, and the kitchen fills with Poppy's smile. I fill the
two mugs with hot water, spoon the teabags into the pedal bin
and go back to my desk. She smiles at me as she walks past back
to her seat.

At four o'clock the show on air is called *Radia*. The sound of
someone doing the washing-up is accompanied by battle cries,
horses' hooves, cheers. I start to daydream, stare at my computer
screen like it's a vortex, and get swept into the world of Resonance FM. When something is so far from normality it can be
best to cast aside cynicism, leave the world you are familiar with
behind you and immerse yourself in this other universe being
offered to you, otherwise you may as well not bother listening at
all. The battle cries continue, as does the sound of running water,
pots and pans being scraped, rinsed. Then the battle stops, sounds
become more mundane, a bumblebee, a piano playing, the sound
of chopping vegetables. *The Archers* without dialogue.

*

It is 5.30, I say goodbye to Alan Medlicott and Craig, unplug my headphones from the computer, turn everything off and look forward to getting home to carry on listening to Resonance FM. I haven't looked at today's schedule, I don't want to know what will happen next. On its website, the station describes itself as 'a box of curiosities' and it is this that makes it unlike any radio I have ever heard. It has the beauty of an overheard conversation, listening to Resonance is like talking to strangers on a train; a conversation begins, you get a brief snapshot of somebody's life before they get off at the next station, their seat taken by someone else with a story to tell.

'I don't know which fader is operating which CD but that's nothing unusual,' says Paul, presenter of *The Art Rocker Show*. 'Here's some high-energy garage rock.' He plays the new single by Muck and the Myers.

'Here's a song by White Denim, bluesy garage rock from Austin, Texas. I've just got back from a big meeting with the editors at *Art Rocker* deciding whether White Denim should be on the cover of next month's magazine. We decided yes.'

He plays songs by Experimental Dental School, Too Hot to Sweat, Water Makes the Blades Blunt, and perhaps the best name of all – Cutting Pink with Knives. For people involved with new music, whether it's a show on radio or a magazine, I imagine they have hundreds, if not thousands of CDs to get through, and so if a band has a name that makes them stand out, or has songs with eye-catching titles or artwork, then they are more likely to get listened to. If I was preparing a radio show there is no way a band called Cutting Pink with Knives would lie in the box untouched. I might not like it but it would definitely get first listen. I would love to be in the position where I could lean towards a microphone and say 'That was the new single by Super Furry Animals.' To have a box of records to listen to, to be able to refer to headphones as cans.

'Hello, I'm your floor,' says a voice at 6.30. 'This is a weekly show, recorded from the perspective of the floor,' continues the voice, which I imagine belongs to a teenager who wears Dr Who pyjamas and is allergic to soya. 'I am currently lying down, my head is about seven inches from the ground. It's a wooden floor, laminated. I'm wearing shoes and corduroy trousers that make a swish sound. I might half watch a film later. I'm going to say goodbye now, and leave you to your floor.'

Which is exactly what he does. We hear footsteps, the faint blare of a TV, murmurs of voices in another room, the words inaudible. This goes on for half an hour. I can't work out whether it's the weirdest show I've ever heard, or the work of genius.

'It's probably polite to fade out now so there can be a jingle or something and another programme can start. Today's floor has been my living room. Goodbye from me, and goodbye from my floor. Or by now, your floor.'

Slum Dum is on at seven o'clock, a show in which a new album is featured each week. Today's is *Let Your Xs be Ys* by the Brazilian soul jazz duo Tetine. I am so enthralled with Resonance that I don't want to miss out for a minute, especially after spending so much time with stations and DJs that don't seem to care about what they are doing. These people at Resonance love radio, they know how exciting it can be. I decide cooking is out of the question, there's nothing in my fridge or cupboards other than jam and Rice Krispies. On my kitchen noticeboard takeaway menus are displayed like treasured family photographs. I take one down for a local Indian. I want to order the meal deal of chicken jalfrezi, pilau rice, plain naan, onion baji, but it sounds too lonely to ask for a 'Meal for One'. You know you spend too much time by yourself when even people who work in local takeaway restaurants let out a sympathetic 'aah' when you place your order. So I get a vindaloo.

At eight o'clock, waiting for the doorbell, I listen to Stephen Ball present *Breath: Polymers and Pneumatics*.

'This was specially recorded yesterday,' Ball tells us. 'A breathing performance by Australian artist Irene Barberis, a collaboration between the Royal Melbourne Institute of Technology and Saint Martin's College, London. The exhibition brings together artists exploring cultural movement, a re-imagining of space, movement as part of everyday life.' Barberis takes over from Ball.

'This exhibition is a snapshot of contemporary urban space, a lens with which to view the interaction between social, cultural, political and psychological forces of globalization,' she explains. 'We all have a first and a last breath that are remembered; other than that, they all disappear, are forgotten. In life, we are all sharing breath. I am surrounded by fluorescent pink polymer tubes. I'm inflating the shapes so that my breath is captured. By blowing up these forms I am instilling a measure of my life into a defined area.'

After using a lot of this precious breath to explain a slightly baffling concept, Barberis blows up one of the PVC tubes. And

then another. And another. And when I get back from the door
after paying the man for my food and putting the complimentary
onion salad straight in the bin, she is still blowing up these
mysterious tubes. By the time I have finished eating she is
still blowing them up. I sit, listening, wondering whether anyone has just tuned in now and is baffled to hear nothing but
what sounds like balloons being blown up. When Irene Barberis
explained the concept I thought it can't be . . . she can't just . . .
it is, it's just a woman blowing into things. But once you have
started listening to something like this you can't just stop, you
have to find out what happens, what the pay-off is going to be.
In the end she blows into tubes for twenty-five minutes. At
times, when she is out of breath, it sounds a bit like sex noise.
But sometimes that's just not enough.

The next example of someone obsessed with sound is
Riccardo Iacono, whose artwork revolves around making strange
noises. We hear a clip of him throwing wet clothes around the
entrance to the Elephant and Castle Tube station, and another at
the same location, throwing frozen peas. We hear a clip from a
video on his website.

'What are you doing?' an onlooker asks.

'Throwing peas.'

'Why?'

'It makes sounds,' he explains. 'It's like drumming.'

'What kind of sound does it make?' he asks, bewildered.

'It depends what it hits.'

'Why are you doing this?'

'Art.'

*

'I've got a new bank account that lets me have infinite money,' Tom Bell reveals during *Indie Cops*, on at nine o'clock. 'There's a special infinity button on some cashpoints, and when you press it, you get infinite money.'

'Yeah, I've been stuck behind someone getting infinity out of a cashpoint before. It took ages. I missed my train.'

Comedians Tom Bell and Terry Saunders create whole worlds in the comfort of the Resonance studio. Today is a repeat of their *Hallowe'en Special*. The rain is pouring down, they are walking down the street, and hear a cat meow.

'It's funny how the rain stops as soon as the cat meows.'

'Well I can only play one special effect at once. They're all on the same CD.'

'Or maybe it's a cat that controls the rain? Listen . . . it's stopped meowing, and the rain has started again.'

'Hey, Tom. Let's go in this haunted house which has probably got a door that creaks when you open it.'

The door creaks.

'Wow! Look at all this food. Let's eat some. What are you having?'

'Bread. You?'

'Grapes. Lovely grapes. What are you eating now?'

'Some salad. You?'

'Grapes. Lovely, lovely grapes.'

'I'm having tiramisu now. What are you having?'

'Well, I suppose I could do a switcheroo, but I'm going to stick with grapes.'

A clock strikes midnight.

'Wow, look at all those ghosts! That's a heck of a lot of ghosts!

This is really scary! Have you brought your ghost-busting equipment with you?'

'No. It's really heavy. Remember last time when I carried it all the way across that big field and didn't meet any ghosts. That was a waste of time.'

'Look. There's the ghost of a pirate.'

'Are you sure he's a pirate? He's carrying a receipt saying "Pirate Costume". And they don't traditionally wear white trainers.'

'I think we could have been more scared in this episode.'

'Look! There's a lot of dead bodies!'

'And in this cupboard is the band Architecture in Helsinki.'

Tom and Terry close the show with a track from the new Architecture in Helsinki album, then say their goodbyes.

At 11 p.m. is *The Glass Shrimp* which plays obscure music, a lot of it from Finland, Iceland, Germany. This is what I want to be doing, I don't know how many listeners Resonance has at this time of night, but even if the only person who has tuned in is me then the time the two presenters have put into choosing which songs to play, putting the show together, leaving their house, getting on the Tube, bleeping their Oyster cards is all worthwhile. I assume they have jobs, careers, live lives as routine as the rest of us, but in the evenings they play Half Man Half Biscuit on the radio. They are doing exactly what I want to do. I decide that my challenge set down by Sandra, to do what you want to do, has to involve radio. I look on the Internet for how to apply to volunteer at Resonance FM. But then I have a better idea, think more locally and see if there are any community stations in

Norwich. I find Future Radio, a station that began broadcasting last year and is within walking distance from my house. I email them, tell them I'm a big fan of radio and would love to get involved.

The thought of being involved with Future Radio excites me and I look forward to opening up my emails tomorrow, staring at my inbox, clicking on refresh, waiting to hear from them. I open a bottle of beer and listen to obscure German electro followed by two teenagers with guitars in London and time seems to stop still; it's just me and loud music. I go to bed during Max Tundra's show, who plays the Butthole Surfers and John Cooper Clarke.

'I'd like to dedicate this show to a woman I saw crying on the Tube today,' he says. 'I hope she's all right.'

8

THE JAZZ

'I'm Digby Fairweather, excited about spending a couple of jazz hours with you.'

After spending another Saturday afternoon listening to Liverpool lose at football on Five Live, I get a phone call inviting me to a party tonight in London. I say I'm not going but when I look at the state of the kitchen I decide a party will be more fun than doing the washing-up, scrubbing the hob, ironing work shirts. Three hours later I am at Liverpool Street with a bag of beer and a big smile on my face.

I have fun at the party and am glad I went, but by six in the morning most people still haven't been to bed and I can't face spending any more time in a room that smells of Jägermeister, my head resting on empty beer cans where a pillow should be. I make my way out of the house, walk through the cold streets of Shoreditch, and arrive at the deserted station, negotiating the departures board through squinting eyes that want peace and quiet. My train home leaves at 7.32 a.m., and with the help of bus replacement services I arrive back in Norwich almost four hours later. I was really pleased I got to hang around Ipswich train station for an hour, that is exactly how I wanted to spend my morning.

Back in my flat I feel too awake to sleep, yet at the same time too tired to do anything other than curl up in my bed and feel sorry for myself. With drawn curtains thick enough to block out the concept of daytime, my last task before closing my eyes and waiting for everything to be better is to put the radio on. No station seems appropriate though, I am in no mood to hear voices and certainly not the sound of laughter, in fact noise of any description is pretty unwelcome. I find a station called The Jazz and listen as I lie rocking under my duvet in the foetal position.

The Jazz launched on Christmas Day 2006 and its aim was to build up an audience in a similar way that its sister station, Classic FM, had done years earlier, playing songs people recognized without being pretentious. The market existed due to Jazz FM being forced to rename itself at the insistence of Ofcom. There had been complaints from listeners who had accused Jazz FM of pandering to more accessible music; playing too much soul and R&B at the expense of scat and bebop. In 2005 the station rebranded itself as Smooth FM to give it more scope with the music it played. When the DAB multiplex was formed, Ofcom declared that one station should cover jazz properly, and The Jazz was born.

With a mixture of rum and red wine continually pumping through my bloodstream, I listen to Claire Anderson and as she plays Peggy Lee and Frank Sinatra I am lulled into gentle sleep. I can hear the music, but take a welcome break from the twenty-first century, lyrics like 'Two for tea and tea for two' mean that there is no way I can be in the same era as I was this morning, eating falafel at Ipswich train station and listening to MP3s on my mobile phone. As Louis Armstrong blows his trumpet my digital radio morphs into a gramophone, my boxer shorts and T-shirt transform into a tuxedo and Ella Fitzgerald takes my hand and leads me to the dance floor. Barbershop quartets woo groups of girls, a starlet with blonde ringlets is spread atop a grand piano and I'm dancing the tango with the girlfriends of American soldiers.

At eleven o'clock it is *Legends of Jazz* with Ramsay Lewis, featuring music from what he calls the Great Performers. Lewis is a jazz legend himself, with three Grammies to his name and having been personally invited to perform at the White House by Bill Clinton. His show is not recorded for The Jazz, it is a syndicated programme to over sixty-five US cities. He tells us he will be playing Quincy Jones, Miles Davis, John Coltrane. Lewis's voice is gravelly and oozes Chicago charm.

He speaks to legendary crooner Tony Bennett in his hotel room in New York.

'You sound very peaceful,' Lewis tells the man he describes as the 'youngest 81-year-old in the world'.

'It is very gratifying to be accepted,' Bennett tells us. 'I sell out every venue I play.'

'And do you feel the love from the audience?'

'Yes.'

As conversations go it isn't making me want to rise from my stupor. The interview seems to do nothing other than confirm that Tony Bennett is still alive, and to remind both Bennett and anyone listening that he is very successful.

After two of his records the interview continues. Tony Bennett moans about record companies not supporting jazz, and after a version of 'I Left My Heart in San Francisco' he reveals that he has founded a school in New York to help young people find their way in the arts. It hasn't had a single dropout, every person who joined the school has ended up in college.

'We take the kids to the Louvre,' he tells Lewis. 'We give them the chance to sing at Carnegie Hall. One day we will be the best school in the world.'

Lewis plays another Tony Bennett song, then closes his show with the theme tune to *The Pink Panther*.

'Happy birthday to my mum,' Jacqui Dankworth says to start her show. 'Here she is performing at the London Palladium a few years ago.' Dankworth's mum turns out to be Dame Cleo Laine and we listen to her singing 'I'm Going to Sit Right Down and Write Myself a Letter'.

The show plays new songs as well as old, and after being treated to the best jazz songs of the last fifty years by Ramsay Lewis, Jacqui Dankworth seems keen to emphasize that the future of jazz is every bit as exciting, rich and varied as its heritage. I am snoozing again and still haven't fully roused from my slumber. Every time I think I am awake it is a false start, my eyes close again and I lie there thinking that I should be doing something useful with my day. I picture families tucking into their Sunday dinners, couples taking long walks in the countryside, groups of mates watching football in the pub. I am under my duvet and need a poo.

*

'Three tracks in a row to start the show while I take my coat off,' Digby Fairweather says to start his 1 p.m. programme, followed by a vaguely threatening trailer, urging us to listen to The Jazz. Digby started off as a jazz performer, becoming a fan of jazz in the 1960s when the likes of Louis Armstrong and Duke Ellington were still performing live. He talks about them affectionately, as though beloved family members. Fairweather had been an outspoken critic of Jazz FM before its re-branding, describing it as a station that 'despite its worthy beginnings was later responsible for both the attempted rape, and (fortunately aborted) re-definition of the music'.

Part of his show is called Dixieland Corner. He treats us to twenty minutes of Duke Ellington and I manage to stay awake for the duration, puffing out my cheeks to the sound of the trumpets.

At five o'clock it is The Jazz's regular interview slot where a guest plays their favourite jazz music. In the past the show's host Helen Mayhew, who also presents a weekday evening show on the station, has spoken to Michael Parkinson, Herbie Hancock and Diana Krall. This week it is the turn of eighties pop star Rick Astley, who has sold 40 million records worldwide. An interview about the jazz in Rick Astley's record collection is not something I would normally expect to tune in to. I would turn the radio off right now, if only I could feel my fingers.

'I've learnt to laugh at myself,' Astley tells Mayhew. 'If you were a pop star in the 1980s you kind of had to.'

The first song played on the show is 'Never Gonna Give You Up', Rick Astley's debut single that went to number 1 and immediately changed his life.

'How did you get into music?' Mayhew asks.

'My sister took me to see a band called Camel when I was about ten and that had a massive impact on me. I only saw my mum at weekends because when my parents split up I was brought up by my dad. He was very musical, there were always records playing in our house and me and my brothers and sisters all loved *The Jungle Book*. Even now if we all got together we'd be able to sing along to every word.'

This segues into 'I Wanna Be Like You' by Louis Prima and for the first time all day I find myself singing along to the words.

'We lived in Newton-le-Willows, near Manchester, and my dad owned a garden centre. He used to let me play drums in one of the greenhouses and every day after school I would sit there drumming for hours.'

'Were you in bands?'

'Yeah. The first band I was in was called Give Way, because our guitarist had nicked a Give Way sign from the end of his road and we propped it in front of the drum kit. I used to both play drums and sing, but in the end we had to get another drummer in because it wasn't really working, so then I was just the singer. I was a very average kid and for the first time girls were interested in me because I was in a band.'

'What song would you like played next?' Helen Mayhew asks in her best Sue Lawley voice.

'The other week I was in Las Vegas,' he says, and immediately backtracks, insisting that his life isn't as glamorous as that statement had implied. 'I went into a shop and this was playing, I hadn't heard it for years and it brought back very vivid memories of watching Charlie Brown and seeing Linus playing piano.'

Mayhew plays 'Linus and Lucy' by Vince Guaraldi and Astley seems genuinely moved to hear it again.

'I left school on the first day I was legally allowed to,' he says, continuing the story of his adolescence. 'I was still in the band and Pete Waterman, who was becoming a big producer at the time, had a girlfriend who lived in the same town as me. She worked in a hairdresser's below a venue we used to play in; he came and watched us one day and invited me to London. Stock, Aitken and Waterman had just had their first number 1, but they were still not established. I signed a deal with them, they released my first single "Never Gonna Give You Up" and it went straight to the top.'

'And your next record?'

'This is by a band that doesn't exist any more, but their jazz influence cannot be disputed. It's called "Selfless, Cold and Composed" and it's by Ben Folds Five.'

I sit bolt upright. Ben Folds Five are one of my all-time favourite bands. Their best-known song 'Underground' is one of my favourite songs. Maybe me and Rick Astley are more similar than I thought.

'What does the future hold for you?' Mayhew asks.

'Well my wife is a producer . . .'

'. . . she was nominated for an Oscar.'

'Blimey. You've done your research. Yes, my wife's a producer of short films and she suggested I write a musical film. So far I'm really enjoying it. Also, I am touring again. It's more fun than ever before. I went straight from doing pubs to performing at Wembley Stadium and so missed out on average-sized gigs. Obviously I wouldn't be able to get close to selling out stadiums now, nor would I want to, but smaller venues are more important, more enjoyable. When I was performing at Wembley it might as well have been my brother on stage, no one would have been any the wiser.'

'And your final choice of song?'

'"Cry Me a River". The best song ever written.'

Listening to Rick Astley was the stimulus I needed, to hear voices rather than saxophones, conversations rather than riffs. It was also nice to have an hour-long programme that did not pause for adverts. At one point I even got up from under my duvet and ate a yoghurt.

At six o'clock it is Margherita Taylor who presents *Easy Jazz*. Within half an hour though I start to find the continuous jazz music tedious. At its best jazz can be beautiful, emotive, with saxophones that put a beaming smile on your face. At worst it sounds like the music people hang themselves to. I have not been the most attentive of listeners today, what with the snoozing and trips to the toilet, but I have managed to educate myself in the world of jazz and am almost starting to feel like an aficionado. Listening to Margherita Taylor under my duvet, I realize that this isn't the way jazz is supposed to be listened to. In fact, I'm not sure this is the way a 25-year-old should be behaving. Jazz had not sounded right in my bedroom. It did not make me want to take a trip to Ronnie Scott's in London, look up Norwich jazz cafés in the *Yellow Pages* or track down the records of Weather Report, but it struck me that perhaps it wasn't the music that was the problem, it was me; I was not giving jazz a chance. I open my curtains and let some fresh air into the flat. I shower and change my clothes. I look in the mirror, my eyeballs are the colour of malt. I flex my muscles, stretch my limbs, and, taking deep breaths, realize that I have survived the afternoon, and so I turn up the radio and look forward to a whole new evening ahead. I bebop out of my bedroom, recover my phone from last night's trousers and decide to make a few calls. I will continue listening to The Jazz for the rest of the day but need to change things around a bit. I scroll through my phonebook and invite people to my flat. I switch on the radio in the living room, find a pack of dog-eared playing cards in the drawer where I keep bottle openers, Sellotape and pencils that need sharpening, and set up a poker table, using Monopoly money as chips.

Half an hour later my friends turn up at my flat, hand me their bottles of wine and sit down at the table. I invited four people round; if you listen to enough Duke Ellington you find yourself doing everything in quartets.

'We're going to be listening to jazz,' I tell my guests, motioning towards the radio in the corner of the room. The music fits in with the surroundings; we add our own percussion with corks squeezing out of bottles, splashes of wine and the clinks of glasses.

I shuffle the cards to the sound of Cole Porter, and as the Monopoly money is thrown around the table, Dizzy Gillespie and Miles Davis cheer us on. I tell my guests what I can remember from last night's party, reveal my day of hibernation and that I now like Rick Astley.

At nine o'clock Courtney Pine takes the ropes with his weekly hour-long contemporary jazz show, *The Courtney Pine X-Perience*, which Digby Fairweather described this afternoon as 'one long sixty-minute groove'.

At 9:40 Courtney reads out the week's jazz calendar, an eclectic mix of events in theatres, wine bars, sculpture exhibitions and hotel lobbies held in places like Aylesbury, Winchester, the Barbican. That is where jazz is meant to be appreciated, not in my bedroom muffled under a duvet. At ten o'clock Pine is finished and I decide to turn off The Jazz. It has been playing in my flat for almost twelve hours now. I lost at poker after a series of unwise bluffs. But the defeat is made sweeter by the fact that when he thought no one was looking, I saw my friend Paddy, long out of the poker game, engrossed with the music, plucking at an imaginary double bass.

9

THE *RADIO TIMES*

*'Hardly a day passes without someone in the house shouting
"Anyone seen the Radio Times?"'*
(John Peel in his introduction to *The Radio Times Story*)

In 1923 a magazine was launched to advise the public on official BBC programmes available on a newly invented gadget called the wireless. The *Radio Times* was an immediate success with a weekly circulation that soon exceeded 600,000. Issue one already had a letters page, still present today, printing not only correspondence of support but also criticism, never more than when the magazine has its revamp, often at the arrival of a new editor. Regular readers do not like change; any typographical adjustment, decrease of column space or change of colour will result in letters signed 'Yours, disgusted'. A 1984 relaunch provoked one man to write in saying, 'The new *Radio Times* is an impregnable mess.'

When my dad brought the *Radio Times* home every Tuesday it provided a new sense of optimism in our house. No matter how bad school had been that day we had something to look forward to. Me and my sister would be excited about fresh programmes on offer, never-seen-before episodes of *Neighbours*, pages of film reviews, the week mapped out ahead of us in a pristine, glossy magazine. By the end of the week the corners were dog-eared, the staples were hanging on a thread, the crossword wrongly filled in, and it lay neglected as soon as the next shinier, glossier issue was out. The most exciting edition was always the bumper Christmas Special, which had specially commissioned artwork with a festive drawing of a snowman, Santa, mistletoe or Del Boy. No matter how much tinsel there was in our living room at home, regardless of how many fairy lights were on trees down our road, how many times I had heard Slade and Cliff Richard, for me it was always when I saw the festive edition of the *Radio Times* resting on a chair in our living room that I was hit with the realization that it was Christmas again.

Over the years the publication has become a national institution, and to be featured on its cover is as much a status symbol as being asked to appear on *Desert Island Discs* or being honoured by the Queen. Past front covers of the *Radio Times* display a history of broadcasting. You can watch the ageing process of those famous enough to have graced the front cover several times: Terry Wogan, Delia Smith, Jonathan Ross, Deirdre Barlow. The publication has lived through wars and strikes and has been at the centre of massive world changes, including the invention of television and shortly afterwards, Channel Five.

Even though other listings magazines are available, as the

BBC is obliged to issue reminders, the *Radio Times* continues to be as important as ever. Despite competition from the Internet and weekend newspaper supplements, the publication is still as relevant today, in a world of Sky Plus and *Big Brother's Little Brother*, as when it was first launched, in the days when people said 'hullo' and read by candlelight.

After a speculative email to the *Radio Times*, I am invited to meet its editor, Gill Hudson, at her BBC office to talk about her involvement with radio. I ask Alan Medlicott for the day off and he checks his diary, scratching his head like a *Countdown* contestant during the Conundrum.

'Do you need to know now?' he asks. I don't know whether to let him know I never really do anything at work, that my continued employment is baffling. With the date Hudson suggested two weeks away, I tell Alan Medlicott he can get back to me. It seems bizarre that it's easier to arrange a meeting with the editor of the *Radio Times* than to get someone to cover my data input for one day.

I feel like a tourist as I arrive at the world-famous BBC Television Centre in sparkling sunshine and think of all the names to have trod the same path I walk along. I watch black cabs zip through parking barriers and wonder about the cast of characters that have been driven in and out of this car park. I walk into the building I have seen so many times on television, announce who I am to the man with spiky hair behind the desk, and, reading from the printout I pull out of my pocket, state the name of the assistant who is to meet me and accompany me. The receptionist tells me I am in the wrong building, and BBC Worldwide is up the road just beyond the flyover. I turn and walk back outside thinking that I should be back in Norwich, I am out of my depth.

I arrive at the right place fifteen minutes later, wet from a burst of rain, and already late for my appointment. I apologize and am escorted from the reception desk, up the stairs, along corridors lined with celebrated *RT* covers, Stephen Fry, Paul McCartney, Dr Who, Pudsey Bear. We walk through open-plan offices bustling with people meeting deadlines, editing interviews, and into a little room where the *Radio Times* radio critic Jane Anderson is waiting with Gill Hudson. I recognize both immediately because their photographs are in the magazine every week alongside their columns. After I've plucked my Dictaphone and a list of questions from my bag they ask me the not unreasonable question of who I am.

'What is your connection with radio?' Jane asks, once the introductions have been dealt with.

'I listen all the time,' I tell her. 'I listen to a different station every day and am trying to learn about people that work with radio.'

'Okay,' Gill says, nodding her head. She seems to accept my explanation rather than call for me to be escorted back into the rain.

I begin with my first question. 'To what extent has digital radio changed your listening patterns?'

'For me, not at all,' Jane Anderson tells me. 'But for a lot of people it has made a huge difference. Fifty-five per cent of people listening to radio are aged fifty-five or older. They like to be able to book an appointment with a certain show. Schedulers are very aware of the listening patterns of the majority of the audience – hence putting *Front Row* on after *The Archers*, that way it creates thousands of extra listeners. The drawback of picking and choosing your radio programmes, as more and more young people who have been brought up in a different technological world are doing, is that it denies the possibility of finding programmes by accident. People like the eclectic mix. They like doing the ironing not knowing what's going to come on next.'

'I listened to a show the other day about Mexican pottery,' Gill Hudson chips in. 'There's no way I would ever choose to download a programme like that. I wouldn't have picked it out as something to listen to. And it was one of the best shows I've heard for weeks.'

'And that is why people listen to Radio 4,' Jane Anderson says. 'It has a sense of community. The joy of discovery is something that most digital stations can't touch.'

'Are there too many radio stations?' I ask.

'That's like asking if there are too many books. A radio station has to have quality or a function or a genre group that it appeals to so that there is a point to it. If there are lots of stations doing the same kind of thing then it is pointless. But as long as there are radio stations that serve a role then there isn't really a limit.'

'That's when things like the *Radio Times* become useful,' Jane adds, gesturing to next week's copy, hot off the press on the table between us. 'The more stations there are, the more guidance people need. So there isn't really an exhaustible amount of stations.'

'I can imagine having a radio station on every street if there was the demand for it,' Hudson says. 'The point is, is it any good? Does it have a function? Do people want to hear it? This is why things like hospital radio and student radio survive and flourish. If there was this micro radio station in your own street, people could call and say "I've got a leak, can anyone help?" and someone would come round or phone to give advice. The show wouldn't necessarily be of a high quality but it would have a function, a clear target audience. This is what the management at radio stations need to be aware of.'

'On XFM for a long time they had no presenter between ten in the morning and four in the afternoon. Do you think commercial radio is in decline?' I ask.

'Commercial radio is in a tricky state at the moment,' Jane Anderson says. 'It is easy to forget how strong a position it could find itself in if they got it right. The BBC needs something to respond to.'

'Instead of having a presenter, they played an automated voice,' I explain to a confused-looking editor of the *Radio Times*. 'It was like the speaking clock, simply stating the name of singer and song.'

'I'm not convinced that getting rid of a presenter is the best step forward. But it's because of the cutback in funding that these stations are being forced into big decisions. The problem with a lot of commercial stations, particularly the genre music stations, is that they aren't particularly billable, they are very difficult to review. With stations like The Jazz, all you can say is "they play lots of jazz".'

'Do you think radio gets enough media coverage?' I ask.

'Don't get me started!' Jane says, laughing.

'The only thing that has made it sexy recently is that technology has finally caught up. We have been the poor relations for a long time. One of the issues we have at the magazine, and we practically invented the genre and helped it grow, is how difficult it is to produce a front cover relating to radio. When someone is at a news-stand the decision to purchase is taken in less than two seconds. You must have an immediately identifiable face. There aren't as many instantly identifiable figures on radio as there are on television for obvious reasons – you see them on telly, you don't see them on radio. A picture of John Humphrys on his own on the front cover, you can maybe do it once, but you can't do it regularly, so there's an inbuilt problem with the lack of visibility of some of the presenters.'

'Another problem radio has,' Jane Anderson says, 'is if you listen to something like *Front Row*, they will give you the breakdown of what's on at the cinema, the theatre, art galleries and on the television, but you do not get any feature about radio.'

'What is very interesting to me,' Gill says, 'is that you don't have to look back too many years ago to when viewing figures for some of the soaps would be twenty million plus. Twenty-four million viewers watched *To the Manor Born* one Christmas. You can see why television commanded such attention. Now look at the figures. People say a show is a success if it attracts around five million. Compare that with the listening figures for radio and they're pretty much matching TV figures now. *The Afternoon Play* can pull in around two million. Afternoon television shows would be thrilled at that kind of response. Surely there is a reason now to give radio a bigger share of the limelight. There has been a shift recently, a massive shift.'

'What about national newspapers? How well do they cover radio?'

'It's non-existent in the tabloids,' Jane says, spitting the 't' word out like corked wine. 'Broadsheets do a good job. But the radio section is always tucked away . . . You need to get television viewers to say hold on, I watch Jonathan Ross on TV, I'll give his radio show a go.'

According to Jane: 'One of the really lovely things about this job, and it sounds like I'm name-dropping now, but I've had people like Helen Mirren phone me in my office. Big stars would not normally speak to the likes of me, but because she's appearing in a play on Radio 4 she's phoning me from Hollywood and is so enthusiastic, even though it's for no money. There is something about radio that can attract that calibre of personality. It isn't about big fees.

'It's because they can have more control. There is no interference, they can just get on with it. Whereas TV is a nightmare. People have a genuine affection for Radio 4. We've had Sigourney Weaver and Ian McKellen in specifically to talk about their new radio projects.

'Look at Bob Dylan. The most private man in the world. But my God when he does his radio programme he's terrific! It's riveting, so eclectic.'

'What changes would you make in radio?' I ask.

'There aren't enough women on the radio,' Jane Anderson says, without the need to chew the question over. 'I'd like to change that. We need more female voices. I have to say that Radio 1 is extremely good at getting women on the radio. Also I was pleased with the choice of Kirsty Young as the new host of *Desert Island Discs*.'

'One thing that sticks out in my mind,' Gill says, 'is the *Desert Island Discs* with Yoko Ono. The chat show is dead but with things like *Desert Island Discs* you really find out about people, it reveals much more about personalities than any chat show ever could. That's why it continues to work so well. The Yoko Ono interview was extraordinary. Extraordinary. When she was pregnant at forty-two she decided she would have Sean Lennon aborted. She's not talked about this before, ever. It was so moving when she talked about her husband dying in her arms.'

'What's your most memorable day of covering radio?' I ask.

'For me it is the day I got a phone call asking me to comment on the death of John Peel. For years he had a regular *Radio Times* column, it was one of the most popular features of the magazine. But I wasn't aware he had died. So I rang the BBC press office to check what had happened and they were all in tears. And so were my colleagues. It was bleak and depressing but it was certainly the most memorable.'

This seems a good place to end the interview. I have already been with Jane and Gill longer than I anticipated and do not want to outstay my welcome. I thank them and they give me a copy of next week's magazine, hot off the press, and a book about the history of the *Radio Times*. I head to a nearby café to get some lunch, making the most of my day off, Broadcasting House behind me in glorious sunshine, and I think of Alan Medlicott and Craig hunched over at their desks while I eat a panini on the promenade with a renewed desire to know much more about radio.

10

BBC RADIO HUMBERSIDE

'A few knocked-over birthday cards.'

It's Monday, 27 February 2008. The bookshelves start shaking, the walls wobble, my cup of tea does a hiccup. If I had had any ornaments or vases in my living room, they would probably have smashed.

'What was that?' I ask. Living alone, the question is immediately rhetorical. It is one in the morning, I check the windows to make sure no one is trying to break in; double-lock the door and when I am satisfied there are no men in balaclavas trying to steal my valuables, I switch on the radio as I clean my teeth.

'If you felt the earthquake, please phone in,' Ian Collins urges on his talkSPORT programme. Earthquake? I swirl and spit. Soon Collins is using words like tremor and Richter scale and I realize that the thing making my books bounce on their shelves was not subsidence or terrorists, but what the guys in San Fran call a quake. I quit studying geography in year nine, can't tell a cumulus cloud from a nimbostratus, an estuary from a peninsula, but even I realize that an earthquake is unusual for the UK. A man from Birmingham phones in.

'It was so loud I nearly fell out of bed.'

A lady in South London calls. 'I thought someone was breaking in. My dogs won't stop barking.'

It is late at night and I want to go to sleep, but still haven't made tomorrow's sandwiches. As I get a slab of cheddar from the fridge, more information filters through. People as far apart as Brighton and Darlington have been affected.

'The earthquake's epicentre is Market Rasen, twenty miles south of Hull,' Collins announces.

The cheese grater drops out of my hand, cheddar shavings fall to the floor. I grew up ten miles from Market Rasen, lived there until I was eighteen when I went to university in Norwich. It's where my mum and dad still live. They won't like to be at the epicentre of an earthquake. They don't like inconvenience.

I switch off Ian Collins in favour of revving up my computer and listening to Radio Humberside online to get more localized information. The only time I have ever listened to Radio Humberside was on the rare winter mornings when I woke up and saw the roads covered in snow. Me and my sister would listen, waiting for our school to be mentioned on the list of school closures for the day. I haven't listened since, in fact it is surprising that the station is still going. Humberside as a county ceased to exist in 1994, local MP Michael Brown saying he wanted the word Humberside to be expunged from the English language. Listening to reports coming in it seems the whole region was almost expunged about ten minutes ago.

Steve Redgrave is on air. The radio presenter, that is, not the former Olympic rower. I am only assuming this. He is talking to a representative from Humberside Fire and Rescue Service, who urges people not to phone the emergency services unless they feel there is a genuine problem.

The earthquake shook three minutes before the end of Redgrave's late-night show, just as the station was tidying up bits and pieces, preparing to link up to Radio Five Live's output for the night. They had to make an instant decision, and it was decided that Redgrave would stay on air for as long as necessary, that this was a time when people would be switching on their radios for information, that they needed to serve their community. It seems I wasn't the only one to seek Radio Humberside for reassurance:

'The phone lines have lit up like crazy and calls haven't stopped coming in,' Redgrave says through my tinny laptop speakers. He is the reassuring presence, the local voice that people need in this type of situation, and the emails and phone calls are clearly appreciative of his overtime. One lady calls from the increasingly high-profile Market Rasen.

'I thought a plane had landed on the top of my house.'

'Here in Hull it sounded like the air-conditioning had broken,' Redgrave tells her. As the calls continue to come in, it seems that after the initial concern and confusion, people have started to settle down and are responding in a very English way.

'It must have been loud. It woke the missus up.'

'I live in a semi-detached house. I woke up and thought it had become detached.'

'I was terrified. Then I had a cup of tea.'

I could have listened to updates on Five Live or talkSPORT,

or switched on rolling news coverage on television, or even gone to bed and forgotten about it all, but I chose to listen to Radio Humberside because I wanted to hear how the quake was affecting people close to home, Grimsby, Scunthorpe, Goole.

'If you know of anyone on your street who is alone and might be scared, please do the neighbourly thing – knock on their door, make sure they're okay. Check that your own family are okay,' Redgrave tells us. I decide not to phone my mum and dad though. Sleeping through an earthquake only to be woken by a phone call is the kind of irony that happens regularly in our house.

Bennett Simpson from the British Geological Survey in Edinburgh is in touch with the show. Clearly not only Steve Redgrave is working into the night, the producers must be frantically trying to find information, experts, clarity that they can relay to the listener.

'The preliminary information from our instruments is a measurement of 5.3 on the Richter scale, which is a considerable amount,' Simpson says. 'It has been felt throughout the UK, and is definitely a quake, not a tremor,' he confirms. 'It was timed at 00.56 this morning and is the largest UK earthquake since 1984 in North Wales, when it measured 5.4. This is a very significant earthquake,' he reiterates.

'How does this compare with the Mediterranean, and further afield in Asia?'

'In a worldwide context this is very small. They happen every day throughout the world, but for the UK it is huge.'

'What are your responsibilities when this kind of thing occurs?' Redgrave asks.

'We've spoken to the media and liaised with the police. When earthquakes occur people panic, they are not used to this kind of thing. People assume it is something much worse.'

'Do these things come in waves? Is it likely to come again?'

'Aftershocks are very common. After the incident in Wales there were repeat quakes, but much smaller. We'll have to wait and see.'

Bob calls from Pocklington.

'It lasted eight or ten seconds. I thought it was my wife having a fit. She thought it was me having a fit. My daughter's stereo fell from her shelf, but I've had a look around the house, there's no more damage. It's on television now, Sky News says it's affected Leicestershire, Bedfordshire, Norfolk.'

'So were you in bed?'

'Yeah, my wife needs to be up at ten-past six, I need to be up at seven. But the ground started going de-de-de-de-de-de, the bed started shaking, like in *The Exorcist*. A few lights came on around the street. I walked downstairs and out to the yard and stood watching the lights turning on, and then off again. I've checked gas and water and everything's fine, so fingers crossed.'

'It's very unnerving, isn't it?' Redgrave says.

'Mercifully there's been no one injured so far, according to Sky,' Bob says.

'Well, sleep safe,' Redgrave tells him, then repeats the phone numbers, the email address, the radio frequency.

Redgrave is now growing comfortable updating news, saying 'This is Radio Humberside' in his newsflash voice, telling people tuning in that Something Has Happened.

Dave is in Anlaby.

'It's a bit strange really, I've never experienced anything like it.'

'Was there any damage?'

'Not that I'm aware of. I was concerned though because my wife's just had a baby, born six weeks premature. She rang me from the hospital. It was a bit frightening to be away from her and the baby.'

'Of course. And are they both okay?'

'Yes, well the little one's in special care, so we were a bit worried, but everything seems fine. It was just weird. I don't know how to explain it really.'

'Unnerving, I think is the word I would use.'

'That's right.'

'It's just worrying how much the house shook. I'm not sleeping much anyway, what with everything going on with the baby. But she's improved a lot now, should be coming home soon.'

'You've got a lot on your mind! What's your daughter's name?'

'Lily Elaine Simpson. Born on Sunday morning.'

'Well that's something to tell her about when she's older! The earth shook the day you were born!'

'Thank you ever so much,' Dave says.

'All our love to your family. Hope everything is back to normal for you soon.'

'We're now getting little bits of information coming through,' Redgrave informs us. 'We've spoken to Five Live who say they're being inundated with texts from all over the country. We haven't heard from anyone in a high-rise building yet . . . not wanting to worry anybody,' Redgrave quickly adds. 'There seem to be no major problems but a lot of people are shaken up by it all. Glenn Ramsden from Humberside Fire and Rescue is on the phone. Glenn, tell us what's going on.'

'Well, it woke me up. I immediately called Control, they said they were being swamped with calls. There are only so many incidents that we can mobilize to. Right now we're out looking at dangerous tiles in Bottesford and a chimney stack in Hull. There are hundreds of jobs, we can only attend if we know we can give practical assistance. A lot of people are very frightened, and need somebody to talk to, but we can't attend to all these people. Our appeal would be to wait until daylight breaks to examine your house, don't go out with a torch if it puts you into danger.'

'Do you have any special training for this kind of event?'

'To be brutally honest we have no knowledge, really. We have training in emergency planning, and mass evacuation. But with something like this that could have caused a huge amount of damage, it would be difficult to know where to start.'

Malcolm in North Newbald, west of Beverley, phones in.

'Hello, Malcolm. Most people have reported not too many problems, a few broken ornaments, knocked-over birthday cards. How are you?'

'There is a large crack across my bedroom wall,' he says. He sounds elderly, his voice frail, and tells Redgrave he lives alone. 'The coving has come down and most walls are slightly cracked.'

'It sounds like quite severe damage?'

'Yes. It was very eerie, the whole house shook.'

'Did you see the cracks appear?'

126

'No, I heard the coving fall from downstairs. I phoned the non-emergency number for the police to see if there had been any reports of a tremor, but there was no answer. I'm going to call the insurance company first thing in the morning,' Malcolm says.

'You sound remarkably calm!' Redgrave tells him. 'Compared to other listeners your damage seems fairly severe. Is it a new house?'

'Fairly new, it was built in the last fifty years.'

'Things will be okay,' Redgrave replies, although he clearly has no more inside knowledge than anybody else; he cannot say with any conviction that there will be no more tremors. 'You seem to be coping okay now. Is your house safe to stay in?' Redgrave asks.

'I hope so. Thank you for being on air,' he says, before saying goodbye.

'Well, take care. I'm relieved that you're safe. Have a proper look round when it gets light.'

Other callers describe slightly post-apocalyptic scenes: tiles slipping off roofs, animals howling, neighbours standing on the road in their dressing gowns and slippers, shaking their heads, shrugging their shoulders. Others phone in who begrudge the interruption of their night's sleep, annoyed that they will be tired at work tomorrow, that they know they are going to spend the next couple of hours wide awake, counting sheep, turning their pillow round like a Rubik's Cube, trying to get comfortable.

It is already 2.30 a.m. Hazel is on air in Scunthorpe.

'I looked out of the window, but no one came out on the

street. But I think that's just because people are antisocial in Scunthorpe!' she says with a chuckle. 'I was sat on the settee with my cats. I'm in my eighties. I can't believe the windows could shake so much without coming in. And the front door flew open. For one horrible moment I thought someone was breaking in. I've got to this age without ever being as frightened as I am right now. The main thing is not knowing what is happening.'

'You must remember as far back as the war.'

'We were never frightened in those days,' Hazel says, stoically. 'My cats flew off the settee almost before it had happened.'

'They can sense these things, can't they!' Redgrave says. 'Well, let's hope that this is the end to it. Are you all right?'

'Yes. I daren't go outside, but I'm okay. I'm amazed the house is still standing.'

As 3 a.m. approaches it is clear that the panic has calmed down. Fears of repercussions have subsided, and people are going back to sleep. There is nothing more to add. People calling in have started to relay the same information. Redgrave's work here is done; he summarizes the night's action, recaps key information, thanks people who have been in touch, and wishes his listeners well. Glenn Ramsden is back on the phone with an update from the Humberside Fire and Rescue service.

'The incoming calls have decreased. We have a picture that everything is okay. There have been no problems with gas or electric. We've rung round all the major utilities and there seems to be positive feedback. We've had nothing serious, just chimneys and roofs. We've had to evacuate a few houses, move them in with friends and family.'

Redgrave signs off, plays some gentle music before switching back over to Radio Five Live for the rest of the night. I turn off my computer, go back to bed, and look forward to my four hours' sleep.

11

BBC RADIO 4

'When I die I would like Radio 4 piped into my coffin.'

(Damon Albarn)

My alarm wakes me and immediately I think about calling in sick. I go back to sleep. Then I wake up and consider giving up my job, finding something new, never seeing Alan Medlicott again. Then I get dressed and catch the bus. Much like every other day then.

The earthquake is the main story on the *Today* programme, presented this morning by Edward Stourton and Carolyn Quinn. I decide that Radio 4 will be the best place to hear what actually happened with the earthquake. Ever since I started listening to different radio stations I knew that one day would involve this potentially exhausting challenge; listening to the relentless cleverness of what must be the most treasured radio staion in the world. For many, Radio 4 is one of the cornerstones of British culture, along with *Fawlty Towers*, the Beatles and David Attenborough. There is a report live from Market Rasen, which has never been at the epicentre of anything before, other than an occasional farmers' market. Despite only having had a couple of hours' sleep I have never been so awake on my way to work before. Radio 4 gives you no time to yawn, stretch, wipe sleep from your eyes. There are too many facts to digest, opinions to absorb; clerics talking about religion, the views of botanists about the National History Museum, doctors diagnosing the best way for drug addicts to recover. The Home Secretary Jacqui Smith is challenged on this subject. She says drug addiction is like having a crippling disease, but over the next ten years there will be noticeable improvements for those recuperating. Smith has recently suggested a change in the law, that if drug dealers don't attend recovery sessions they will have their benefits cut.

Possibly the most contentious part of Radio 4's schedule is *Thought for the Day*, which today comes from John Bell of the Iona religious community.

'I spent an enjoyable gap year in the seventies working in child care,' he tells us. 'Few people wanted to be involved in it, the hours were long, the pay poor and there was no training, which meant it was possible for the wrong people to get a foot in the door. Staff members would be allowed into children's bedrooms. It is with hindsight that we are able to see the flaws of the past. But hindsight is present in every era. So in thirty years' time what will people consider to be the mistakes of today? Perhaps it will be pester power, we will look back and remember a time when parents were afraid to say no, when they would give their children a computer game when they needed a conversation, microwaved food when they needed a meal. We should never forget that children are God's gifts.'

Tom Daley will be fourteen years old when he represents the UK at diving in the Beijing Olympics. The *Today* programme interviewed him a few weeks ago as he was set to become the nation's youngest competitor in the history of the Games. In the studio Ken Lester has some bad news for young Tom.

'I was thirteen in the 1960 Rome Olympics,' he reveals. 'My date of birth was misprinted at the time so I never got the credit I deserved.' He shows Edward Stourton the trilby he was awarded by the Olympic Committee for his achievement and reminisces about walking around Rome alone as a thirteen-year-old boy.

'I feel as if I've taken something away from Tom,' Lester says, 'but he does still have the opportunity to be the UK's youngest ever medal winner.'

Back to today's big issue of drugs and the *Daily Mail* columnist Peter Hitchens is in the studio with Matthew Taylor, former adviser to Tony Blair. They are reacting to this morning's interview with Jacqui Smith.

'Most drug users are desperate to come off drugs,' Taylor claims.

Hitchens is immediately riled. 'The idea that drug taking is a disease is fatuous rubbish. Those people are breaking the law. Celebrities are continually being exposed as drug takers yet nothing ever happens to them. People need to realize that the effects of drugs are catastrophic!'

The two guests continue bickering like two kids arguing about whose go it is next on the PlayStation. They both speak at the same time, meaning the words of neither can really be understood.

'He won't let me finish!' Hitchens complains to Stourton, who grants him the platform to continue. 'Perhaps Mr Taylor would care not to interrupt me on this occasion,' he pleads. 'No one is letting me speak!'

Stourton ends the discussion, neither party particularly happy with its conclusion, and off air I am sure Hitchens and Taylor continue to bicker until *Book at Bedtime*. There are certain guests that shows such as *Today* know make good radio, whether they are journalists, politicians or former Coventry City goalkeepers who claim to be the Messiah. They are clockwork guests – the presenter knows exactly how to wind them up, then sits back and watches them do somersaults.

At nine o'clock Libby Purves says hello to the nation and I say hello to Alan Medlicott and Craig. Alan Medlicott is cleaning his glasses, Craig is Tipp-Exing. *Midweek*'s first guest is Teri O'Leary, who runs the country's only homeless theatre.

'I became homeless through bereavement,' she tells Purves, the show's presenter since 1983. 'I spent five years in hostels. I know what it is like to be oppressed; I am aware of the boredom of the streets.'

'And has anyone from your theatre gone on to bigger things?' Purves asks.

'Well, we've had three actors who later worked with the Royal Shakespeare Company. It's not about that though,' she adds, bluntly. 'It's to give people something to think about other than being homeless. The chance to do something as simple as mix with other people.'

Chris Turner is a BAFTA-winning sound engineer who releases albums of noise he records.

'Could we call it sound, please? Not noise,' he interjects.

Sorry, Chris.

He has worked with David Attenborough on countless documentaries, and most notably recorded black howler monkeys from Venezuela. I'm sure they've done a session for John Peel. Purves asks him about his latest project.

'I saw lions mauling a zebra and thought it would be interesting to capture the sound of the vultures swooping down and devouring its carcass. So I attached the microphones a newsreader may clip on his lapel to the ribcage of the zebra and the sound was incredible.' As the devouring of the carcass reverberates around my headphones I can't help but grimace. Alan Medlicott looks up, he must think I am in pain. Turner continues with news of another of his favourite projects. 'I made a CD recording of vast Icelandic glaciers, capturing the sound of their movements by using underwater microphones. Over the course of a few weeks the creaks and groans became audible.'

I've never listened to *Woman's Hour* before. There is something about the title that has always made me feel detached from it, although that never stopped me buying the album *Young, Gifted and Black*. Today's show is a mothers' special, prompted by the surge of calls after yesterday's show where a young mother confessed she had difficulties loving her newborn baby. Today, caller after caller talks about their experiences as mothers dealing with post-natal depression and feelings of inadequacy in regard to their children.

'It took me a few months to be able to love my daughter,' admits one young mother, who will remain anonymous as I can't remember her name. The next caller reveals that she has an eleven-year-old and a six-year-old.

'I coped very badly with pressures and expectations from friends, colleagues, society in general.'

'How long did it take for you to love your children?' asks Jenni Murray.

'I'm still not sure I do,' the caller confides. 'I'm a terrible mother.'

People continue to call in, always with reassuring words for previous callers. Two fathers speak to Jenni, saying that feelings of inadequacy and anxiety are by no means restricted to mothers.

At eleven o'clock is a programme called *Three Men in a Float*, an account of the journey three friends took from Lowestoft to Land's End in a second-hand milk float.

'It's too obvious to climb a mountain,' Dan Kiernan says, as though that alone is explanation for their journey. Kiernan is deputy editor of the *Idler* magazine, a publication devoted to the art of loafing. He quotes J.B. Priestley, who says that in this time of excessive speed we rush about from one place to the next so quickly that the place you have left and your destination are becoming identical, and in the future it is going to become even more so.

Their main obstacle is recharging the vehicle's battery. They have to stop off in Bungay, Suffolk, because it is almost dead and they need to use somebody else's electricity supply.

'I did drive for about a mile with the handbrake on,' designated driver Dan admits.

'The first few people we asked to help us said no,' Prasanth Visweswaran, the group's electrical expert says. 'Then we decided to start using the word 'recharge' rather than 'hotwire' and we found help straight away.'

It is important for their adventure that they are at the mercy of strangers. 'We all live in the city, we don't know any of our neighbours. The point of travelling is to meet nice people,' Prasanth says. One person who helped them out was Pete, a local tour guide. At first he told them he was unable to help them with their request to 'hotwire' from his cooker socket as there wasn't any parking by his house. But after a phone call home he had good news, his wife was standing outside, saving them a space.

'Men of a certain age love getting their teeth into a problem,' Ian Vince, the milk float's navigator tells us. As their journey towards Land's End continues they relish the pace of proceedings. 'The only problem with travelling at 15 miles per hour is that we get a long, lingering look at roadkill. Other than that it's magical.'

On completing their journey they question why people feel the need to rush around all the time, speaking to a friend who has avoided motorways for twenty years. 'People see us and suspend their cynicism of the world,' Ian says, bringing the programme to a close. 'If I'm ever on a motorway, I'll fill with regret at all the things I'm missing out on.'

I wonder whether this programme will be featured on Sunday's *Pick of the Week* show, a programme that features the best of the week's radio, often with a Radio 4 bias. One show that certainly won't be featured is *You and Yours*. Although I have heard interesting things on this show before, today's is a little tedious, with subjects ranging from dentists, to bogus shares, to the lack of new housing available in Manchester.

'Did you feel the earthquake?' I ask Kate in the kitchen, our empty mugs next to each other, waiting to be filled.

'No,' she tells me, 'I seem to be the only one who missed it. Andrew Hodgson's chimney fell off!' she says, giggling, then glances at the door to make sure that Andrew Hodgson hasn't snuck into the kitchen undetected. The kettle boils, Kate reaches for two teabags. 'How's your day?' she asks. 'Boring?'

She expects me to say yes.

'It's been really good, actually. I'm listening to Radio 4 on my headphones.'

'Radio 4! It's all right for some. I'm on the phone all day.' Kate deals with customer complaints. She has one of the few jobs worse than mine.

After a walk to Comet during *The World at One* I am back at my desk for *Britain in a Box*, a profile of *Rising Damp*, described by TV producer Paul Jackson as 'ITV's most successful sitcom . . . ITV's only successful sitcom'.

Eric Chapel, the show's creator, reveals he was working at East Midlands Electricity Board when he read a newspaper article about a black man who pretended to be a prince to get good treatment in a hotel. He quickly developed the idea into a script and eventually it was on stage in the West End, titled *Banana Box*, starring most of the cast who went on to be among television's best-loved characters.

TV executive Sir Paul Fox suggests one reason for its success was that they tackled racism in a more sophisticated way than other programmes in the seventies, such as *Love Thy Neighbour*. Morals and politics were openly discussed, but above all it was well cast and funny.

The Afternoon Play is called *Poetry for Beginners*, written by the poet Kathryn Simmonds, and set on a residential writing course in Shropshire. The two teachers Celia and Fran clash over everything, Celia embraces formal poetry and thinks line breaks are very important. Fran likes rap and uses it as a workshop exercise to get the elderly clientele to dance. Their main clash is over their feelings for Nick, an artist who is completing his first collection of poetry. Another rhymester attempting to woo Celia is a headmaster, William, who writes a poem about her called 'The Shepherdess of Poetry'.

We learn about the developing feelings of the teachers through their diary extracts, but it is left to William to shatter everyone's dreams and reveal the truth: Nick is a married auditor and the artistic career he has duped them into believing in is all made up.

It is three o'clock and I am at the filing cabinets listening to *Gardeners' Question Time*, praying for an earthquake, any divine intervention that means I can go home and get into bed. My only consolation is that the show is presented by Peter Gibbs, my favourite weatherman.

Again, this is a programme of little relevance to me, I don't have a garden or even any pot plants, the only evidence of horticulture you'll find in my flat is a jar of mixed herbs I sometimes put in mash. Nevertheless the show has a peculiar appeal, someone emails on behalf of their 89-year-old gran Ethel, about how best to maintain her peace lily. Although these problems pale in significance to those on *Woman's Hour*, these are still things that people need help with. Their problems are watered down compared with those earlier today, their worries are seedlings. Janet emails to say her cherry plum tree is confused about seasons, that it had already flowered by January. The unlikely named expert Bob Flowerdew tells her that cold spells last summer have made flowers think they've missed out on autumn and that it is already winter again. Other calls enquire about organic flowering and growing chickpeas. Even though I know for certain that none of this will ever be relevant to me as I will never be wealthy enough to own a garden it's hard to begrudge people on their allotments taking an hour out of their day to lie back on a deckchair, rest their feet on a bag of compost and listen to *Gardeners' Question Time*. These are people who leave their wellies by the back door, bake crumble while *The Archers* is on, and Sellotape pound coins to birthday cards.

Thinking Allowed is a show looking at how society works. Today's subject is 'the hoody' – young people wearing hooded tops. The criminologist Jack Fawbert has been following the subject of 'hoodies' – in the last twelve months, 'hoody' has been used thirty-six times in *Mirror* headlines:

> Hoody Gang Stabbed Mother
> Dad Killed for Chasing a Hoody
> Hoodies Bit Off My Nose

Fawbert has devised a 'hoody graph' which peaks during what future generations will refer to as 'The Bluewater Shopping Centre Ban'. Within a week of the Kent shopping centre banning anyone who entered wearing a hood, there was a 26 per cent increase in shoppers, and the notable change in shopping pattern was that sales of hoodies increased enormously. More recently, however, the hoody graph has shown a steady fall, revealing a decline in their popularity.

I walk home relishing the fresh air. My brain is starting to repel the knowledge Radio 4 is trying to spoonfeed me. There have been too many facts and opinions for my simple mind, the poor thing doesn't know what's just hit it. There has been too much information, not enough loud distorted guitar. Eddie Mair presents *PM*, his voice is piped daily into cars in traffic jams throughout the country. *PM* is followed by the six o'clock news, where again the earthquake is being discussed, as well as a Palestinian rocket attack, a threat of a new Cold War and protestors on the roof of the Houses of Parliament.

In the evening 6.30 is always time for comedy on Radio 4, what I've always thought of as the *Just a Minute* slot. Tonight is a new show, *The Museum of Curiosity*, co-hosted by Bill Bailey and John Lloyd. Three guests are invited to nominate something they would donate to the fictional museum. The first submission is a pineapple, courtesy of TV presenter and author Fran Beauman.

'I am fascinated by pineapples,' she tells the nation. 'I'd like to publish a history of the pineapple. I'd write twenty volumes if I was asked to.'

'Do you think you'll ever be asked to?' Bailey wonders.

'No.'

She reveals that when they first arrived in the UK, pineapples cost the equivalent of five thousand pounds and were considered a sign of status, people would take them to dinner parties to display their wealth. You could even hire one for an evening.

'Also,' Fran says, getting even more excited, 'you can die if you eat too much pineapple because it contains a flesh-eating enzyme.'

'That's why people who work in pineapple factories lose their fingerprints. The bromelain wipes them off,' Lloyd adds.

Professor Gary Sheffield is a military historian and I imagine the only professor in the world called Gary. His exhibit of choice is the Anderson shelter.

'It is a symbol of hope and survival,' he says. 'It portrays British toughness.'

John Lloyd asks him about the military. 'Is it true that when they are firing, most soldiers shoot to miss?'

'I'm not sure. I know it's a fact that 2 per cent of soldiers are clinically psychopathic. They revel in death and torture.'

'There is a saying that war is God's way of teaching Americans geography,' Lloyd adds, amusing the studio audience.

Last is Ben Elton, whose submission is the concept of privacy. Trust Ben Elton to go metaphysical.

'Privacy is now old-fashioned enough to belong in a

museum,' he suggests, and says he identifies with Winston Smith, the central character in *Nineteen Eighty-Four*.

'Twenty per cent of the world's CCTV cameras are in the UK,' Lloyd reveals. 'There are 5 million here, one for every twelve people.'

'We will put privacy in the museum,' Bailey announces, 'but we won't tell anyone where it is.'

Seven o'clock was always a sacred time in our house. Even now when I phone home, I check the time to make sure I'm not interrupting my mum listening to *The Archers*. She is an *Archers* addict. In fact, she is an *Archers Addict*, she subscribes to the newsletter. Whenever I have listened and there is a scene with two people on the farm, I've found it impossible not to imagine the two actors standing with their wellies on in the middle of a muddy field. If two characters were lying in bed, about to go to sleep, I would be convinced the two actors would be doing exactly the same, wearing pyjamas, an alarm clock on their bedside table, a glass of water in case they are thirsty during the night.

In today's episode, Ruth and David go on a shopping spree. I'm not sure what has gone on between them. Ruth says she is glad to be 'me again'. Why is David treating her? What has happened? Why is he taking her to the seafood place in Darrington and asked Heather to look after the kids?

In *Front Row* there is a treat for Mark Lawson, who spends much of his time interviewing distinguished thespians, accomplished novelists, art historians, as today he gets to talk to

Hollywood actresses Scarlett Johansson and Natalie Portman about their roles in the new film *The Other Boleyn Girl*. They speak of their mutual respect for each other and the lack of juicy female lead roles.

'Have you ever turned down a role because of who the actor is?' Lawson asks.

'It's the other way round,' Portman tells him. 'I'll read a script for a film, but if I'm then told that, say, Samuel L. Jackson is in it I'll agree straight away.'

Lawson recalls a part of the film he enjoyed.

'I love what you British find funny!' Scarlett tells him, giggling.

Lawson is brought back to reality with Johansson's polar opposite, Clive Anderson. He is there with fellow *Whose Line is it Anyway?* stars Josie Lawrence and John Sessions to promote its release on DVD. Anderson tells Lawson that the improvisation show was originally on Radio 4, but the BBC were so slow to respond to suggestions of making a television version that by the time they were in contact to say 'Possibly we may have some interest at some stage in talking about maybe making a pilot' the team had to respond by saying 'Actually, we're starting filming a thirteen-part series for Channel 4 on Monday.'

'Did you ever cheat on the show?' Lawson asks. 'Were you ever told in advance what subjects would come up?'

'There would have been no point,' Sessions replies. 'It's much easier to be spontaneous. Faking it would have achieved nothing.'

'There are reruns on the digital channel Dave at the

moment,' Clive Anderson says. 'For the first time my children's friends are saying "Wow, I never knew your dad was on telly!"'

'I was walking to my flat one night and there was a group of lads with their hoods up, staring at me,' Josie Lawrence says. 'I was a bit scared, they were definitely talking about me, and then one of them came up to me. I almost stopped breathing but he just said "*Whose Line*, respec"!'

The Moral Maze is presented by former newsreader Michael Buerk. Each week they discuss an issue, and different witnesses relating to it are grilled by a panel. Tonight the subject is prostitution and the debaters include Michael Portillo, Melanie Phillips and Clifford Langley. The first person to be put under the spotlight belongs to a group called Feminist Coalition against Prostitution.

'It is male violence against women who are vulnerable and disenfranchised. It affects women of colour and migrant women.'

'That's a huge generalization,' Portillo claims, interrupting her spiel. 'What about high-class prostitutes? They choose to be in the business, they make a lot of money and are happy. Do you deny they exist?'

'Well, I have never met someone in this position.'

'That's not really the same thing,' Portillo tells her.

'It is bleak and unhappy to be a prostitute. It is a symptom of an unequal society.'

'So you are going to drive these women into further desperation?' Portillo asks.

'What about gay prostitutes?' the columnist Melanie Phillips asks. 'Would you criminalize those involved with gay prostitution?'

'Yes,' the feminist replies. 'It is morally wrong for one individual to derogate and exploit another.'

'So it's not a gender problem at all,' Phillips says, dismissing her witness.

The next person to be Portilloed is Sebastian Hawsley, a former male escort who regularly uses prostitutes.

'Do you have any moral qualms about buying and selling sex?' Buerk asks.

'No. We all have the right to buy and sell parts of each other. For some people sex is a compulsion. It is as difficult for an attractive person not to have sex as it is for an unattractive person to have sex.'

'Are you any different from an animal?' Melanie Phillips asks. 'Erm . . .'

'Clearly not,' she snaps, appalled at the hesitation. 'Do you ask the women you use about their life? Ascertain whether they need help, whether they are vulnerable?'

'Of course,' Sebastian says, an answer greeted with a collective snort of derision. 'Everyone around this table is a prostitute!' he reveals. 'Everyone listening at home is a prostitute! Who says you cannot fuck in a church and pray in a brothel?'

'It depends what meaning of "pray" you are using,' Phillips quips.

'It's the other word he used I was more concerned about,' Buerk adds.

'Are you projecting your own self-disgust on to other people?' Clifford Langley asks.

'You don't know what you're talking about, Clifford!' Hawsley tells him. 'You are a journalist, journalism is a profession which people hold in much lower regard than prostitution. Have you ever been to a prostitute?' he asks.

'No.'

'Have you ever slept with a prostitute?'

'No. I have spoken to them though, and know that 90 per cent of them are addicted to hard drugs.'

'I've spoken to prostitutes. They don't feel frustrated and exploited. And they certainly don't welcome middle-class intellectuals sitting around reading the *Guardian* formulating their opinions for them.'

'All the prostitutes I've met have been heroin addicts.'

'Well, I'm sure you've got terrible vices yourself. If you do not have vices you are not worth talking to.'

After the excitement of *The Moral Maze* I decide to phone home, find out how the earthquake affected my mum and dad.

'It woke us up,' my dad says. 'I thought it was a lorry but your mum checked Teletext and found out it was an earthquake.'

'Can I speak to Mum?' I ask. He hands her the phone. 'Mum, why did David Archer take Ruth to a seafood restaurant?'

By the time I have had something to eat, and learnt about Ruth Archer developing breast cancer and then considering having an affair, my evening has come to a close. I make tomorrow's sandwiches, shower, get changed, turn my light off and listen to *Book at Bedtime*. Dervla Kirwan reads me a story by Anne Enright and throughout the country people kick off their slippers, make sure their alarm clocks are set and drift off to sleep.

12

MARK RADCLIFFE

'There is no great secret to being on the radio. It's just talking.'

(Mark Radcliffe)

'Do you want some cheese?' Stuart Maconie asks, opening his desk drawer. I nod, he cuts off a block and hands it to me.

'What kind of cheese is it?' I ask.

'Expensive cheese,' he says, slicing some for himself and placing it back in the drawer.

I would say that it was good of Stuart Maconie to agree to spend time with me in the Manchester office he shares with Mark Radcliffe, but the first he knew about my arrival was when I took my coat off and sat next to him on the chair that Radcliffe pointed at.

'Shove your stuff on the floor and don't mind Stuart,' he tells me. 'Are you sticking around for the show?'

'If that's okay?'

'Stay for as long as you want,' he says, then explains to Stuart that I will be spending the evening with them. The Radio 2 show they co-present starts in less than two hours: Maconie is on Wikipedia, Radcliffe is texting. I take my notebook and pen out of my bag, and sit still, nervous excitement running through my body. Despite having never met either before, I do not feel that I am in a room with two strangers. Both have mastered the art of making radio a personal medium to such an extent that I feel I could walk into either of their homes without even knocking at the front door. That is one of the beauties of radio, that you feel you know people just because their voices are so familiar in your own home. Radcliffe and Maconie have forty years of broadcasting and journalism experience between them, Maconie was assistant editor of *NME*, Radcliffe was one half of Mark and Lard, who took over from Chris Evans on Radio 1's prestigious *Breakfast Show*, which makes cobbling together a show like this as routine as a Michelin-starred chef peeling potatoes, and rinsing them under the tap.

'I started on late-night radio,' Radcliffe tells me when I ask about his background. 'I used to do a show called *Cures for Insomnia* on Piccadilly Radio and then me and Lard did *Hit the North* on Radio 5. It was on the ten to midnight show on Radio 1 that people really became aware of us. We used to call it the "graveyard shift". Late evening was always deemed to be the least desirable time to be on air, that's why Smashy and Nicey were moved to the *Mumbling around Midnight* slot: "Hello to all you truckers out there." But me and Lard were very excited to get it. We used to work on it all the time, adding little bits all day. Radio 1 gave us our own studio and never really bothered us. People always assumed that the two of us had this deliberate policy to distance ourselves from the rest of the station, which we never intended. We didn't think "let's be different". We just thought, as listeners, which bands would we want on, who would make us laugh? It was never more clearly thought out than that. At that time, when Matthew Bannister was controller, the stock of what a DJ was had fallen pretty low. It was before the super DJs like Fatboy Slim, so that style of DJ didn't really exist. Apart from Peel and Annie Nightingale, Radio 1 mainly consisted of DJs who were just waiting to be quiz-show hosts. And we thought that was a shame, there was so much more you could do, there was a world of interesting music out there. Poetry was described as the new rock and roll at the time and that worked perfectly on a radio show.'

'Has there ever been a reluctance to having poets like John Cooper Clarke and Simon Armitage as guests on your show?' I ask. Maconie picks up a ukulele, starts to strum it gently.

'On these Radio 2 shows you just think "Who is interesting to talk to?"' Radcliffe tells me. 'Poets are perfect. They tend to be intelligent and funny and very observant. So rather like comedians, wherever they've been, they pick up detail. If Simon Armitage has been to, say, Bristol, that weekend, he won't say the weather was good, the people were friendly. He'll use a couple of details that bring it to life. And then you can always finish the show on a poem. It's good to end on something, it structures the show. Comedians never want to do part of their act. I've always found poets to be great for the radio, it's a gift. To say the obvious, on the radio there are no pictures, so the words become incredibly important. People like Armitage, Ian McMillan and John Cooper Clarke are the guests I really like. With the best will in the world, when you are talking to Jagger or McCartney, they are never going to say anything to amaze you.'

'What about the music you play. Is that all chosen by you?'

'Radio 2 send us some playlist stuff,' Mark says, looking over his shoulder to see what Maconie is laughing at on the desk behind him.

'What are you doing?'

'I just typed prog rock into YouTube,' Maconie replies.

'The good thing about Radio 2,' Radcliffe continues, leaving his colleague to make his own entertainment, 'is that they have a playlist but by and large they let us pick what we want. If Barbra Streisand is on the playlist, there's no pressure on us to play it. Common sense seems to prevail. The head of music is a reasonable bloke. At times I had terrible trouble with the head of music of Radio 1. What he was doing was broadly right, and I was wrong, but I was absolutely right to have the battle anyway. It's always good to fight for these things.'

If Mark and Lard didn't like a song they were never shy in letting their listeners know, certain bands, particularly the Stereophonics, were notable recipients of regular slatings. Radcliffe's view that a lot of music on the playlist wasn't very good was backed up by the rare occasion when he was given the chance to choose his own records, and then the show suddenly had an extra dimension.

'We're both enthusiastic about music, that's the point of the show,' Maconie chips in, sliding his chair across the room to join us.

'We try and pretend otherwise, but we do have great respect for each other's tastes,' Radcliffe continues. 'If either of us says "I'd really, really like to play this", we'll probably put it on the show, particularly if it's a new record. We argued the other day about soul. I think it was the Detroit Spinners. Stuart thought it sounded great but I didn't think it would be right in the show. If either of us really doesn't feel comfortable with it, then we'll put it to one side as there are so many records to go through. It would be easy for a couple of middle-aged guys like us to play a lot of guitar bands we grew up listening to, so we do try to mix it around. Otherwise we'd just fill the show with Smiths records.'

'It's important to play music for reasons other than it makes you seem cool,' Maconie adds. 'It's important for our show not to fall into that trap. But then you get the old Peelites who think that unless a song is tremendously obscure it's not worth playing. I have a great respect for Peel. Because his tastes were so extreme he set the benchmark so wide that it allowed other people to operate within it. He played music from out here,' Maconie says, spreading his arms out wide, 'so that we could operate from within here,' he says, bringing his hands much closer together.

I make notes in my notebook, furiously scribbling every word I hear, very aware of the privileged position I have been granted. I don't want to mess this opportunity up.

'I'd have loved to have heard Peel play stuff from *The Perfumed Garden*,' Radcliffe continues. 'Psychedelic tracks in the middle of all the new music. For me, that's what I'd have liked from John's shows, a context. He had been there for so much and experienced so many things, that it would have been nice for him to occasionally say "This is from when Marc Bolan came in, wearing a duffel coat and slippers."' Maconie laughs at Radcliffe's Peel impression.

'Have there been any stand-out incidents on any of your shows?' I ask. 'I remember Damon Albarn saying "fuck" a lot.'

'He did do, yeah. But there's never really been problems. When you're making the kind of radio we do there isn't much that can go wrong. You can forget to put a record on, I suppose. But you tend to get away with slip-ups: your audience can relate to it, they accept that it's all going out live.'

'We wanted to create something with this show that didn't already exist,' Maconie adds, reaching across for the ukulele from his desk. 'If a new Radiohead or Nick Cave album comes out, where would you hear a discussion about it?'

'There's *Front Row* on Radio 4,' Radcliffe continues as I continue scribbling in my book, 'which is terribly academic, and not really the way that people talk. We wanted to do something that was meant for fans, but wasn't too up its own arse and dry. A show has to have context and muscle to it, but it must still be entertaining to listen to, like people talking in a pub, but at the same time done by people who know what they are talking about. We wanted to have discussions without getting too formal. The brilliant thing about doing this slot is that this used to be seen as a dead time to be on air. It's interesting how much radio has changed over the last few years. So many opinions have been entrenched; people at large have become much more fluid; mornings aren't just for housewives any more, late-night radio isn't just for truckers. This idea that evenings were dead airtime was borne from a world when everyone clocked off work at five, had their tea at six and settled down to watch TV at seven. And four things have changed. 1) Not everyone finishes work at five any more, they finish at any time. 2) People eat a lot later.

3) There's nothing on telly anyway. And 4) a lot of people listen on the Internet. There's been a global revolution in terms of listening habits; I don't think people are hunched over watching their radios as they listen to us. They might decide to open a bottle of wine, read the papers, do the crossword, and put Radcliffe and Maconie on in the background. Also, people do the most peculiar things. Last night we had a request from Roddy, listening to the show while plucking cockerels in Aberdeenshire.'

'Anyway, should we take John down to the studio?' Maconie suggests, checking his watch, laying his ukulele on his chair. I had noticed that the time was sneaking towards eight o'clock, the start of the show, but liked the idea of keeping them to myself. If your hero is Madonna or Bono then meeting them would be an odd experience and almost impossible to arrange. But my heroes have always been more tangible; I don't like the world of celebrity, with layers of ropes and big guys wearing shades, arms folded, guarding someone off the telly. I'm just glad that despite his millions, constant Hollywood exposure and paparazzi pressure, I can sit side by side with Stuart Maconie. It is Radcliffe, though, who I have grown up listening to and when I found out I would be meeting him I went all wobbly. Sitting on the train to Manchester I felt an excitement and optimism that I thought data entry had wiped out of me for ever. Arriving at the station I found the nearest pub to the BBC and sat in there, impatient for it to be time to walk to reception and say: 'I'm here to see Mark Radcliffe.' One of the reasons I like him is his dry, self-deprecating humour, regardless of whether he is talking to Lard or Maconie or Sir Paul McCartney. When interviewing Kylie Minogue on Radio 1 he asked her if she

154

wanted to come round to his house, telling her 'the wife's at Book Club so she won't be back till late'. He sees a great affection in people, it is not rock and roll anecdotes that interest him as much as what they had for their tea. When Mick Jagger was on his show Jagger ended up telling him about how Keith Richards has a shepherd's pie before every Rolling Stones gig. One night Ronnie Wood saw there was only one left, and so ate it, infuriating Richards.

The Radcliffe and Maconie show reveals domestic vignettes of listeners doing very ordinary things, and therein lies its beauty. Another person on last night's show emailed to say 'Can you tell the wife I was right; her and the kids didn't finish the jigsaw puzzle in time and it's still on the living-room floor.'

'There's not much to show you really,' Radcliffe says apologetically, as he holds the door to the production room open for me. Already seated behind a control panel is Nick the engineer. Radcliffe says hello, then shows me into the studio. An oil painting of him and Lard has pride of place on the wall.

'This is where I've sat for the last twenty years,' he tells me, making himself comfortable in his chair. In front of him is a computer, where he can play jingles on the touch screen, and a record player.

'This has been newly installed,' he says, spinning the turntable, 'because I wanted to be able to play vinyl.'

He finds a chair for me next to Nick the engineer and Viv the producer. I am offered a cup of tea and Nick puts the Liverpool match on the television in the corner of the room. Nick flicks a switch and we hear Radio 2 going out live, watch proceedings from behind a glass panel, the ultimate webcam. The old adage states that you should never meet your heroes, they will only disappoint you. But what about if you know your hero is nice? I've been listening to Mark Radcliffe for years, I've read his books, I've seen him on telly, I knew as soon as he agreed to meet me that I would probably get on with him. Mike Harding, on air with his folk show, says 'Next is Radcliffe and Maconie' and during the news the two presenters take their seats. They chat to us as the news is played, and soon they are talking not only to Nick and Viv but to the whole of the country.

Radcliffe thrashes his desk with drumsticks along with the opening song of the show, 'Sylvia' by prog rockers Focus. Maconie ties his shoelaces and then they chat about how they have just been watching the YouTube video in their office.

When they play their next track Maconie walks through to our room to apologize for talking too much, and collects emails that are printed out from the computer next to me: requests for songs, listeners telling them about their day.

'They are supposed to do a quick link before playing their second song,' Nick tells me when Maconie returns to his seat. 'That was about fifteen minutes,' he says, with mock annoyance. Viv coughs, clearing her throat.

'You ought to quit smoking,' Nick says to her.

'I know.'

'Or quit coughing.'

I look at Nick the engineer watching the football, chatting to Mark and Stuart during the records, and think what a dream job he has, but then he tells me he spent three hours this morning in a meeting about risk assessments and I realize that ultimately, all jobs become routine, being responsible for a show that goes out to millions of people is as everyday as me photocopying and stapling for Alan Medlicott.

It is hard to tell when Radcliffe and Maconie are on air as their personas do not change whether they are sitting in the office, talking to the nation or asking Nick what the football score is (1–0 to Liverpool). It is so relaxed, in fact, that Radcliffe does not notice a song has finished because he is having a chat with Viv and his face resembles a parent who has just realized their baby is still on the bus as he launches himself at the CD player to press the stop button. For all the off-air chat, drumming and reading *NME* in between records, though, there is a slickness about the show. A song finishes as the second hand is strolling towards the hour and time for the news. I think of all the people sitting at home or in their cars listening as I watch, sipping their wine, lying in the bath while the news is on. Meanwhile, Radcliffe and Maconie talk about which Nick Cave track to play to open the second half of the show.

During the last record a man with a beard appears in our studio, asking Nick if he can borrow . . . whatever it is that men with beards need to borrow at ten o'clock at night. Nick disappears to help him look through cupboards of plugs and cables, Radcliffe signs off and puts on the last record and Maconie puts his coat on.

'Nice to meet you, John,' he says to me, shaking my hand. 'I've got to get a cab.'

'What are you up to now?' Mark asks as I thank him for letting me watch the show.

'I'm meeting my friend Simon in a pub.'

'I drive past there,' he says when I tell him its name, and he offers to give me a lift to save me getting a taxi. I wait for Radcliffe as he locks up the office and goes to the toilet.

'I've spent my whole life on this road,' he says, driving out of the underground car park on to the Oxford Road. 'It would be odd to work anywhere else.' He pulls up on a slip road, I thank him, shake his hand and look forward to telling people in the pub what a nice man Mark Radcliffe is. His car is blue.

13

FUTURE RADIO (1)

'As long as there are cars and there are people too lazy to download, we will have radio.'

(Ira Glass, presenter of *This American Life*)

After meeting people involved with radio I've felt I have oozed a confidence I'd almost forgotten I was capable of, it's put colour back into my cheeks and zapped an energy into me. The version of me that sits alongside Stuart Maconie, Mark Radcliffe, Gill Hudson is a much more confident, assured person than the one who sits on his swivel chair at work opposite Alan Medlicott and Craig. There are, however, certain clues that reveal I am far from being the consummate professional I sometimes pretend to be, with a Dictaphone slipped into my suit pocket and a diary full of scheduled appointments. Still pumped up from my day in Manchester at the BBC I started to panic when I woke up to find out that I didn't have the notebook I'd used during my meeting with Radcliffe and Maconie. The scribbled notes I had made to document the day were not in my bag when I woke up, presumably left in one of Manchester's bars, taxis or fried chicken outlets. On the train back to Norwich I was frantically trying to rewrite my notes from memory, attempting to recall every nuance, every aside, every minor detail when my phone rang, and I heard a familiar voice at the other end.

'Hello, John. It's Mark Radcliffe.'

'Hi,' I say, slightly confused.

'You left your notebook here.'

'Aah.'

'We read through it all, naturally.'

'Oh.'

'"Feeble punch lines"?'

'Did I write that?'

'Yes. Quite right too. Anyway, let me know your address and I'll post it back to you.'

There was a chuckle in Radcliffe's voice as he dispensed the information about the whereabouts of my book. I didn't know whether to be relieved or embarrassed, but as I thought of Radcliffe and Maconie sitting in their office, reading my thoughts about them, a secret diary that was never meant to be opened, I couldn't wait to tell people what had happened, tell my friends what an idiot I was. I shouldn't be allowed to meet important people.

While the rest of the country has been recovering from an earthquake that turned out to be a bit of an anticlimax, and while I've preoccupied myself with going to Manchester, I have heard back from Future Radio. Back in Norwich I walk to their studios to meet Simone, the station's volunteer coordinator, who has agreed to talk to me about getting involved with the station.

'You must be John,' a woman who must be Simone says, greeting me at the front desk. She is around my age, short hair, wearing bangles and flipflops. She beckons me to follow her, and we slalom through narrow corridors and into the kitchen.

'I was just making a cup of tea, do you want one?'

I nod. I like it here. Sometimes when you walk into a room or building you immediately feel at home, relaxed, that you know this is somewhere that is going to make you happy. Brewed up, we go to her office and Simone pulls across a chair for me to sit at. A man at a computer in the corner waves. Terry Lee I say to myself, somehow recognizing his smile even though I have never seen him, only heard him on the radio. He is the presenter of the *Breakfast Show* that I have listened to a few times and was surprised to actually enjoy.

'This is Terry,' Simone says, 'he's one of three full-time members of staff here at Future.'

'I really like your show,' I tell him, and he seems genuinely pleased at the compliment.

'So what makes you want to volunteer here?' she asks as I sit down, take off my coat.

'I listen to radio a lot,' I tell her, deciding it may be best not to tell her exactly how far my radio obsession has escalated. No one likes someone who is too keen. 'I've got a boring job and would like to do something productive with my spare time.'

'That makes sense,' Simone says, nodding. 'What interests you most? Producing? Editing? Presenting?'

'Music,' I tell her. 'I'd like to do something that involved making playlists, or listening to new bands.'

'Well, we're always being sent CDs by record labels, but no one ever has time to spare to go through them all, or to get in touch with feedback. Maybe that is something that would suit you?'

I sit in my chair resembling the nodding Gromit perched on Craig's computer.

'What about in terms of presenting?' she asks. 'Is that something you'd like to do?'

'Maybe,' I say, thinking of the two presenters playing Half Man Half Biscuit on Resonance FM. 'Only if it's a music show though,' I say, perhaps throwing around too many demands considering my tea is still too hot to drink.

'At Future we focus very closely on music,' Simone tells me. 'We play indie, alternative, but not the same songs that other stations play because we simply can't afford to compete with the bigger stations directly. So we differentiate by playing songs by bands that you know, but wouldn't necessarily expect to hear. On our playlist, for example we have Kings of Leon, the Cure, Primal Scream. But songs are intended to take you by surprise.'

Simone continues with the background of the station. Future Radio launched full-time in Norwich in August 2007 after running on a part-time basis for a year. Although community stations aren't always held in high regard, mainly due to negative associations with pirate radio, they can provide a valuable service. A licence will not be granted unless the station is clearly making a difference to a community, not just on air but also behind the scenes, training people in broadcasting, offering incentives for young people. Sometimes community radio can be an invaluable resource. In Bolivia in 1949 miners gave a percentage of their salary to fund the miners' radio station. Over the next fifteen years more and more radio stations were created. Bolivia was not always at peace, and so the miners' radio was where announcements of births, burials and deaths would be made. It was the best place to hear reliable information about political upheaval. Norwich doesn't have a prosperous mining community, and political upheaval is thin on the ground these days, but its community radio station seems to be in good health.

'I'll give you a tour,' Simone tells me. She holds open the door beside Terry Lee that leads to the two studios, one of which has a bearded man speaking into a microphone, his listening audience denied his extreme hand gestures. As we go through to the vacant Studio 2 he is punching the air with both fists. The equipment looks expensive, top of the range, as slick as anything Christian O'Connell has ever touched. I follow Simone through the corridors to the opposite end of the building. We pass a state-of-the-art computer room with twenty flat-screen PCs and we sit down in the training room, which has a mocked-up radio studio with the same equipment.

'This is where we run workshops for people interested in radio. Schools come here a lot, and if you decide to volunteer with us you can come here, you'll be taught how to use the equipment, and can book the room to practise putting shows together.'

She teaches me how to create playlists on the computer and shows me the touchscreen that plays jingles for each show. Simone reaches up for a folder to give me the relevant application forms and I want to fill them in straight away, but fold them up to take home.

'The schedule is quite rigid,' Simone tells me, 'but we are always keen to hear new ideas for programmes. And if you want to get involved directly, you can do a *People's Playlist*. This is an hour-long show every week where a listener comes in and creates their own show, choosing twelve records and explaining why they have chosen them. It would be really great if you wanted to get involved with that.'

Simone walks me to the main doors. The computer room has filled with a group of children, two teenagers sit in the office with Terry Lee, and I look forward to coming back here, sitting in a room listening to a box of records, maybe even presenting my own show. Back in my flat I make some food, eggs on toast with mushrooms and spinach. I pour a glass of red wine, read newspapers, and feel at ease with the world. I do things I have been trying to avoid – putting clothes on hangers, CDs back in their cases, soon my messy flat is tidy again, and I feel less stressed. I feel comfortable in my own home. I look through the Future Radio forms, fill in the boxes: educational details, reasons I want to volunteer, times I am available. When all four pages are covered with my Biro scribble, I think about how much I'd enjoy being involved with radio, having my own show. As long as I get to play Half Man Half Biscuit.

14

KISS FM

*'Every morning I gargle with Cristal, then spit it out and throw
away the rest of the bottle.'*

(Logan Sama)

Pirate radio stations have always fascinated me. I think I relate
to the shambolic, the unordered, the anarchic; some of my
CDs are in the wrong cases and I am not exactly sure how
much National Insurance I'm paying.

It was listening to John Peel on Radio 1 that made me aware of
the existence of pirate radio. Peel described *The Perfumed Garden*
show he presented in the sixties on the pirate station Radio London
as 'a sacred little corner of hippydom magically unsullied by commercial forces'. He read out listeners' poetry and played the type of
music that people had never heard before: Captain Beefheart, Marc
Bolan. Despite never having heard the show I was captivated by it.
Peel wanted his listeners to know that they were not on their own,
that solitude can be something to be cherished rather than feared.
It was a mantra later adopted by Nintendo Wii.

Peel's show went hand in hand with the birth of flower power and the Summer of Love. It was a photograph of John F. Kennedy's teenage daughter Caroline which gave the Irish entrepreneur Ronan O'Rahilly the desire to create a radio station inspired by the teenage girl's visage, whose youth, excitement and optimism he wanted to capture, preserve and use as inspiration for the newly founded Radio Caroline. O'Rahilly vowed to bring the 1960s Chelsea swagger to the radio sets of the UK. London was swinging like it had never swung before, Chelsea was awash with rock stars, models, raconteurs and designers and somewhere on the North Sea waves were the ships which Radio London and Radio Caroline operated from. At the time the pirate stations were crucial to popular culture because the BBC gave such low priority to music. Elvis Presley, Little Richard and the Beatles had ensured that music would never be the same again, but the BBC's stance was a refusal to acknowledge that there was a much cooler party just around the corner that everyone was invited to, and instead carried on playing orchestra music, perhaps frightened to unsettle its audience. Radio London was ultimately closed down by the Marine Offences Bill in 1967, but pirate radio stations had already made their mark and were crucial to the development of music on the radio, and as a result of the pirates' popularity local stations were created, which ultimately led to the birth of Radio 1 only months later.

What appealed to me most about pirate radio was the image of DJs broadcasting in force-ten gales and snowstorms. The pirates had certain songs they would play if they got in trouble which would be coded messages to people on land who would realize that help was needed. I liked the idea of the presenters being seasick in between records, playing the Velvet Underground by candlelight, standing on the crow's nest listening to Donovan. It seemed to me an idyllic life, all the DJs were there purely for their love of the music, they were so passionate about what they were hearing, the records they bought and bands they had seen that they were prepared to risk their lives to be at sea. It's certainly a different approach to making radio than Ben Jones and Russ on Virgin seem to take. These pirates would rather play the Rolling Stones and Jimi Hendrix than get mortgages, wives, jobs in banks. It was not just about embracing an alternative lifestyle and playing cool music, Radio London played new releases by black artists who had no exposure elsewhere. The pirates were revealing a side of the world their listeners had never encountered before.

Until it was granted a radio licence by the Department of Trade and Industry in 2000, Kiss operated as a pirate radio station and even though broadcasting illegally, still attracted over half a million listeners. Kiss first aired in 1985 and broadcast to London, its fan base and credibility were due to acid-house nights it put on at London's Wag Club. The growth of urban music and rap had created a need for a radio station to play the music that was becoming popular with London teenagers and clever marketing by Kiss FM made the station credible to a completely new audience. Kiss was owned by its DJs, who were all shareholders. They attracted a loyal listenership and there was a widely held excitement about the vibrancy and hope of the new wave of UK hip hop and garage.

I develop an unquenchable thirst to be a teenager in the 1960s. I become desperate to be listening to tracks from *Sergeant Pepper* for the first time, using a tinny radio under my duvet when I am supposed to be asleep. Lacking even the most rudimentary tools for time travel, I tune my radio to Kiss FM. I switch on at 9 p.m. when Dynamite MC starts his show, billed as the 'the freshest in hip hop and R&B'. I have never really listened to the music that Kiss FM champions. I don't like hip hop and R&B. I like Cumberland sausages and armchairs.

I sit slouched on the settee playing computer games, still sulking slightly from earlier on this afternoon, when after my lunch break I arrived back in the office after a trip to Comet and saw Poppy had a basket of muffins on her desk, wrapped in a bow. The afternoon was agony; every time I looked round to her desk she was there, smiling with blueberry lips. Mondays at work are hard enough to get through without someone ordering Poppy muffins. Eventually I pull myself together and start to enjoy listening to Kiss, not so much for the music being played but because of the infectious enthusiasm of Dynamite MC. He plays the Wu Tang Clan and Jay Z, but it is his gusto which makes me decide to switch off my Xbox and move out on to the tiny balcony at the back of the block of flats I live in. I turn the music up and make myself comfortable, spreading out over the wooden floorboards. I keep a stash of drinks on my balcony and I pour some supermarket own-brand rum into a mug, mix it with some supermarket own-brand cola and start to imagine that the show is being recorded on a boat in the pitch-black of the late-night North Sea and that I am a teenager again.

'I went to a chilli-eating competition at the weekend,' Dynamite MC tells us in between tracks. 'I bought myself a new cookbook and some of the hottest chillies money can buy. I eat phaal for breakfast!' he boasts while lining up a Lethal Bizzle record. I put my headphones on. Music sounds better with headphones on; that way you do not let any of the vocals seep into the carpet, the guitars don't get soaked up by the curtains, the bass line doesn't disappear into the room's soft furnishings. I've always liked music at a loud volume but suspect that my neighbours might not be of the same opinion, particularly the man at number 22. He's a dickhead. After a song by Ludacris, Dynamite MC congratulates Fran Matthews for passing her driving test. He dedicates a song to Alex, revising, and says hello to Sam and Paul, driving to Dover, all enjoying the same listening experience as me. Next he interviews Blind Alphabetz, who sing about gun crime, violence and being threatened in the streets.

'How did you come up with the name Blind Alphabetz?' Dynamite asks.

'I was touching a sheet of letters from the Braille alphabet. It had a real resonance with me,' Abdul Rahman, one half of the duo, says, before praising the Prophet Mohammed as being his hero and biggest influence. They rap about terrorism, about troops abroad. They are angry but articulate and claim to be the future of hip hop.

At eleven o'clock it is time for Logan Sama, who presents 'the world's only 100 per cent Grime radio show' every Monday. I have no idea what grime is and so check out Sama's biography on the Kiss FM website. 'Every morning I gargle with Cristal, then spit it out and throw away the rest of the bottle.' I like the sound of Logan Sama. Grime is still a mystery to me though.

The first track he plays is the new Kano single, 'Grime MC'. 'Text in what you think of it,' Sama tells us, and fifteen minutes later he plays it again. I like the idea of playing the same song twice in the same show, if you buy a new CD you will listen to it more than once before you make your mind up about it. My only problem is how to critique grime. I text in.

Really good. Kano rocks. From John, sitting on his balcony in Norwich.

No matter how grimy you are, deep down all you want is to be appreciated as 'really good' even if it is by a 25-year-old drinking rum alone at midnight. Through the balcony doors I can see I left the television on. Jimmy Carr is presenting a quiz show and I feel a sense of pride in myself, that there is more substance in what I am doing than flicking through repeats on late-night digital television. The viewing figures for Carr's show will be astronomical in comparison to Logan Sama's, but I feel I am achieving something more than if I was sat watching Carr's single entendres and smug glances at camera.

Logan plays a song called 'Six Figure Deal' by Chipmunk. The lyrics include the names of practically every radio presenter who plays new music in the UK, including Logan Sama, John Kennedy, Huw Stephens. The message behind the song is that if any DJ plays Chipmunk now, the band will stick with that DJ when they've got a six-figure deal. They make it sound so simple.

Sama's special guest is Tinchy Stryder, who is in the studio to publicize his much-anticipated album *Soundtrack of Urban*

Streets released earlier today. His album was produced by two mates, who together with Stryder did all of the publicity themselves, appearing in clubs, making the most of their limited budget, an approach rewarded with underground success. Their production values seem to be similar to those of Kiss FM: fuelled by self-belief, a passion for music and perseverance.

'If you want to win tickets to Tinchy's album launch party at Brick Lane tomorrow then text in now and you can be there,' Logan advertises. I reach for my mobile phone and text the number. I have nothing to do tomorrow. Well I do, I have to go to work, but would much prefer to go to an album launch party. There might be free booze.

'Last week we had two hundred and twenty texts in ten minutes,' Sama says proudly. 'Let's beat that today, Tinchy is going to be giving away signed singles to every tenth person who texts in.'

This is exciting. A few hours ago I had no idea who this guy was, but suddenly if I'm not at his launch party in the next twenty-four hours, or don't own a signed copy of his new CD, then I will have to re-evaluate what I am doing with my life. In the first four minutes they receive 300 texts. The thought of 299 other people doing exactly the same thing as me is fascinating. I wonder whether they were as eloquent as me when they texted in to comment on Kano's new single. Tinchy performs a twenty-minute freestyle set and I get out my notebook and think about the songs I would play for *People's Playlist* on Future Radio. Obviously Blur and the Smiths and Half Man Half Biscuit, but it should be more personal. The first album I ever bought, due to inexcusable bad taste as an eleven-year-old, was Status Quo. The first single I ever bought was 'The Macarena'. Looking back at my former self it is amazing that I am now a man of such impeccable taste. I think back to Simone's suggestion that I think of the kind of show I would like to present myself. Logan Sama and Dynamite MC are playing the music they are passionate about, and I wonder whether I could present a show where I play the records I won in the John Peel competition in 2003. I decide to email Simone with the idea at work tomorrow.

'It's not bedtime yet,' Logan Sama reminds us at 1 a.m. as he signs off, no doubt handing Tinchy copies of his CD to sign for the baying mob who have texted in. As Kiss FM is a commercial station, there have been adverts playing all night; for university courses, anti drink-driving campaigns, pleas to join the army. There is an advert recruiting the unemployed to repossess vehicles. It paints quite a picture of those listening to radio late at night.

As I wait for Logan Sama to phone and congratulate me for winning a prize I listen to the Dangerous Minds Crew. It starts to get cold outside so I take off my headphones and relocate to my bedroom. I have completely lost all sense of time and temporarily forget it is the middle of the night and people are asleep in my block of flats, and I almost start on daily household tasks – I think about vacuuming, phoning friends, putting on the washing machine, learning to play the drums.

Dangerous Minds won a Pirate Sound Clash competition and were given a contract for a weekly hour-long show on Kiss FM. They specialize in grime, garage, UK hip hop and bashment. It took me long enough to get to grips with grime, it is far too late at night to try to understand bashment. After playing songs with references as diverse as 'stab wounds' and 'Emile Heskey', the two presenters, who had previously been talking about their tennis injuries, rap for the last twenty minutes of the show. This doesn't happen on the *Today* programme.

15

CLASSIC FM, BBC RADIO 3

'A touch of calm with Brahms.'

(Simon Bates)

At 7.30 I answer the front door in my boxer shorts. The postman hands me a parcel. I open it up to find the signed Tinchy Stryder CD I so craved. Delighted, I switch on my digital radio and scan through the channels. On releasing my finger, the radio lottery decides I will spend the day listening to Classic FM.

I have never liked classical music, and never will, even if I live until I'm thirty. Spending my day listening to Classic FM is the equivalent of someone with a fear of water being stranded in the Pacific; no lifejacket, no rescue boat, no helicopter on the look-out dangling a rope ladder. I don't know a double bass from a cello, wouldn't have a clue what to do with a cor anglais, whether to blow it, suck it, pluck it, hit it with a stick. I like Blur. But that is exactly why I should be listening to Classic FM today – it makes no sense to say you don't like something if you haven't even tried it. Listening to different radio stations every day is the perfect excuse to try out new things, to open up my imagination a little.

Listening to Stravinsky while trying to motivate yourself to get out of bed is difficult, it goes against everything classical music stands for. I need to be up and ready for work but it's cold and I prefer to stay where I am, with my feet on the radiator, my head on the pillow. Outside there is pollution, traffic, swearing. In my room there are violins, clarinets, a conductor in white gloves waving his baton at me, instructing me to sleep.

'For unassuaged pleasure, I bring you Beethoven and Rossini, back to back,' says Simon Bates as my face sinks back into the pillow.

Bates has one of the easier breakfast shifts on British radio. He doesn't have to start until 8 a.m. and some of the pieces he plays are so long it means he can say something about *The Magic Flute* or Gershwin, press 'play', and doesn't have to speak again for ten, fifteen minutes. The most listened-to presenter on commercial radio starts his show with a droll comment about the British weather before treating us to the sounds of Haydn. People text in.

'What a beautiful, relaxing morning.'

'Thank you for the tranquillity.'

'We're having a lovely holiday in Tuscany.'

The references to relaxation are ceaseless; it seems that any sentence that does not mention serenity will cause the entire nation to flap around, their blood pressure soaring, panic-buying stress balls.

I stay in bed so long that even though I catch the bus it still means I am late for work yet again. It is 9.15 and the open-plan office ripples with perfunctory hellos, swivel chairs being adjusted, people trying to conceal their yawns. I switch on my computer and say hello to Alan Medlicott and Craig. They are wearing matching ties; their body clocks becoming more synchronized every day. Soon they will be sharing sandwiches, going on day trips to places of historical significance, cutting each other's hair.

'Sorry for being late,' I say. Alan Medlicott looks at his watch. I think about asking how he is, but just get on with my work, let the day pass as normally as possible.

'Moments of calm with Brahms,' Bates says, playing a lullaby, and I am able to take deep breaths again, look forward to the day ahead. I like Bates, his voice is gift-wrapped in tissue paper, scattered with rose petals, double-bowed with red ribbon. Before long I find that data entry can be soothing, it is nice to have no responsibility other than making sure Caps Lock isn't on. I start to relax, to forget about unopened bank statements on my bedroom floor, the tedium of the route to work, the fact that bit by bit, day by day, data entry is killing my brain cells.

'Hello to Emma who is back from her holiday in Bali and waiting for her photographs to be developed,' Bates says. 'Andrew is at work in his art gallery. And a big hello to Heather who is at home, baking.' Right now I would swap places with any one of these people. I don't know how they manage to be so relaxed with the constant interruption of adverts which are a stumbling-block in this utopian paradise. It is hard to enter a Zen-like consciousness when ads for insurance companies and breakdown services keep jingling every five minutes like alarm clocks on snooze. Voices tell me to buy jeeps and anti-wrinkle cream. I feel I am being targeted by windscreen repair companies. I can't even afford windscreen wipers, never mind a car.

Classic FM has 6 million listeners, far more than initially predicted at the station's launch in 1992. Its popularity is largely because of the station's accessible playlist that has been carefully put together to appeal to people who work in art galleries, who go on holiday to Bali, who are at home during the day, baking. Their clear rivals are BBC Radio 3, which many people find too serious and unnecessarily stuffy. In turn, many of Classic FM's detractors complain that the station is too populist, panders to an audience that does not understand music, that if you knew anything about classical music you would listen to Radio 3. The most notable enthusiasts are Friends of Radio 3, a listeners group who aim to promote the station, protect its heritage that dates back to when it was the BBC Third Programme in 1946, and make sure it does not become too diluted or dumbed down in the twenty-first century. Despite Radio 3's traditional fans who value the culture and intelligence of the station, Classic FM have three times as many listeners. Part of the commercial station's evolution has involved playing what they call 'popular classics', or what I call songs from adverts and films. To the classical aficionado I'm sure this is something to be spat at, that Rachmaninov would be spinning in his grave knowing that his legacy lives on in a Toyota advert, or in the background of a film while Orlando Bloom is snogging someone. But this is the music people like to hear. Already this morning I have heard the theme tunes to *The Apprentice* and *The Vicar of Dibley*. The listening figures are testament to the way Classic FM brings classical music to the masses without being pretentious. After dedicating a piece to Anna at home writing a dissertation on Voltaire, and Emma, a pianist listening to Classic FM for inspiration, it is time for Bates to go home. At 11.45 he says: 'The next voice you hear will be Jamie Crick.'

After more adverts, 'Come to our hotel', 'This is a nice car', 'Buy our magazine', Crick presents *The Most Wanted*, where listeners choose pieces from a pre-selected list on ClassicFM.com. Crick is a likeable presenter, whose youthful air fits in with Classic FM's game plan. He genuinely seems excited that Schumann has made it to number three in the top five, 'his highest ever entry', beating Bach and Elgar but losing out to Vivaldi at number two and Tchaikovsky at number one. It is important to have favourites, so from now I choose Tchaikovsky as my favourite composer. My favourite painter is Van Gogh. My favourite in *Friends* is Chandler.

From one o'clock Crick presents *Classic FM Requests* and urges us to send in our suggestions. It's my dinner hour and I eat my sandwiches while walking to Comet, as for the first time this week it isn't raining. The lack of rain clouds does nothing to brighten up the industrial estate. There is nothing inspiring in the names of the businesses that neighbour our office: Mr Clutch, Blockbuster Drain Services, Manufacturers of Polythene Envelopes. These places have plot numbers instead of names, on Norwich industrial estate there is no Cherrytree Meadow, Honeydew Avenue, Scarlett Johansson Lane. There is Plot 38, Unit 14A, corrugated-iron curtains, tin huts, Portakabins with stacks of pallets in their yard. I walk past these places every day; they look bleak but they are putting sausages and eggs on people's dinner plates, selection boxes in stockings at Christmas. I listen to Crick as I walk up and down the aisles, thinking about what I would spend my money on if I had any, frown at people browsing iPods when they could be buying digital radios. People text in:

Mary: 'I'd like to hear *The Merry Widow* because my husband and I are learning it on our clarinets.'

Mike: 'Please play Ravel's *Boléro* for my three children who love it.'

Lynne: 'Can you play something for me and my husband, we are at home decorating, our radio is broken and we can mostly hear crackle.'

I find it interesting that people listen to Classic FM, crackle or no crackle and tolerate the constant interruption of adverts. To relieve the tedium of the day I decide I'll request a song too and think about who the lucky recipient should be. One of my friends? Me? Alan Medlicott? I look at my computer screen, open at the story of Sandra biting the bullet, marrying a man who arrived on her doorstep. I decide on a romantic gesture of my own, and dedicate a song to Poppy.

Hi Jamie. Can you play Pachelbel for Poppy, even though she will never hear it? From John at work in Norwich.

I like Pachelbel. I heard him on an advert once.

It is three o'clock, I check my emails and Simone at Future Radio has been in touch. She really likes my idea about a show where I play the records I won from John Peel and would like me to come in and talk to her about it. I reply to suggest dates, really excited about the prospect of being able to listen to loud distorted guitar and not this classical music I'm subjecting myself to. But ever the pro I stick with the radio, wondering how I will feel about this kind of music when I've been listening to it all day. Alan Medlicott gives me a stack of papers and I spend the afternoon in the filing room. Time stands still in this room; as with casinos there is no clock, no window, no evidence of the transformation of daylight into dusk, just a light bulb swinging from a flex. The only certainty is paper cuts. Classic FM is making time go even more slowly. I am suffering, feeling fatigued and tempted to reach into my pocket, take the batteries out of my radio, fling off my headphones. It is as though the word 'relax' is seeping through the walls, ghouls are whispering 'This is calming' through the air-conditioning. It's like being on a roller-coaster with a man at the front employed to shout 'This is fun!' and another as we go down a steep drop who shouts 'This is scary!'

As I file I listen to *The Afternoon Show* with Mark Forrest, who starts his show with Schubert, and then Ben, a twelve-year-old, emails in to dedicate Gilbert and Sullivan to his dad. I will forever associate classical music with this room, a stack of papers in my hands as I stoop, squint, alphabetize. With nothing else to think about I wonder what Mark Forrest looks like. If I was at my desk I could find out in seconds online. But perhaps radio presenters are best left faceless and mysterious. I imagine every presenter on Classic FM wears a bow-tie and top-hat and tweaks a coiled Brylcreemed moustache. Before the Internet the closest the public could get to seeing what someone on the radio looked like was the popular 'Face Behind the Voice' feature at the back of the *Radio Times*. People thumb through the pages, find the face and say 'Oh, they've got curlier hair than I thought', or 'I never pictured him with a beard.'

And then it happens: 'Can you play Pachelbel for Poppy even though she will never hear it? From John at his desk in Norwich.' I open the door to the filing room and look over at Poppy. She walks to the fax machine and violins start to play.

By half-past five I finish the filing, say goodbye to Alan Medlicott and Craig, who have never left work earlier than me, and walk home and hear another piece I recognize, 'The Sleepy Lagoon', also known as the theme tune to *Desert Island Discs*. My shirt untucked, my tie loosened, I amble down the road in the relaxed way that would make Simon Bates proud. When I get in I decide to switch stations, and tune the radio to BBC Radio 3, giving Classic FM a rest. Before the changeover though I pick up the Tinchy Stryder CD propped up on my windowsill like a trophy and for the first time today classical music is suspended, and as the sun sets Tinchy wakes me up like a cold shower and I feel able to cope with anything Radio 3 has to throw at me. *Performance on 3* comes from the Lufthansa Festival of Baroque Music and the Ensemble Pierre Robert, a group known for its interpretations of French baroque music. I get changed into jeans and T-shirt, switch on the radio in the living room and splay myself across the settee. Within the first fifteen minutes of the show I have already drifted in and out of gentle sleep more than once. The violins are so gentle, so soft; I close my eyes and there are kaleidoscopes. I feel I should be rubbed down by a Swede, or take a glass of champagne to the jacuzzi. I don't have a jacuzzi. I don't even have a bath. The closest I could get would be to fill a bowl with hot water and washing-up liquid and stick my elbows in.

Composer of the Week is Franz Waxman, the twentieth-century composer with twelve Oscar nominations who wrote the music for almost 150 films. Presenter Don McLeod plays a clip of an interview with Waxman, where he talks about a time his wife was in hospital, and after visiting her with their son one day they went for a walk to a nearby temple and heard organ music being played. After listening for a while, Waxman introduced himself to the organist, who said how privileged he was to meet him. Shortly afterwards his wife died, and Waxman commemorated her by writing a piece based on the Book of Joshua, which developed into his best-remembered work, and premiered at that temple.

By now words like sinfonietta and timpani are as much a part of my vocabulary as filing and hometime. At 9.45 I listen to *Night Waves* as I iron my work shirts. The critic Gillian Reynolds talks about a new cityscape of Liverpool, a 128-foot painted panoramic view of the city by artist Ben Johnson.

'People recognize parts of their life in the picture,' the Liverpool-born Reynolds says. 'I looked for the school I went to, the two cathedrals on Hope Street, the church where I was christened. You feel like you are watching it through a dream, that you are waltzing through the city on your tiptoes.'

'You can read this picture like a book,' the historian Tristram Hunt adds.

I go to the kitchen to make some food and the *Guardian*'s Andrew Dixon talks about the recent performance of Henrik Ibsen's play *Rosmersholm*, a story of a Christian minister who loses his faith, which has been revived for a twenty-first-century audience. I feel like I should be nibbling venison and sipping cognac, but settle on eating cereal while listening to a discussion on Ibsen's moral ambiguity.

*

I go to bed during *Late Junction* presented by Verity Sharp, calypso followed by a fourteenth-century folk song, and then West Indian stomp by Harold Boyce and the Harlem Indians. I really like the show but turn my radio off before the end, when I go to a sleepy lagoon of my own. I'd like to carry on listening but need to be fresh for a full and challenging day at work tomorrow. I really wish that was true.

16

JUST A MINUTE

*'The toilet door was nine inches from the ground and somebody
had written "Beware of the limbo dancers".'*

(Peter Jones, in an episode of *Just a Minute*)

I remember being nine years old, in the kitchen with my mum;
she switched the radio on and suggested I might like the programme that was about to start. It was *Just a Minute*, and the
guests for the show included Paul Merton and Wendy Richards.
My mum explained the rules to me as she cooked: that you were
given a subject to speak on for sixty seconds but were not allowed
to repeat a word, hesitate, deviate from the subject. I thought the
show was the funniest thing I had ever heard. I was starting to
watch sitcoms like *Dad's Army* and *Fawlty Towers*, as well as
Merton's Channel 4 sketch show. I was starting to appreciate
comedy for the first time.

It was 1991 and already *Just a Minute* had been running for
twenty-three years. Over the next few months I started to learn
about the show's history. I borrowed tapes from the library and

for the first time heard the voices of people like Kenneth Williams, Peter Cook, Clement Freud, Sheila Hancock. But it was Paul Merton who kept me tuning in; growing up I would watch his every appearance on television, listen to everything he did on the radio. I thought *Just a Minute* was so funny, so special, so unique, but what I really liked about it was that none of my friends listened to it, so I could nick the jokes, pass them off as my own.

One person who has not missed a single episode of the show, which has now celebrated its fortieth anniversary, is its chairman, Nicholas Parsons. After sending emails to his agent saying how much I love *Just a Minute*, he agreed to talk to me, and one day I come home from work not to eat tomato soup or iron my work shirts, but to phone Nicholas Parsons at his home in Buckinghamshire.

'I had done a lot of improvised stand-up comedy,' he tells me when I ask how he got involved with *Just a Minute*, 'and won an award for *Listen to this Space*, which was radio's first improv show, and I then ended up on the panel for the pilot of *Just a Minute*. But it turned out I had to be chairman, and when it was shown to the BBC, they said that although they didn't like certain aspects of the show, one thing they did like was the chairmanship. So I was asked to do it for the series. I would have preferred to be on the panel, but you don't turn down a good job so I thought "How can I make this work for myself?"'

'If you hear some of those early recordings they are quite archaic, the rules hadn't been defined or refined, it was all very haphazard, the rules were loosely interpreted. Two of the original players, Derek Nimmo and Clement Freud, preferred it that way because it meant there were not many interruptions. And then Kenneth Williams joined the cast, and really struggled for the first three series, but soon he made the show his own and said it was his favourite programme to appear on. When Peter Jones joined, we established the four 'regulars' and slowly the show grew slicker. I do take some credit for that as I gradually refined the rules myself; began to make it much more strict. If you want any longevity with shows like this you have to make them slick and sharp and up to the minute. I started giving bonus points to people who made witty interruptions, but the player who was speaking would also get a point and carry on with the subject. I had to go on *Points of View* to defend myself, people said "He's changed the rules!" I simply explained that I was giving more scope for entertainment. Then of course Kenneth died. At the time he appeared on every show, the other regulars would occasionally have a week off and their chair would be filled by a guest. But as Kenneth was part of every recording people thought "It's over." But I fought for the show to survive. I said it would be ridiculous for us not to carry on; Kenneth was brilliant on the show, but he wasn't the show. In fact on occasions he could overpower it because he got so carried away. It was tremendous having him, but we did occasionally need to indulge him slightly. I had to constantly tell people "The show is the interplay and rapport between the four players and the chairman. That's what makes it so popular. It's not about individuals.'"

One of the great things about advancing digital technology is that you can now listen to episodes of *Just a Minute* from the early days and hear the flow of Kenneth Williams, the interjections of Clement Freud, the exuberance of Derek Nimmo. You can close your curtains and exist in a bygone age as you listen, just as with other shows from the BBC's archive such as *Hancock's Half Hour* and *Steptoe and Son*. Occasionally the BBC 7 announcer will apologize for poor sound quality but that is missing the point; the crackle, the fuzz, the static is all part of the enjoyment of listening to these shows just as people did generations ago.

'The World Service said it was the most listened-to show around the world,' Parsons continues, 'and they said to Radio 4, "If you don't want it, we'll have it." So Radio 4 decided to do another series, we brought different people in, changed the format, and Paul Merton came in. I'd been working with Merton in television and had been pushing for him to come on; I thought he was wonderful. And then one day somebody couldn't make it to the recording, so the producer said "What was the name of the young comedian you mentioned?"

'"Paul Merton."

'"Well I've never heard of him. I don't know much about this new generation of comedians. I'll give him one show, if it doesn't work it's your responsibility."

'Anyway, Paul was one of the few people who took to it straight away, he was excellent. It is such a difficult game to play that sometimes, no matter how talented, engaging, amusing people are in the other work they do, the first time they play *Just a Minute* they struggle a little. But the producer was so impressed with Paul that he immediately booked him for two more shows. He soon became an integral part of the show, and he still loves to do it, doesn't need to, but he enjoys playing the game. If he is free he will always come along. There's not much money in radio, none of us get paid very much, we do it because it's fun. The two of us always have fun together, spark off each other, which is communicated to the audience, which in turn is communicated to the listener at home.'

And it is communicated to the audience. At the Edinburgh Festival one year I went to queue up for tickets to watch *Just a Minute*, and the demand was incredible. Even though I arrived an hour before they were being released the queue already numbered hundreds, stretching out of the courtyard and down the road as more and more people joined. I had to check with the man in front of me that I was in the right place, and wasn't accidentally queuing for a Beatles reunion or to audition for *The X Factor* rather than watch Nicholas Parsons present a radio panel show. I collected my tickets but was lucky, as anyone stood just a dozen places behind me, after waiting for hours, had to leave empty-handed as they were told there were none left. As I sat in the audience watching Merton, Greg Proops, Dara Ó'Briain and Clement Freud I thought of the people who had missed out on being able to watch what I was lucky enough to be seeing; I felt a real sympathy for them. But then I thought sod it, they should have got there earlier, and it'll be on the radio anyway.

'Over the years we have accumulated a cast list with every name you could mention,' Parsons continues. 'We always ask different people to be part of it, sometimes they're not free, sometimes they turn us down because the money's so poor. But people tend to do radio because they enjoy it. For a lot of actors, like me, it is our favourite medium of work. When I was younger, as a BBC drama rep I could make a living wage out of radio. Television was still young, but over the years, as TV has become more powerful and dominating, most of the licence money goes straight to them. What I think is the most amazing accolade for BBC Radio is that on a very modest share of the licence fee, it runs not only Radios 1, 2, 3, 4 and 5, but also the World Service and local radio, and the standard of all BBC radio is so, so high.

"To be successful in the show you need to be able to think in a very disciplined way, to have a very thorough understanding of comedy and humour, to be able to listen so you can check for mistakes yourself as you go along. Paul Merton, for example, has a wonderful comic brain. He's very quick, which means that as he's telling a story he can suddenly change direction, because as you talk about something, words you have already used will inevitably come up again, so you have to think of another word without repeating yourself. I only mention Paul because he is a supreme example of how to play the game. When I do my *One Man Show*, I am invariably asked if I have a favourite contestant. But I tell them I can't have one, I have to be utterly fair, otherwise I'll be accused of nepotism. I can recognize the skill of certain players, such as Merton, Clement Freud, Graham Norton, Marcus Brigstock. These are people the public love, which is great for the show. But the point is, you don't need to have a favourite. The excitement is in the way the game is played. For example, in the last series, we had a show that featured Graham Norton, Tony Hawks, Sue Perkins and Paul, who are all very sharp, very humorous, and the fizz, the buzz, was electric. When the show really takes off like that it is a challenge for me, because I am in a position to orchestrate the whole thing, to take control, move it on. That's what makes for the best shows, and if you have the best players involved, it makes for a memorable show. It can't be just one person that makes the show though. Paul Merton is the most generous player, if he feels he has been talking more than the others, he will hold back, give the others a chance to join in. He is one of the most generous performers I have ever met. But obviously he wants to do well. In any job you want to excel, to do the best you can. Not many comedy players have that kind of generosity. But it would be wrong to single out one person at the expense of the others. Graham Norton is incredibly funny too, and incredibly skilled. It's the sharpness of the mind, the ability to create humour that makes these players so popular.

'One thing that is incredibly interesting about *Just a Minute*,' Parsons continues, 'is that the essence of comedy is timing. You use pausing for emphasis, repetition for effect. We're doing a comedy show, making people laugh, but it is the antithesis of what works in comedy. If you tell a joke in normal circumstances, it is impossible not to include a pause or repetition. It's interesting that we are making a comedy show which denies people that opportunity.'

'Is there any guest who has eluded you?' I ask, although I have seen the list of famous people who have appeared and it is a complete guide to the history of British comedy. 'Is there anyone you have wanted on the show but has never appeared?'

'A lot of very skilled performers know they would struggle the first time they were on. Josie Lawrence was someone I had been desperate to have on the show, she's so funny, naturally spontaneous, the most brilliant performer. It's our producer's job to book people, to decide who appears, and she was desperate for her to appear too. But Josie didn't want to do it, resisted it for a long time, saying she was too nervous. Eventually she came on though, and struggled a little to start off with, but I am in the position to twist the rules for first-time players of the game. And we had such fun on that show. She was absolute magic, and when she was back on the show she received no leniency from the chairman, because by then she was settled. I've been doing the show for so long now, I've learned how I can help people, how to play tricks, make jokes that I know people will be able to bounce off. Some contestants, Paul, or Ross Noble, occasionally launch themselves into the realms of the surreal, and the other players know to hold back if someone is on a roll, because it is such wonderful comedy. The generosity of players is delightful. We are working within the realms of spontaneity. And when I introduce the four panellists at the beginning of the show, the audience goes wild, because wherever we go, it is always packed, which is the greatest compliment the show could receive.

'Nothing is planned for the show, nothing is prepared, it is all off the top of our heads as we play, and the audience know that instinctively. An interesting thing about comedy: if you have a scripted show, the audience are on a different wavelength. It might be brilliant, the funniest show ever written, but it is written, so a different style of comedy completely. With *Just a Minute*, the audience instinctively know they are present at a happening, an event. It is psychological, which is why somebody can ad-lib a response and everyone roars with laughter, because it happened there and then. I proved this recently because I came home from a show and said to my wife "It was brilliant, I said this, and Paul replied with this!!" And my wife said ". . . and then what happened?" The proof of spontaneous comedy is that if you repeat it out of context, you have lost the atmosphere generated by the performers and the rapport with the audience, and it isn't funny to repeat it. You can repeat a funny scripted line, because it has been edited, redrafted, thought out as something clever, but an improvised show relies on the spontaneity of the moment and the speed at which the response comes in. It is just a lot of fun, and when you hear the laughter emanating from the players on stage, it is all genuine, we are enjoying it, we are laughing along with the show, and that's what makes the show work.'

And the show does work, hence the queues and ovation at the Edinburgh Festival and the fact that I still listen to it whenever I am home on a Sunday afternoon or a Monday evening. And I still love it now, just as much as when I first heard it, standing in the kitchen on that Sunday lunchtime, nine years old, me and my mum.

17

CAPITAL FM

'Are you distracted by the spot on my nose?'
'Which one?'

(Johnny and Denise)

'I'm so excited to be on the radio!' a caller screams.

'I'm like that every morning,' Johnny Vaughan tells her. 'What's your name?'

'Nikki.'

'Is that one "k" or two?'

'Whatever you like, darling.'

Vaughan presents the *Capital Breakfast* show with Denise Van Outen, reprising their much-loved double act from Channel 4's *The Big Breakfast*. Their comedy partnership is unique, half Peter Cook and Dudley Moore, half Zig and Zag, Van Outen easily matching the quick wit of Johnny Vaughan.

'It's so good to have you back, Den,' Johnny says to her. She has been off work sick all week.

'Do I look rough?'

'Yeah,' Vaughan says, without pausing to consider his answer. 'Thanks!'

'But now you know how we feel. That is how everyone else is every morning. We all sit here at five o'clock feeling sorry for ourselves, and then you walk in, all glam. It's good to see you look a bit worse for wear.'

'On a scale on one to ten, how rough am I?'

'Can we confer? What do you think Welshy?' Vaughan asks the show's soundman in a hushed voice. 'Seven?'

'Eight?' suggests Welshy.

'Seven and a half?'

'Nine?'

'We've decided on six out of ten, Denise.'

Newsreader Emma Corden tells us there are long delays on the North Circular, the M1 is slow southbound, there are severe delays on the Victoria Line. As the commuters of London hail black cabs and wait on Tube platforms, I amble out of my house, walk to work in the Norwich drizzle. I feel more buoyed than usual, partly because I've always really liked Johnny and Denise, but mainly because today at work is Dress Down Friday. When the memo went up on Monday people swarmed around the noticeboard like A-Level results day.

I put on jeans and a shirt, and leave the top two buttons undone. My neck reaches out of the collar like a newborn chick hatching out of its egg. This afternoon I'll be able to walk home from work, clicking my heels, knowing that my fridge is full and I don't have to get up in the morning.

'Guess what police found when they pulled over a car in Texas?' Vaughan asks.

'A panda?'

'No, Denise.'

'A dead body?'

'No, Den. Thanks for playing along though. Police stopped the driver because he was driving erratically, and when they opened the boot . . .' Vaughan adopts the voice of a policeman, 'I don't believe it, a perishing alligator.'

Vaughan switches to the accent of a Texan yokel. '"I couldn't believe what I was seeing," said an onlooker. The driver, Mr Johnson, was charged with illegal possession of an alligator.'

'I didn't know that was a specific law?' Denise asks.

'Mr Johnson was also a wanted burglar and the police found stolen goods in his car. Now,' Vaughan says, 'if you are a wanted criminal, I think it would be best not to draw attention to yourself. Keep your head down, don't drive crazily, remain calm and sensible. And that would include not keeping an alligator in your car.'

'I wonder if it put its head out of the window and stuck its tongue out like dogs do,' Van Outen wonders.

I walk into work. My own version of Johnny and Denise, Alan Medlicott and Craig, have not embraced Dress Down Friday, both wearing shirts and ties as usual. Maybe their mums forgot to remind them, like always happened to at least one kid at the end of every school term.

'Hello to Sharon and Karl working at the dentist's,' Vaughan says. 'To Dennis and his mates decorating. And a big shout out to Big Gay Ray and his bisexual boyfriend Tel.'

'You keep looking at me funny. Are you distracted by the spot on my nose?' Denise asks.

'Which one?'

'Johnny!'

'Do you know what, Denise? It doesn't seem like work any more now that you're on the show with me. And that's the truth, I know it's the sort of thing that always sounds fake, but every morning I look forward to coming in because I know we're going to have a really good time. I loved being here at *Capital Breakfast* before you came, but now it's even better.'

'Aah. Thanks, Johnny. That's really sweet. Now stop staring at my breasts.'

'Sorry.'

The world of breakfast radio is fiercely competitive. Within London alone, Vaughan is just one of several recognizable names. Jamie Theakston on Heart, the affable Alex Zane at XFM, Neil 'Doctor' Fox with Magic 105.4, all talking at once, as well as national DJs like Chris Moyles and Christian O'Connell, who all play similar music, interview the same type of guest – pop stars, people who have been on reality shows, all trying to prove they deserve the big salaries they earn.

'I've presented this show for four years now,' Johnny says, proudly. 'When I started the tabloids said I wouldn't last six months. When I first took over from Chris Tarrant I asked him "What do I do if I run out of things to say?"'

'"Just say it's 7.22."'

'"Why 7.22?"'

'"Because that's what time it will be."'

'And on my first day I got stuck, couldn't think of anything to say, looked up and the big hand of the clock moved slightly and I said, "It's 7.22."'

Vaughan closes the show with 'If I Can Dream' by Elvis.

'All my hopes and dreams are contained within this song. It will give you goose pimples.'

'People keep emailing in saying there is a strange smell in London this morning,' says Margherita Taylor, the station's longest-serving presenter, when her show starts at ten o'clock. 'If anyone knows what it is, do get in touch.' As Capital FM pipes into the offices of the metropolis, Taylor plays the Zutons, Shakira, Kelly Rowland. The first hour goes by with Margherita barely saying a word; on commercial radio brevity can be a virtue, there are far too many presenters too fond of the sound of their own voice, who are far too keen to talk about their day, their opinions, start every sentence with 'Have you ever noticed . . .'. People text in about the smell in London, reports emerge of pongs in Islington, Westminster, Harrow.

'It smells like manure.'

'It's like dead animals.'

'I have to work while holding my nose.'

'It's because the wind has changed direction and smells are coming over from mainland Europe,' Emma Corden tells Margherita from the Capital news desk. 'It's not just London, it's the whole of South East England.' The London stench acts as a motif for the rest of the show, everyone Margherita talks to mentions the smell and how it is affecting them. I leave my desk, go outside, have a sniff to see whether it has spread to Norwich. Unfortunately, my sense of smell is as strong as my commitment to my job and even if there was a gas explosion outside I'm not sure I would detect it. I stay outside for a couple of minutes taking advantage of the fresh air. I walk around the car park pretending I am making a phone call, knowing that I am visible through the window by Alan Medlicott's desk.

Margherita plays another ten great songs in a row, which she does every hour, while I am on my lunch break. I look across the room, Poppy is eating a baked potato. I have never used the microwave, maybe one day I will be more adventurous than eating sandwiches. Poppy's favourite filling is coleslaw. Dress Down Friday sees her in a white dress, sandals, her hair flowing down her back, unleashed from its customary bobble. When she has washed up her plate and cutlery, wiped down her desk, taken a bottle of Fanta from her bag, it is time for Tony Shepherd's show. He also plays ten great songs in a row, Girls Aloud, Kaiser Chiefs, the Killers, and I wonder if maybe they could have pitched the idea slightly differently – because these aren't great songs. They're not bad, I think most of the playlist is okay, but maybe it should be called ten songs that are all right if you're working in an office and are pretty much waiting for half-past five. They aren't the kind of songs I would listen to at home, but they are pop songs that a lot of people like, and by now I've accepted that Tony Shepherd isn't going to start his show with a Bearsuit B-side, or say 'We've just opened a cupboard and found a load of previously unheard Beatles songs.' I've started to like a lot of pop songs that I never thought I'd listen to, but when Shepherd hails the Hoosiers as genius then you can't help but think that hyperbole is at work.

'London still smells,' Shepherd says. 'Apparently it's because of muck-spreading in Belgium.'

I email friends who work in London to see if they have

noticed the smell. As Tony Shepherd hyperbolizes more bands, they reply:

Not really.
London smells of London.
I can't smell anything.

These are also the friends who bring the worst wine to parties.

The ownership of Capital FM has changed hands several times over recent years. After being under the rule of GCap, in 2008 it was bought by the privately owned Global Radio company for £350 million, with the aim of creating a strong brand to rival the BBC, incorporating Classic FM as well as dozens of local stations including XFM, Trent FM and Radio Broadland. Just as 6 Music advertises on Radio 2, Global's ownership of stations such as Capital FM means that commercial stations are able to exploit the same economies of scale. Shepherd's show is an identical format to Margherita Taylor's, playing the same songs on loop, talking about the same things, and is the radio equivalent of eating a baked potato. The playlist comes round as regularly as the Circle Line on the London Underground, but it passes pleasantly enough, and in turn, so does my Friday as I edge ever closer to a Saturday morning lie-in. Greg Burns presents his *Drivetime* show and is aware that everyone listening to him has one eye on the little digital clock in the bottom right-hand corner of their computer screen. You can tell it's a Friday because Burns starts to use words like floor filler, anthem, and Groove Armada. Greg Burns has more to say than his daytime colleagues and like them plays ten great songs in a row. Run-D.M.C., Take That, the Kooks.

'Suitcases are starting to be returned from Terminal 5 after thousands of items of luggage have been lost for three weeks. A lot of the cases ended up in Italy,' Greg Burns tells us. 'How depressing that your luggage has had a better holiday than you have.'

It's getting closer to 5.30.

'The job as a mortgage broker that Leona Lewis had before she won *X Factor* is still open to her. Her former boss has told newspapers that if she wants she can even be given a role in the pensions department.'

It's getting closer to 5.30.

'Chanelle from Big Brother 7 has fought back after being named the least talented celebrity, saying I'm really . . . what's the word? Talented.'

It's getting closer to 5.30.

'Put your windows down and your volume up!' Burns tells us. 'It's the weekend!' And the whole of the open-plan office jangle their keys, close their desks drawers, lean back on their chairs. We all count down like it's Millennium Eve. Ten, nine, eight. Everyone stands up, puts their coats on. Seven, six, five, four. People head for the doors. Three, two, one. Fireworks shoot across the sky, music blares out from speakers, everyone in the office links arms in the car park, singing the Hoosiers, the whole company united on a Friday afternoon.

I walk home and travel updates seem to be every five minutes, there are delays to District and the Hammersmith and City Lines, traffic is crawling on the M3, the whole of the M25 needs to go to the toilet. As London is gridlocked I stop off at the off-licence for a bottle of red wine to celebrate this fabled 'weekend'. When

I get through my front door I don't need to scrunch my shirt into a ball and sling it across the room, don't need to kick off my trousers, Dress Down Friday means I can head straight to the settee. Burns plays dance music now, but still I'm enjoying listening to the radio, I feel fresh, pleased that the week has passed quickly.

At seven o'clock Vaughany is back on air. *Desert Island Disco* is a weekly programme where guests choose their favourite songs. Johnny Vaughan, who interviewed the likes of Madonna and the cast of *Friends* in his days at Channel 4, announces: 'I'm sitting on a sunlounger with Alphonso and Irwin from the English pop band the Hoosiers. The first song you need to choose is the first track you ever danced to.'

After 'Now That We've Found Love' by Third World, Irwin, the band's singer, chooses New Kids on the Block.

'I'd like to dedicate this to your beautiful *Breakfast Show* co-host Denise Van Outen,' Irwin says, 'in the hope I can repair a rupture. I was at an awards ceremony and said to her "That's a lovely dress." She seemed really weirded out by it and said "Are you making fun of me?" I told her that I genuinely really liked it. "I don't believe you." "Seriously!" I said, and she shook her head, looking sceptical. "I do!" I insisted, maintaining that it was a really nice dress. And she suddenly seemed really embarrassed and said "Oh . . . okay, sorry, that's really nice of you to say so." So I said, "Not really, I was joking" and she stormed off. I have no idea why I said it, I love Denise and it was a really nice frock she had on.'

'Don't mess with an Essex bird!' Vaughan tells him. 'All you need to say is "You're well fit" and leave it at that. Your next track is your favourite holiday song.'

'Curtis Mayfield, "Moving On Up".'

'You mean "Move On Up", I take it? Or do you genuinely want M People?'

'Definitely Curtis Mayfield.'

'Good, this is one of my all-time favourite songs. The Hoosiers, it was a delight to have you on the show.'

'*Vielen Dank.*'

'*Dankeschön,*' say these two members of the most played band of the day.

'Your final track is one you are ashamed that you like.' And as 'Summertime' by Will Smith plays, I pick the foil from the cap of my bottle of wine, fetch the corkscrew. Next on air is Des Paul. I throw a pizza into the oven like a Frisbee and listen to the start of his show but Des Paul wants to give me beats. He wants to give me vibes. He wants to start my weekend. He wants to throw out some *tuuuuuuunes*. But what Des Paul doesn't know is that I'm going to sit on my settee and watch *Have I Got News for You*.

18

BBC 6 MUSIC

'Does anyone know where I can buy a comfy pair of headphones?'

(email to Gideon Coe at midnight)

'Which celebrities look like an animal? I think Amy Winehouse looks like an owl.' The studio roars with laughter. I switch my radio off immediately and go back to sleep. Six o'clock on Monday morning is far too early for this nonsense.

At seven I wake again to have a second stab at 6 Music. Shaun Keaveny is on air, following on from the over-enthusiastic Chris Hawkins. He plays 'Rock 'n' Roll High School' by the Ramones as the nation waits for its toast to pop.

'I want to apologize to anyone on my street who was woken up at 4.30 this morning by my car alarm. Please don't put my windows through,' he tells us, apologetically. Keaveny is a likeable Mancunian, and took over 6 Music's *Breakfast Show* from comedian Phill Jupitus, who was the first person on air when the station made its much-anticipated launch in 2002.

'Is it wrong to have milk and sugar in Earl Grey?' Keaveny asks. 'If it's wrong I don't want to be right.'

He plays Pulp and Suzanne Vega, then reads a story from the paper. 'This is from page twenty-six of the *Sun*. In Boldon, a small village near Newcastle, more cold remedies are bought than anywhere else in the country. Ten thousand packets of tablets and bottles of medicine were sold there in the last three months. So if there are any songs you can suggest to go with the story, send them in. I've thought of a couple, "Bad" by Michael Jackson, or "Still Ill" by the Smiths.'

After playing Blondie, he is back on air. 'Fight! Fight! Fight!' he chants merrily. 'I love nothing more than a good old North versus South fight, I start one whenever I can.' He reads out emails.

'It's because us Northerners buy medicine and get on with our day while poncey Southerners would stay in bed feeling sorry for themselves.'

'Isn't it just that the North is colder than the South?'

'I've had an email about Earl Grey from Joe in London. It was marked as high importance so it's clearly a subject close to his heart. It says: "No milk. Definitely no sugar. Maybe a bit of lemon."'

Keaveny pauses for a moment and takes a slurp of his tea. 'Do you hear that? Do you hear that? That's the sound of a man enjoying a cup of Earl Grey with sugar and milk. Joe also says he's had to start taking his iron to work with him because it's the only way he can stop being paranoid that he hasn't left it switched on at home,' Keaveny says, laughing heartily as he puts on a Morrissey song.

More emails come in suggesting tracks relating to flu symptoms: 'Night Nurse' by Gregory Isaac, 'Dr Jones' by Aqua, 'Hit the North' by the Fall.

'I've decided to play this song though. Every time I play this band we get so many appreciative emails, and the title of the song is very relevant to the texts we've been getting in about this rivalry between the top and bottom of England. It's by the Wedding Present, and it's called "I'm From Further North Than You".'

After the eight o'clock news is 'Toast the Nation', a daily feature where a caller tells Keaveny about where they are from and why it is special. 'Whether it is a town, a village, a postcode or a hamlet, tell us about it and we will put our hand on our heart, face in the direction of Buckingham Palace and swell with pride.' Today's caller is Vicky, calling about Mitcham, on the border between South London and Surrey.

'It used to be a lovely village with lavender fields and a cricket ground,' Vicky tells us. 'Now it's a one-way system. Queen Elizabeth the 1st used to travel for miles just to visit. Now people just use the A23 to go to Ikea and Croydon.'

'Are you still happy there?' Keaveny asks.

'Yes, I still like living here, I feel bad being negative about it. I'm six months pregnant and it will be a nice place to bring up children.'

'My partner Lucy's six months pregnant too,' Keaveny tells her. 'I'm sure our children will become firm friends. What song would you like us to play that you can dedicate to Mitcham?'

'"We Gotta Get Out of This Place" by the Animals.'

'There's a story in the paper today,' Keaveny reads, 'saying that the main reason people leave their job is friction with work colleagues. Having to sit all day with people who sniff and click their ballpoint pens. Producer Louise really hates one of my bad habits. Turning up every morning. She hates it when I do that.'

Louise does not speak on air, which means that unlike his breakfast show rivals, Keaveny does his whole show as monologue rather than conversation. The show fits perfectly into 6 Music's ethos, which is completely based around music rather than having the chattier nature of its sister station, Radio 2, and the station it hopes to tease listeners away from, Radio 1. New songs played alongside music from the archives are much more important to the station than having DJs talking about what happened on *EastEnders* last night. 6 Music's audience seems to be people who feel too old for Radio 1 but too young for Radio 2, something I can firmly relate to.

'Another story from the *Sun* today has the headline "Vast Bee Attacks Three". A big bee has stung a mother, her son and a passer-by. It is described,' Keaveny says, laughing, 'as a two-inchlong monster. I've used that expression myself a few times. We had a bee at our house the other day. Lucy trapped it in the bathroom and didn't dare open the door until I came home. Sadly I had to squash the bugger dead.'

It's nine o'clock and as I sit at my desk my interior monologue is saying 'tired, tired, tired, should have had a shave, tired, tired, tired'. I switch on my computer and say hello to Alan Medlicott and Craig. Craig has had a haircut. Alan Medlicott is blowing his nose.

Keaveny interviews Janet Street Porter – the former editor of the *Independent on Sunday* who is credited with revolutionizing television in the 1980s.

'When you wake up in the morning you need to say to yourself "I am great, I am the best person in the world",' she tells him.

'Positive affirmation,' Keaveny says. 'You can't beat it.' He does not seem to be intimidated interviewing someone with such a fierce reputation of speaking her mind.

'Men and women have their brains set to different radio frequencies,' she tells him. 'Men do things at one speed, women operate and function completely differently.'

'Well that's pretty much what it's like in our house,' Keaveny says. The programme draws towards a close after three hours of gentle chat, lots of good songs and nothing too irksome.

If you go on to any radio discussion forum on the Internet you will find George Lamb's name mentioned on more threads than any other. But if you are his auntie or an old primary school teacher wanting to coo over his achievements I would hesitate before you type his name into Google; the topics tend to be along the lines of the worst person on radio. He wins convincingly, knocking into a cocked hat of defeat the likes of Dotun Adebayo and Richard Bacon. He is described at various points as 'a moron', 'a penis', and 'utter shit'. I would be naive to only believe what I read on the Internet, so I look forward to judging for myself how bad George Lamb is.

I am a similar age to George Lamb but he speaks in a language that I'm sure doesn't exist; I don't understand most things that he says. Perhaps this means I'm not cool enough. But I don't think that's the case, I know someone who's got a motorbike and one

of my friends once had a trial with Nottingham Forest. On the
6 Music website there is a page that lists words in Lamb's lexicon
that need a translation, including: 'I'm feeling it' – 'I like it.' 'A
Don' – someone who has achieved something – 'Lewis Hamilton
is a proper Don.' 'Wackola' – 'the worst'. For example, 'The Manic
Street Preachers are wack but the Zutons are wackola.'

He says *Shabba* in every sentence, Shabba is hello, Shabba is
goodbye; he uses Shabba as an adjective, a noun, a subordinate
clause. Just minutes of listening to him is enough to drive you
crazy.

Every show is dedicated to a different listener who Lamb
speaks to for the first and last ten minutes of the show. Today it
is Stephen O'Brien, a sales manager from Driffield.

'Okay, Stephen, let's get to know you a bit more. What's six
times six?'

'Erm . . . thirty-six.'

'Do you like pineapple on pizza?'

'No.'

'Would you ever order a surf 'n' turf in a restaurant?'

'No.'

'Excellent. You got them all right. Stephen, if you are ever in
a mugging situation, do you know what you should do? Rub a
kebab in your face! The person mugging you won't be expecting
that!!' Lamb tells him, apropos of nothing. Stephen roars with
laughter.

'What type of kebab would you choose?'

'Doner kebab.'

'Let's applaud that!' Lamb declares. There is applause.

'Let's Shabba that,' Mark Hughes, his colleague, suggests.

'Shabba!' they all say together.

'Shabba, Stephen?'

'Shabba,' Stephen agrees.

'Ting wap Shabba?' Lamb asks.

'Ting wap Shabba,' Stephen agrees.

Lord Reith will be turning in his grave. I feel like unplugging my radio for the rest of the day. I look at the desk opposite me; suddenly Craig doesn't seem so annoying. At least when he is asked to do overtime he says 'yes' rather than 'ting wap'.

The redeeming factor of Lamb's show is that he plays good music, although you sense that if he was left to his own devices he would be playing Shabba Ranks' back catalogue rather than Elvis Costello and Joni Mitchell. 6 Music's unique selling point is that it has such an eclectic mix of songs. There are over 40,000 records in the BBC Music Library and it makes sense to utilize your resources rather than just play the same songs from the charts on continuous loop in the way Virgin and Capital FM do with the Scissor Sisters and the Hoosiers. Presenters will come and go, styles will change but as long as 6 Music has this diversity of music as its backbone, the station should be a success. It just needs to make sure that presenter ego does not seep into the pro-gramme's content.

After the news at eleven, Lamb reads out facts about action hero Chuck Norris.

'Chuck Norris doesn't believe in Germany.'

'Chuck Norris once ate a whole cake before realizing there was a stripper inside.'

'It takes fourteen puppeteers to make Chuck Norris smile, only two to make him burn down an orphanage.'

'Do you think Chuck Norris could beat Steven Segal in a fight?' Mark asks George. They debate it, leaning towards Segal emerging as victor. I'd like to see Chuck Norris beat George Lamb in a fight.

'There's an email here saying that in India, Fanta is called Banta.'

'No way!'

'Yeah. Imagine that. Banta! "Can I have some Banta please!"'

The studio laughs, I imagine they carry on laughing well into the next song, the new single by PJ Harvey.

Lamb interviews Stewart on the phone. He is the president of an Internet Biscuit Society.

'Let's get to know more about you. What is six times six?'

'Forty-two?' Stewart answers with uncertainty.

Laughter. 'No. Do you like pineapple on a pizza?'

'Er, no.'

'And would you order a surf 'n' turf?'

'Er, no,' says Stewart, who seems ill at ease in his role as guest on the show. He talks about the importance of dunking, the hierarchy of biscuits, class connotations of the jammy dodger, the Mint Viscount, the custard cream.

The Hub is 6 Music's studio for live music. Today the featured band is the Scanners who perform songs from their new album *Violence is Golden* – a concept album about meeting George Lamb in a car park late at night. George speaks to them.

'Do you like pineapple on pizza?'

'Yes.'

'Oh no! What about surf 'n' turf?'

'What's that?' Sarah the singer asks.

'It's having lobster and steak on the same plate.'

'Sounds a bit expensive for me.'

'We don't like it on this show,' Lamb explains. The Scanners speak for the nation with their indifference towards this fact.

At one o'clock Nemone starts her show by playing the Inspiral Carpets. A former Radio 1 DJ, she got her big break working as a receptionist at Kiss 102 when her genial telephone manner secured her work on the night-time show. Although she does not possess George Lamb's incredible ability to stumble over words and be constantly confused about what record he is playing, she still does not cover 6 Music with glory. Nemone plays Morrissey and James Brown, the Stone Roses and Echo and the Bunnymen, but despite that the show just plods along without ever being interesting.

'Today we're asking you to send in your favourite band name that is just made up of initials. REM or AC/DC,' she suggests. 'If you can think of any, text them in. Also, let us know if anything exciting has happened to you recently.'

Nemone plays CSI and ABC. I email in my suggestion of B. It's what I abbreviate Blur to.

'Emma's emailed with something exciting that's happened to her,' Nemone announces, excitedly. 'My best friend asked me to be godparent to her baby girl. If anyone has got any good god-parent anecdotes, send them in.' I think Nemone may be clutching at straws slightly.

I reach into my bag for my sandwiches. Except my bag is empty. I backtrack through the last twenty-four hours in my mind. No recollection of buttering bread, of double knotting a polythene bag, of opening the fridge door this morning. I've been expecting that this day may come. I forgot to make my sandwiches.

I think about going on the scrounge, get the admin ladies to empty their handbags of Polos and biscuits, ask if anyone can spare a crust, if I can have a bite of a baguette, maybe Poppy will let me have a forkful of potato, but I lean back in my chair and try not to think about food.

Once I have negotiated the afternoon of Nemone and filing cabinets, combined with crippling hunger, I have high hopes for the rest of the day. It is nearly four o'clock and I have survived both George Lamb and Nemone, and it's time for Steve Lamacq's show. I never thought I would be so relieved to hear his voice, he's like a responsible grown-up taking control from two unruly babysitters. I used to listen to Lamacq religiously when he presented Radio 1's *Evening Session*; it was the mid-nineties and he championed Britpop while I was doing my homework. 6 Music seems as though it could have been made entirely for Lamacq; the opportunity to play records he loves is something he clearly relishes, he plays tracks recorded live from his old *Evening Session* show as well as from Peel and Mary Anne Hobbs. He opens his show with the Super Furry Animals and the Doors, and his style of presenting has not changed since Blur and Oasis were the biggest bands in the country and my French homework was not good enough, according to Mr Flewker.

'Text and email in if you have ever been to a gig that was cancelled when you got there,' Lamacq suggests. 'I say this because I got the train to watch Colchester United against Hull City on Saturday and the referee called it off an hour before kick-off. It was all right in the end though, it meant I could go to the pub to play quiz machines.'

People email Lamacq their own stories:

'I hitchhiked all the way from Weymouth to London only to find out I had the wrong night to see the Clash.'

'My friend's dad drove us from Colchester to London to see Wham, but when we got there we found out George Michael had bronchitis. It was okay though, my friend's dad took us all to White City to watch greyhound racing.'

'I've turned up to Paul Weller twice and the Manic Street Preachers once and all the gigs were cancelled minutes before they were supposed to start.'

I email Lamacq my own story.

Hi Steve

I lived in Germany for a year, and one day made a two-hour trip to watch Oasis in Hamburg, only to find a handwritten note on the venue door saying OASIS, CANCELLED. It was the day after Liam Gallagher had been punched in Munich.

From John, hungry at work because he forgot his sandwiches.

At 5.30 I am out of the door like a schoolboy on the last day of term. I don't have any money so have to wait until I'm home before I can eat. In my kitchen I cook everything in the fridge, eat cereal as eggs fry, sausages sizzle, toast pops, beans go dry and tasteless in the microwave. As I eat Lamacq introduces *Good Day, Bad Day*, where people call in if they are having a particularly good or bad day. Up until now I would have said the latter, but as I wipe ketchup from my chin and pat my stomach I realize the day hasn't turned out too badly at all. On today's show it is the turn of Peter Brooks, a music teacher in Bracknell.

'What are you up to at the moment?' Lamacq asks.

'I'm in the middle of a lesson,' Brooks tells him. I remember music teachers at my school being slack but I don't remember any of them interrupting the lesson to be involved in a radio phone-in.

'Who are you teaching?'

'I've got two lads here, Dan and Sam, learning to play "The Pink Panther" on keyboard.'

'Well, which of them would like to play for us now, live on radio?'

'They can do it together. Go on lads, turn the volume up a bit for Steve.'

And they play the familiar theme tune live on air. It is their first session for Steve Lamacq.

Tom Robinson was the singer of the imaginatively titled Tom Robinson Band in the 1970s and is the presenter of tonight's 7 to 9.30 p.m. slot.

'Last week I played you the first record I ever bought,' he tells us. '"Twist 'n' Shout" by the Beatles. Since then you haven't stopped sending me emails detailing the first record *you* ever bought. So tonight I'm going to play as many of them as I can.'

The first is 'No More Heroes' by the Stranglers, the first purchase by Michael Campbell. 'It cost 45p and two bus rides,' he tells the presenter. Next is Mike in Southampton, who texts that his 'first' was 'Spaceman' by Babylon Zoo, which is followed by 'Crazy Horses' by the Osmonds, the first record bought by another listener. Already it shows the diversity of people tuning in to Robinson's show, with records spanning three decades.

The next song is 'Mmm Mmm Mmm' by the Crash Test Dummies from 1994, one of the greatest records of all time, and I immediately decide to lie for the rest of my life and claim that this was the first record that I ever bought in the hope that people will be impressed. They must never know it was 'The Macarena'.

Lawrence bought 'Uptown Top Ranking' by Althea & Donna from W.H. Smith's in Luton.

Rob bought 'Loving You' by Minnie Ripperton.

David bought 'Baker Street' by Gerry Rafferty.

Tom Robinson recalls the story that Stuart Maconie, in his time as assistant editor of the *NME*, started the rumour that the saxophone solo in the song was played by the *Blockbusters* presenter Bob Holness, a conspiracy theory that has been passed on as true ever since.

The live band in *The Hub* is the Hoodlums, who had their very first radio airplay two months ago on this show. At the time they had only done three gigs and were unsigned, but now they are signed up to a record label. 'You restored my faith in new music,' Robinson says to them when talking about the first time he heard the MP3 they sent him by email, and it must be gratifying for any young band to hear that someone like Tom Robinson is prepared to play songs by unsigned bands, and that success can follow as a result.

Gideon Coe starts his show with a session by the French band Herman Düne from a 2000 *Peel Session* and then plays Stereolab and the Teardrop Explodes. Coe has what I consider one of the best jobs in radio. I would swap places with him in an instant. I can imagine him sitting down cross-legged in the BBC Music Library, a pile of records in front of him, his beaming smile radiating enough energy to power the whole of the BBC. He's won three Sony Awards and only recently switched to the evening; previously he had presented the lunchtime Shabba slot now occupied by George Lamb.

Coe plays recordings of live performances from the Wedding Present live in 1988 and his tracklist tonight includes the Fall and Kate Bush and before I'd ever listened to 6 Music, this is exactly what I imagined it to be, and why it is potentially my ideal station. Listening to Gideon Coe makes me excited about the possibility of presenting a show on Future Radio; he shows that you don't have to try to be constantly entertaining in the way that Scott Mills and George Lamb do, or be as cynical as Gaunty or Chris Moyles. Instead of trying to be funny or controversial, Coe is self-deprecating, dry, intelligent, and as a result is much more amiable and listenable-to than most DJs. The most endearing part of his show is Duffers; aware that his average listener is perhaps of advanced years, he likes to hear examples of people behaving in ways they would never have expected when they were punks or mods or hippies, when being young felt like it would last for ever. People who as teenagers rebelled against their parents and teachers, rode to Glastonbury on the back of their mate's motorbike, smoked at parties while talking about infinity. They are now worried about inflation and the credit crunch. They are the parents of grown-up kids, have jobs as civil servants, deputy headmasters, depot managers.

'I just sent in a correction to the BBC website,' one duffer admits.

'Does anyone know where I can buy a comfy pair of headphones?' another duffer asks.

'Am I a duffer?' Phil from Aldershot asks Coe in an email. 'I enjoy Battle of Britain re-enactments and my camera still uses film.'

'Of course you are a duffer,' Coe tells him. 'Revel in it.'

I decide to revel in not being a duffer, turn off my radio and go to the pub for last orders. I've earned it, I've had a day where I've had to listen to George Lamb and then starve. I walk into the bar, order beer and scampi fries, knowing that there is always the chance something will happen that will change my life. Maybe I'll meet some bohemian types who will throw me a motorbike helmet, tell me to hop on, and as the throttle revs up they'll give me a bottle of Jack Daniel's that I'll glug down like Strawberry Yop.

19

TEST MATCH SPECIAL

'I prefer cricket on the radio to on television. The pictures are so much clearer.'

(letter to Brian Johnston on *Test Match Special*)

Although John Peel and Mark Radcliffe are the two people I have listened to most regularly on radio, no show has clocked up as many listening hours as *Test Match Special*. If I was to draw a graph of my listening habits (and that's not beyond possibility; I have a lot of free time on my hands) then *Test Match Special* would tower above any other show.

The programme, one of the jewels in the crown of BBC Radio, is perhaps at its best when England are playing abroad. I remember when England played in Sri Lanka in 1993, I set my alarm for 4 a.m. so that I could listen on the radio. By that time I had started going to watch matches live and playing cricket for local teams, spending every evening bowling at a stump, practising cover drives against next door's wall, losing cricket balls in conifers. As soon as I woke I would sit on the floor next to the radio with the volume down so I didn't disturb anyone in the house, listening to cricket commentary in my pyjamas, covered in goose pimples, waiting for the heating to come on. I was undeterred by the fact that I had to go to school, that my radio had a bad signal and I could mostly hear crackle, and that in the early nineties, England were rubbish at cricket. Even now I still listen as much as I can. The day England won the Ashes in 2005 I was on a train to Norwich, and the reception on my radio started to disappear just as it was getting tense and exciting, so I got off the train at the next stop, Diss, and sat on a bench at the station, listening to the winning moments without even pausing to consider that jumping off that train meant my arrival home was delayed by at least a couple of hours. I was happy, me and my radio, England winning at cricket.

I love the fact that some people manage to pay their mortgage by commentating on cricket. There's something I really admire in people who make a living doing things they love: Stuart Maconie plucking at his ukulele before a show, Logan Sama playing grime on Kiss FM, John Humphrys grilling politicians. The warmth and enjoyment in the commentary box, with lascivious talk of pork pies and chocolate cake, are crucial to the success of the programme and is what makes it so endearing, the reason people like me are prepared to listen to it for hours at a time, day after day. The commentators manage to break down the complexities of Test Match cricket into digestible chunks, and are able to be impartial in a way that other sports do not manage. They are there to talk about cricket, rather than to anticipate an England victory. It is enjoyable to listen to the radio even if England are losing and there are rumbles of laughter from all corners of the commentary box. Brian Johnston, perhaps the most loved commentator in *Test Match Special*'s history, described the appeal of the show as 'a bunch of friends going to a match and talking about it'.

Ever since Johnston was first on air in the sixties, practical jokes have been prevalent in the commentary box. 'Johnners' would tempt a commentator with a large slice of cake and as soon as their mouth was full would direct a question at them live on air, then sit back and watch them struggle to articulate an answer. He was famous for some of the most famous moments in sports commentary, most notably as Peter Willey ran in to bowl to Michael Holding, when he told his listeners 'The batsman's Holding the bowler's Willey.' On another occasion, when Ian Botham trod on his stumps, Johnston could not control himself after Jonathan Agnew said that Botham 'couldn't get his leg over', resulting in the most uncontrollable and infectious giggling fit radio has ever known.

The newest recruit to *Test Match Special* is Arlo White, who has commentated on cricket for the BBC since 2005. There have been very few changes in the commentary box over the years. For home tests, Agnew, Christopher Martin Jenkins and Henry Blofeld have been irremovable, and there hasn't been enough live cricket to allow much room to experiment, so White is in a privileged position and manages to combine his *Test Match Special* duties with reporting on football for Radio Five Live. Lucky bastard.

'I didn't go via the usual route of local radio,' he tells me when I ask him about how he became a commentator. He is on the speakerphone in his car, driving back to his hometown near Derby. 'At the age of twenty-seven I decided that selling plastic to the sign-making industry wasn't really what I wanted to do with my life and I needed to do something more exciting. As a kid I had taken a tape machine to sports fixtures and talked into it as the game went on. At home I would do mock-up commentaries on American football games. But I never really had the confidence to apply somewhere, to take a course or just turn up at a radio station and say "Here I am." Me and my girlfriend decided to travel around the world, so we both quit our jobs and off we went. I had just got in to Radio Derby to do short thirty-second match reports on Alfreton Town and they didn't win any of the thirteen games I had been part of, so I guessed that alone was an indication that I wasn't going to be kept on. I managed to get a show when I was in Sydney and so prepared the tapes to apply for a position at Five Live and luckily I got the job.

'My first day working for *Test Match Special* was in Multan, during the 2005 tour of Pakistan. The night before I sat down with Jonathan Agnew in the hotel bar to ask his advice. Prior to then there had been very few opportunities for anybody to try their hand at cricket commentary, so other than a couple of One-Day Internationals I was fairly untried. Agnew said to me: "If there is a wicket and you don't know who has caught the ball, who took the run-out, don't worry, bide your time, tell the listeners that the batsman will be disappointed, that it is an important breakthrough and so on, wait for the replay on your monitor, don't commit yourself too early."

'So on my first day I had to commentate and sat beside Geoffrey Boycott, which put the fear of God into me. I thought "He doesn't know who I am! I haven't played cricket at first-class level, I've never commentated before." I decided to just say what

221

I could see, leave the coaching and technical side to Geoffrey. And then Younis Khan was out and I commented that the position of his elbow was too high, and out of the corner of my eye I could see Geoffrey backing away, staring at me, and I thought "Oh my God, what am I doing? Stop coaching." And Boycott came up to me later and said in his own unique way "Have you ever played cricket?" I thought it was the end of my *Test Match Special* career before I'd even finished my first day.

'They've all been very welcoming in the commentary box. Aggers and I get on very well, we've worked on a few tours together now. For what it's worth I think he's the best sports commentator in the country. I think he is outstanding, his journalistic nous and reporting are second to none and he is treated with great affection on the circuit. Henry Blofeld is an excellent raconteur, really good company. He didn't know my name for the first six months so I was "my dear old thing" all the time. It is amazing how many different styles can exist on one programme. It's important that I don't replicate any of their styles.'

'And what about football?' I ask. 'How much time do you spend preparing for a game?'

'I always try to isolate around three hours on a Friday afternoon for preparation. You never know what is going to happen. Although you're not commentating you're always likely to be called upon, for a penalty or if your game is particularly exciting or goes into extra time. You may have to do stop-start commentary so that they can use the audio on *Sports Report*. That's when every time the ball is near the goal you have to start commentating in case it goes in. I normally turn up an hour and a half before the game, establish contact with "base", then go into the media room to speak to other hacks, particularly the locals, to find out what is happening with either side. They've always got a tale to tell, and the quirkier the better. Just as an example, last week I was told that Tony Mowbray the West Brom manager had banned his side from buying new suits for the FA Cup semi-final, saying it wasn't appropriate until the final. You don't pick up on things like that if you are just searching on the Internet.

'If it's a Premier League game you are involved regularly over the Saturday afternoon. You have a thirty-second preview, although that has changed slightly; it isn't just doing a voice piece any more, whoever is in the studio presenting the show will ask you a question, which you then answer, making it as newsworthy as possible. In Premier League games you really have to be on the ball, in The Championship you don't have to be that focused on the journalistic side, you can afford to bring a bit more colour into the way you report things. You have to buzz in when there's a goal and speak for ten seconds, it's a great way of listening to what's going on around the country. It's what I would be doing anyway if I was sat at home, but this way I get paid to do it. Then after the game you are told what is required.

'The Saturday evening game for television is a real pain for a lot of reporters because it's at around five o'clock, so we don't get to craft decent voice pieces any more, there isn't enough time; they have to get round all the grounds before the game kicks off which is a real disappointment to a lot of reporters. It takes the edge off the end of the game, spoils one of the most enjoyable things about the job, that we are not able to speak for forty seconds about what we've seen that afternoon. But if I am told we need an interview with Rafa Benítez or Martin O'Neill, it means

I have to hot-foot it down to the press area and hope I can get a one-on-one.'

'What's the most memorable moment of your career?' I ask Arlo.

'There have been so many special moments. Obviously there was the first time I was on Five Live, and working with Boycott for the first time. I also commentated on the World Series live at Wembley, which was really exciting. One memory that particularly stands out though is during the quarter-final of cricket's 20-20 competition. The game ended in a tie, the umpires, commentators, players and crowd all thought it was over. So I described the end of the game and went back to the studio. Suddenly the players came back on. The Warwickshire scorer was the only person in the ground who knew the rules. So I buzzed in and commentated on the first bowl-out in radio history.'

It is a long way from cricket's origins on the radio, when the BBC's Howard Marshall wasn't even allowed to broadcast from within Lord's during a Test match. He had to find a quiet place nearby to tell the country what was happening in the game. The cricketing authorities were at odds with the game being featured on radio, they thought that the game being broadcast would damage attendances. Now people happily sit in the crowd with their radios tuned to the commentary on Radio 4 Long Wave, the commentators keeping them company for the day's cricket. What makes it so listenable is that for every conversation about the technicalities of reverse swing or laments about England batting collapses, there is something much more trivial, Jonathan Agnew talking about the time he met Ulrika Jonsson, or wondering in between overs what name he should give his new dog.

Out of everyone on radio, including Mark Radcliffe and Terry Wogan, it is perhaps Arlo White whose job I am most envious of, and while talking to him it is clear how much he loves his work, that he is aware of the position he holds. I wonder whether he ever thinks about people he used to work with at the plastics factory. As I say goodbye to Arlo and let him continue his journey home I look forward to spending hours of the summer listening to him on *Test Match Special*. I look out of the window and it is starting to rain. He truly is part of English cricket.

20

RADIO BROADLAND

*'Can you play "Billie Jean" for Martin Robinson who is
stressed at work?'*

(email to Chris Marston's afternoon show)

I decide to listen to Radio Broadland, the favourite radio station
of the taxi drivers of Norwich. 'I bet they're playing a song by the
Hoosiers,' I say to myself as I switch off my alarm and turn on the
radio.

Yep. Bloody Hoosiers. Their songs are played more times than
'Happy Birthday'.

I shower, shave, gather my belongings: sandwiches, batteries
for my radio, hankie. This is not how life was supposed to turn
out for me. Rob and Chrissie present the *Breakfast Show* on
Broadland, the local commercial station that goes out to Norfolk
and Suffolk.

'Have you read about Duffy?' Rob asks after adverts for mobile
phones and Toyotas. 'Duffy says her ambition is to sing on the
moon,' Rob says, then plays her single 'Mercy', fading it down

after the intro. 'Do you think that means it will be a cheesy song?!?! Because that's what the moon is made of!' Rob fades the record back up, and, more importantly, his microphone back down.

Walking to work I see the man walking his Alsatian, the schoolboys with their hands in their pockets and one with a bicycle, the lady in a red coat waiting at the pedestrian crossing. But when I arrive at work everything is different. Craig is not there. Alan Medlicott looks worried. I turn the volume down on my radio in case there's a call of 'man down' and I have to jump into action and share the workload.

'David Beckham is going to appear in an episode of *Sesame Street*,' Chrissie says. 'He's already filmed his scene with Elmo.'

'There's someone who works on this show,' Rob says, 'who has an Elmo in their car that she fastens in with a seat belt every time she goes anywhere.'

'It's not me!' Chrissie adds quickly, laughing. In our office there is no such laughter; Alan Medlicott looks anxious, like a teenager on his first date. Every time there is movement at the door he looks up, and when it isn't Craig he feigns nonchalance, continues with his work. I start to worry. Is Craig okay? Is he ever coming back? Has he had an accident? Do we need to go and look for him? Has he done a Reginald Perrin? Will I get his chair? It looks comfier than mine.

'Guess the year,' Chrissie challenges us, and plays 'What's Up?' by DJ Miko. 1992, I say to myself. I remember the song coming out, and am pretty sure it was during my last year of primary school. I do the maths with my fingers. Definitely 1992. She then plays 'Young at Heart' by the Bluebells and 'I Would Do

Anything for Love' by Meatloaf. I am tempted to twist, but I stick. Definitely 1992.

'1993,' says Jim in Sprowston.

'1993,' says Lisa in Bowthorpe.

'1993,' says Scott in Spixworth. 'The best year ever.'

The Internet has ruined this type of game. I bet these people just typed DJ Miko or the Bluebells into Google. They're spoiling it for us traditional players of the game.

Rob and Chrissie play 'Dreams' by Gabrielle and confirm the year was 1993, but don't confirm whether it was in fact the best year ever.

More travel news: temporary traffic lights on the ring road, a broken-down bus on Duke Street. But it's 10.30; no matter how bad the traffic is this morning that is not what has caused Craig's tardiness.

Six Degrees of Separation is a quiz that appeared on Rob and Chrissie's show and now Gary Stevens, on air until two o'clock, introduces the next contestant, Dave from Southwold.

'The game is based on the theory that everyone in the world is separated by just six connections. Your chain starts with Shane Richie and ends with Cameron Diaz. Are you ready?'

'Yes.'

'Shane Richie appeared as Alfie Moon in *EastEnders*. Which star of *Little Britain* played the part of the vicar when Alfie married Kat?'

'David Walliams.'

'Which ex-*Dr Who* star appears in every episode of *Little Britain*?'

'Tom Baker.'

'And which Aussie singer starred with David Tennant in a *Dr Who* Christmas special?'

'Kylie Minogue.'

'Kylie appeared in *Moulin Rouge* with which Scottish actor?'

'Ewan McGregor.'

'And finally, Ewan McGregor starred in the film *A Life Less Ordinary* with which glamorous Hollywood blonde?'

'I don't know.'

'Really?'

'No idea.'

'Well, the game is to connect Shane Richie to Cameron Diaz.'

'I know, but I don't know who stars in *A Life Less Ordinary*.'

'Cameron Diaz.'

'Oh,' Dave says, the penny dropping.

Stevens plays Kylie and Take That, the two songs segued by a jingle saying 'Broadland . . . the best music variety'. It seems the more homogenous a station's playlist, the more variety they claim to play. I don't remember F F Friction or Radio 3's *Late Junction* boasting of variety, even though each song they played sounded like it could have been the first time it had ever been played on the radio, and was introduced by presenters desperate for their audience to hear it.

'Yesterday, I was watching the snooker on TV,' Gary Stevens says, seemingly boasting that his working day is over at two p.m., 'and during the Ronnie O'Sullivan game there was a guy sat in the crowd wearing a Norwich City top. It was two or three seasons old probably, you could tell because it had a different sponsor to the kit they wear now. But I thought, wouldn't it be brilliant if we could speak to him? Find out what he's like, what he was up to at the snooker. And then I thought what if he had phoned in sick to get the day off work just to go to the snooker! And then he was on telly! If anything similar has happened to you, if you've ever been caught skiving, please tell us about it. And if you know the guy in the Norwich shirt, please get in contact,' Stevens begs, 'or even better, ask him to contact us. We'd love to speak to him.'

Stevens plays Adele and Goldfrapp, then brings us an update on Snooker Man.

'We've had his brother-in-law on the phone! The guy in the Norwich shirt watching Ronnie O'Sullivan is called Ian and he lives in Sprowston. Please get in touch, Ian.'

While the twelve o'clock news is on I decide to go outside, walk to Comet. Alan Medlicott looks like he would appreciate time on his own.

'Norwich Union is to be no more,' says the newsreader, with the gravitas of the death of a member of the royal family being made known. 'It was announced this morning that the brand name will be changed, and the company will now be known as Aviva.' The people of Norwich are asked their opinions:

It's really sad.

It's the end of an era.

It's a shame the name of Norwich will no longer be permeating the globe.

Aviva sounds a bit foreign.

But the main news is in the office when I come back, nourished after my ham and cheese bagel, because Craig's mum has phoned to say he won't be coming back. Alan Medlicott still hasn't asked me to help with any extra work, he has just sat there, his face getting redder and redder, tapping the space bar with a bit more aggression each time he uses it. And so Craig is gone. All is transient. As I get on with my work and put my headphones back on, I look at Craig's empty chair and start to mourn his absence like a *Telegraph* obituary, start worrying about why he's decided to leave, and ponder about the ephemeral nature of life. And then Radio Broadland plays the Hoosiers again and all is back to normal.

At two o'clock Chris Marston is on air, playing Six Degrees of Separation with Hannah Moore from Norwich.

'Okay, you have to connect James Nesbitt to Whoopi Goldberg. James Nesbitt presented a Brit Award to which London singer?'

'Kate Nash.'

'And she attended the Brit School with which rehab star?'

'Amy Winehouse . . .'

'Who sang "Valerie", produced by . . .'

'Mark Ronson.'

'Ronson was the DJ at whose wedding to Katie Holmes?'

'Tom Cruise's . . .'

'And on which show did Tom Cruise declare his love for Katie Holmes?'

'*Oprah* . . .'

'Who starred in *Sister Act* with . . .'

'Whoopi Goldberg!'

'Well done, you're the first person all day to get all the questions right! You win £100.'

'Wooooh!' Hannah screams. 'My heart's in my throat.'

'You should see a doctor then.'

'We've had an email in,' says Chris Marston, 'asking if we can play "Billy Jean" for Martin Robinson, who is getting stressed at work.' As Michael Jackson sings to East Anglia I start to worry about Martin Robinson getting stressed at work. It is one of the saddest things I've ever heard. I wonder what his job is, why he's stressed, whether he's got a girlfriend, whether he's going to be okay. If only I worried about myself as much as I worry about strangers.

I walk home from work, still thinking about Martin Robinson. At seven o'clock it is *Music Control* with Kevin Hughes, which isn't made by Broadland, it's a Network Radio show that is broadcast across multiple stations.

'On today's show we're going to give away a hi-fi and a satnav,' he tells us, as I make sandwiches. Sandwiches at lunchtime, sandwiches in the evening; this is how Martin Robinson probably lives his life. 'A hi-fi and a satnav,' he repeats, excited by the prospect. It would be nice to win prizes that don't sound like they've been nicked.

'What's your name?' he asks the contestant.

'Kevin.'

'Great name! Are you a Kev or a Kevin?'

'Kevin.'

'Yeah, me too. Now for every correct answer you win ten free music downloads. Who is the lead singer of the Foo Fighters?'

Kev(in) wins £50 of free downloads. How very noughties. I'd prefer gift vouchers. I bet Martin Robinson would, too.

'Here's the new single by the Jonas Brothers,' Hughes says, before inexplicably screaming 'MAKE SOME NOIIIIIIISE!'

*

'Is it true that love is blind?' asks Graham Torrington, host of *Late Night Love* at ten o'clock. 'Let me run that past you again. Is it true . . . that love . . . is blind?'

Marie is on the phone.

'I don't know whether to go back to my boyfriend,' she tells Torrington. 'He lives in Greece. I moved over there so I could live with him. I ended up with a black eye, cracked rib, broken collarbone.'

'And where did you get those from?' Torrington asks.

'From him. So I cut my losses, moved back to England and started my life over again. But in the last couple of weeks we've had contact, spoken a few times, and he's asked me to go back over there so I'm considering it. Although being over there had so many difficulties, it made me a strong person because I know I can get through difficulties now.'

'So what did he do to give you these injuries?'

'Basically he disagreed with something I was saying. I'm quite an opinionated person. When I have something to say, I like to voice it.'

'So he beat you up?'

'Yeah. I know. If it was one of my friends in the same situation I would say "Don't go back, don't even consider it, you're crazy."'

'So why are you doing what you're doing?'

'Because love's involved. And when you love somebody you'll do what you can to try and get over these problems. Won't you?'

'Are you trying to convince yourself or me?'

'I know it's completely crazy to consider it, but when there's so much feeling involved it's difficult to walk away.'

'What's he said about what he's done to you?'

'He apologized.'

'He didn't mean to do it?'

'He's just got a bad temper. He knows he took it too far and he's apologized.'

'How old is this guy?'

'Forty-two, I'm twenty-two. He has a son who is eighteen and his daughter is sixteen. Which is another difficulty, as well as not understanding each other's language properly.'

'What do your parents say about all this, then?'

'My mum's obviously not impressed. She was devastated when I came home in the state that I did. But when there's so much feeling how can you just say no?'

'So you're still considering going back to him even though he beat you up?'

'Yes. I know I can cope with it. And he's promised he won't do it again.'

'Okay, let's try and help Marie tonight,' Torrington suggests after saying goodbye to her. 'Phone in if you have any advice for her.'

Torrington, half-Jeremy Kyle, half-Alan Partridge, plays 'How Deep Is Your Love' by Take That.

'Is it true that love is blind?' Torrington asks again, and recaps Marie's story. 'Kate is on the phone. You have had a similar experience?'

'Yeah, I've been in an abusive relationship similar to the caller. It's very easy to say leave him, he's no good. I think that love really is blind. I was with the same guy for five years and he continually beat me up, and I ignored all the advice people tried to give me. But she shouldn't put herself in that situation again. It would be a massive mistake for her to go to Greece. The best thing I ever did was get out of that relationship.'

Torrington plays tonight's classic love song, played every night at midnight, 'Hard to Say I'm Sorry' by Chicago.

Freya calls in.

'I was psychologically abused by my boyfriend,' she tells Torrington.

'So how do you feel about being in relationships now?'

'Well, I react to certain situations very abruptly. I don't handle things well, I frighten people off. I spend most of my time single.'

'How old are you?'

'Twenty-one.'

'Twenty-one! So young! Someone's put you through so much already? How do you feel about that guy?'

'I still love him to bits.'

'Do you feel sympathy for him?'

'Yes. I would love to hear from him again.'

Torrington plays 'Guilty' by Blue.

There are adverts for air-conditioning units, Dinosaur Adventure at Banham Zoo, the bus route from Yarmouth to Norwich, late-night chat lines. After 'Don't Wanna Lose You' by Gloria Estefan, Susan is on the line. 'I believe you went back to an abusive partner several times?'

'That's right. It started when I was fifteen. He was twenty-four. I moved in with him, but then he kicked me in the face and the police became involved. He ended up in court, but when I saw him stood there in the dock I felt so bad and so dropped the charges. I went back with him, we had a child, but then he demanded sole custody of it, said that he would sort me out if I didn't agree. He would lock me in my room, give me a bottle to do my toilet in. He made me phone my parents and say nasty things to them and so my family ended up hating me. He got me to rob a bank. That went on for five years, him threatening me that if I didn't do what he wanted he would grass me up, tell them what I had done. In the end I ran out one night after he'd beaten me up. I went to the phone box, told the police everything and gave myself in. I got two years' probation, but in that time I became pregnant with a little girl. My husband had beaten me that much and kicked me in the stomach the night before I gave birth. She died of microcephaly, which is an undeveloped brain. I've remarried since, but he still bothers me.'

'What do you mean, bothers you?'

'He phones me up late at night talking rubbish because he's drunk.'

'My God, there's a catalogue of stuff you talk about there.'

'It is a lot and I've never been able to talk to anyone about it. One night he punched me, knocked me out and when I woke up he was stood over me, pouring the kettle over my chest, and I had blisters for two weeks. He slashed my nose with a bread knife and I needed plastic surgery.'

'Do you still feel sorry for him?'

'I do.'

'No. Don't tell me that. Please.'

'But he's been through so much. I have a lot of regrets for going back to my violent partner. I remarried and recently my new husband hit me. And I said to him "One more time and I'm out."'

'Do you mean that?'

'Yes, I do.'

'Good. Because if you've not learnt anything after that . . .'

'I have. Next bloke who hits me I'm gonna stab them.'

I switch the radio off when Susan has finished speaking. I don't like hearing about violence. I forget that some people lead such complicated lives. That there are people who spend time worried, scared, angry. And at the same time other people just plod on with their lives, keeping out of trouble, watching *Match of the Day* and listening to Blur. People like me. Me and Martin Robinson.

21

BBC RADIO 1

'This is by Death Cab for Cutie. It's for Willie in Kent. If ever there's a name you don't want to mispronounce, that must be it.'

(Colin Murray)

I wake at 7.30 and Chris Moyles is talking about his recent painful dental surgery. He makes the *drrrr* of a drill through his lips. The words pliers, string and doorknob aren't what I want to hear at this time in the morning. I decide not to put sugar on my Rice Krispies.

'Graham Norton is on the show later,' Moyles says. 'Aled's just spoken to him. Apparently he arrived really early and has been sat in his car since six.'

'Has he been listening to the show?'

'He didn't say so. I imagine he's more of a Wogan man though. We've got to publicize his Saturday night show, because I got a really snooty email moaning at me for slagging it off.'

I've got mixed feelings about Moyles. I listened to him all the time when he presented an afternoon show when I was in the sixth form, but that was before he was a household name, best-selling author, television personality, saviour of Radio 1. I really liked him, but since then either I have grown more cynical, or he has grown more cocky. I think it's likely that both are true. I feel more at home with Wogan. I'm much happier listening to Shaun Keaveny or Johnny Vaughan. When Moyles joined Radio 1 he was hailed as the new Chris Evans, but I always thought he was more like the new Danny Baker, which perhaps sounds slightly disparaging but Baker is radio's forgotten man, effort-lessly making the kind of exciting, spontaneous radio that Moyles always claims to. Baker knows exactly what good radio is, he claims to have never had a meeting before or after a radio show, never read from a script, he just turns up with a box of records, makes the show up as he goes along. He represents the old-fashioned broadcaster who likes to speak and has something interesting to say. I remember listening to him once when some-one who had phoned his show had to answer the door to the video-repair man while on air.

'Put him on the phone,' Baker urged him. 'Hi, it's Danny Baker, here,' he told a bewildered-sounding repair man when the phone had been passed across. 'You're live on the radio. Please don't swear. I just wondered, you know when kids put things in the video like spoons and biscuits – is there a techni-cal name for that?'

'It's time for Rob DJ's Monday night pub quiz,' Moyles announces. 'These are questions taken from the quiz my mate Rob runs on Monday nights in Leeds,' Moyles clarifies to those like myself who are not regular listeners. Moyles's colleagues in the studio take part: producer Aled, sports reader Carrie, news-reader Dominic, sidekick Comedy Dave. Moyles has more people working for him than Richard Branson.

'When I say pub, you say quiz,' he shouts. 'Pub.'

'Quiz.'

'Pub.'

'Quiz.'

Aled reads out the first question. 'Which cartoon character did Sylvester chase?'

Silence, as they obediently write down their answers.

'Question two,' says Aled, who has worked on the show since 2002. 'What does CAD stand for?'

'What?' they all ask, as one.

'In what context?' asks Moyles.

'Curry and doughnuts,' quips Comedy Dave.

'I don't understand the question,' Moyles reiterates.

'Carry a dolphin,' adds Hilarious Dave.

'Question three. What is the capital of New Zealand? Question four, what is the Paris Underground called?'

'Le Underground?' Moyles asks.

'And the last question, what is one third squared?'

The Radio 1 crew all look at each other blankly, before bursting into flames.

Aled runs through the scores. Carrie wins with four points. Dominic comes last with one; his only right answer that Wellington is the capital of New Zealand. Moyles's answer was Queensland.

'That's an Australian state,' the newsreader tells him.

'Well Australia and New Zealand are full of old convicts and

I've no business to ever go there,' the self-proclaimed Saviour of Radio 1 replies bluntly.

'Hi Graham,' Comedy Dave says to Norton. 'I don't think we've met before.'

'No, I don't think we have. It's weird to see you with a face,' Norton tells him.

'How's Lord Webber?' Moyles asks.

'He's very well,' Norton replies. 'Have you ever met him?' He and Webber are colleagues on *I'd Do Anything*, a BBC 1 show that auditions people to play the role of Nancy in a stage version of *Oliver Twist*.

'No, my girlfriend has though. They were on the same table at the Brit Awards. It was Lord Webber, Jimmy Nesbitt, David Tennant, Sir Ian McKellen, my girlfriend and her friend Abbie.'

'That's an odd mix,' Norton laughs. 'David Tennant would have been the social glue that held that table together, I imagine. He likes a chat, David.'

'McKellen thought that Jimmy Nesbitt was a singer,' mocks Comedy Dave.

'Well, if you don't know who someone is, and you're at the Brits, I think it's a reasonable guess,' suggests Norton.

'I wonder if the Lord has ever heard our show?' Moyles wonders.

'He asked to be on it,' Aled says.

'No, he didn't, don't be stupid, Aled. That would be ridiculous, we wouldn't have turned down Andrew Lloyd Webber!'

'I think we did,' Aled whispers, slightly embarrassed.

'I know nothing about this! That's unbelievable! Have you seen the type of guest we've had on the show this year! I'd love to meet the Lord. That's a disgrace!'

'You'd like him, you'd get on well. I've been to his house and it's lovely,' Norton says. 'Normally I don't like the homes rich people live in, but it's a really nice comfortable family home. And it's been built by happy money. His houses are paid for by singing and dancing.'

I walk into work, say hello to Alan Medlicott. He waves a hand without raising his eyes from the folder his head is buried in. I think about asking if he needs any help. Maybe I'll offer later. Poppy is at the photocopier. She is wearing her bright-red tights. I look over and she smiles. I bet she likes Chris Moyles.

'Since you've been doing the *Oliver* show has anyone asked who Nancy is?' Moyles asks.

'Actually, when I arrived this morning, Aled told me he didn't know who she was. Then he told me that he'd appeared in *Oliver Twist* when he was younger! What sort of numpty are you?' Norton asks him.

'Aled isn't a very observant person,' Moyles explains. 'He is easily distracted. One time he had really good seats for one of the England qualifying matches, and missed a goal because he was MMSing a friend on his mobile. Also, he didn't realize the teams swapped ends at half-time.'

Moyles reads out a text. 'Please play some songs and stop talking, it's like listening to *The Archers*.' After 'Backfire at the Disco' by the Wombats, Aled runs through today's Radio 1 schedule.

'At ten, Jo Whiley will be on air, speaking to relationship expert Tracey Cox.'

'I love that,' Moyles interrupts. 'She's a relationship expert and her surname is Cox!'

*

'Do you like Chris Moyles?' I ask Kate in the kitchen, mugs of tea warming our hands.

'Not really,' she tells me, pulling a face.

'I hate him,' adds another voice, and a lady peers round the back door, cigarette smoke coming from her fingertips.

'Oh I like him,' her friend next to her says. Suddenly I am conducting a straw poll. If only Poppy could see me now. I am centre of a hub. An anti-Chris Moyles hub.

'Where's that boy that sat opposite you gone?' Kate asks.

'Just didn't turn up one day,' I say with a shrug.

'Probably the best thing he's ever done,' Kate says, and tosses her teaspoon into the sink.

Back at my desk Jo Whiley plays Kanye West and Duffy, and tells us that she spent last night watching *Lost* on DVD.

'If you've seen any good TV please text in. This is the new single by Black Kids, I think it's really good.'

Jo Whiley gets excited about every new band that seems even slightly cool. It is hard to dispute her pedigree, she worked as a band booker on *The Word*, the Channel 4 programme that gave Nirvana and Oasis their first television appearances, but it is a long time since those bands were the cutting edge of new music.

'I was nearly late for work today. I had to go to the bank because my credit cards stopped working. It's annoying when your credit cards don't work.' It's frustrating to listen to something so banal on national radio.

Tracey Cox, the show's relationship expert, is in to help listeners with their problems. Somewhere in London there is the roar of Chris Moyles still laughing at her surname. Whiley reads out the first dilemma.

'My boyfriend has suddenly started being overprotective with his phone. He even takes it to the shower. Is something going on or am I being paranoid?'

'Unfortunately, it looks like something is going on,' Cox tells the listener. 'The most common way for people to get caught cheating nowadays is by text message. It's so easy to start flirting with someone by phone. You can't be sure he's having an affair unless you confront him, he could be planning a surprise for you, or it could be something personal that doesn't relate to you, regarding a family or close friend. But in this kind of situation, a woman's instinct tends to be right.'

Whiley reads out the next problem, emailed in by 21-year-old Lauren.

'My best friend slept with the guy I split up with six weeks ago. I was really hurt, but at the same time, they are both single. But I haven't heard from either of them since. Am I right to be upset?'

'Well, it doesn't sound best-friend behaviour,' Cox tells Lauren. 'It's disrespectful for her not to contact you. They shouldn't have done what they did, six weeks is still too fresh to be doing any-thing like that.'

Geoff in Hull emails. 'I've been seeing a girl for three months, but am a transvestite. How do I tell her?'

'Tricky. You need to be armed with literature. A lot of people don't know the exact definition of what a transvestite is, there is always confusion over whether it's a cross-dresser or a trans-sexual and whether or not it means you're gay. Be prepared for a horrible response; she will not necessarily comprehend it at first. Talk her through it calmly. It can work, but brace yourself.'

Ina emails the show. 'I'm thirty-one years old and have just found out my boyfriend has been cheating on me. I can't face starting all over again.'

'Take a break,' Cox advises. 'Learn to enjoy your own company before you start dating again. When you do find a guy, be honest about your past. Tell him that you can't afford to be hurt again. Give him the chance to get out early if he isn't prepared to commit, in the long run it will save a lot of pain. When you've been on a couple of dates with him, bring a friend along, get her to suss him out. It sounds awful but it will work.'

When Jo Whiley's show is over it is time for *Newsbeat*, a dumbed-down version of *Newsround* on Children's BBC, where newsreader Hannah breaks the day's news down into digestible chunks: Gordon . . . Brown . . . has . . . done . . . something . . . unpopular.

I walk through the automatic doors at the entrance to Comet. Almost every day I come here now, wanting to spend as little time in the office as possible. There is a lot of tension building up, voices are constantly raised from all corners of the room. Lots of men with clipboards keep coming in, shaking hands with people in management, talking in hushed voices:

'Hello, Andrew.'

'Hello, Ray.'

'How was your journey?'

'Fine thanks. Should we head to your office?'

'Of course. I'll get Jane to bring coffee.'

Something is going on. I pace the aisles of Comet when I see a familiar face. Alan Medlicott is by the big tellies, his hands in his pockets. I dart to the exit like a prizewinning greyhound, terrified at the possibility of us coming face to face. He looked like a little boy lost, as if he was hoping his name would be called on the tannoy, so that he could be met and taken home, given a piggyback to the car park.

'I LOVE baked potato with tuna! LOVE IT!!' Edith Bowman says at the start of her show when I am back in the office. I feel old listening to Radio 1, technically I shouldn't be doing this – I'm twenty-five years old now – Radio 1's target audience is eighteen- to twenty-four-year-olds. The BBC has detector vans hunting down people like me. If they find me it'll be prison. I look out of the window, nervously. No sirens so far.

'In Korea they have national Being Single Day,' Bowman says in her thick Scottish accent. 'You know how exciting it is when there's a Day day. National Chips day, you get to eat chips! Yay! Well if you could invent your own day, what would you choose? I'd have National Snowboarding Day. Everyone is forced to go snowboarding! Woo!'

People text in:

National really bad hair Day.
National be rude to your mother-in-law Day.
National fake Australian accent Day.
National students' Day, where everyone eats Pot Noodle.

'They're all hilarious!' Bowman says. 'Text in if you can think of a song that would be appropriate for our day. For example, 'Perfect Day' by Lou Reed. Because if you had your own day, it would be perfect, wouldn't it?'

In many ways I find Jo Whiley's and Edith Bowman's shows just as bad as George Lamb and Gaunty. Their shows are so dreary, their topics so dull. I don't care if Jo Whiley watched *Lost* on DVD last night. I don't care if Edith Bowman likes baked potatoes. Perhaps I'm being over-critical, but when I was growing up I listened to Radio 1 and it felt exciting, there was Mark and Lard, Chris Evans, Lee and Herring. There doesn't seem to be anything that today's teenagers could find exciting about the schedule now, nothing to listen to under the duvet when you're supposed to be asleep. No one plays the music that will become the soundtrack to people's lives.

The winning suggestion to Bowman's competition is 'Have a Nice Day' by the Stereophonics, and as it peters out Tim Westwood joins Bowman in the studio to talk about movies.

'When was the last time you went to the cinema?' Edith asks.

'Not long ago. It was to watch *300*, but my girl fell asleep, so I felt I'd wasted my money a bit.'

'What's your all-time favourite movie?'

'I think *Training Day* is my all-time favourite. Guns, violence . . . plots. And *Scarface* is the ultimate hip hop movie.'

Westwood, who is in the building because he presents a weekly show tonight at nine, speaks with enthusiasm, verve. I have never listened to any of his shows, watched any of his TV work, but he is instantly likeable.

'Who would play you in a film?'

'Denzel Washington,' replies Westwood, who is often mocked for his adopted black persona when he is actually a fifty-year-old Bishop's son from Lowestoft. 'I think that shows the real me trying to get out!' he laughs with a firm sense of self-awareness.

'And what kind of films do you hate? I can't see you being a fan of chick flicks.'

'Well, when you're out with your girl you have to watch that type of thing now and then. I'm a massive *Desperate Housewives* fan. When you're watching something at home with your girl, just the two of you on the settee watching a programme you both really like, that's the best feeling in the world.'

'Have you got the box set?'

'No, I Sky Plus them all. When I was offered a Sunday show on 1Xtra, it was really exciting, and I agreed to do it, but part of me was thinking . . . what about the new series of *Desperate Housewives*?'

'Ha! That's hilarious. Westwood is a *Desperate Housewives* fan! And what would be your guilty DVD pleasure?'

'The Westwood DVD.'

'You have your own DVD?'

'Yeah. From a while back.'

'Did it do well?'

'It didn't . . . recoup.'

'Was it bad?'

'Career-threatening.'

As Bowman finishes her show I have to take off my headphones, pretend I am doing work, because Alan Medlicott comes round to my side of the desk and pulls up a chair. This has only ever happened twice before: once, on my first day, when he taught me how to use the database, and the second time on my second day, when he had to teach me again, because I hadn't really been paying attention. I immediately fear the worst, that he is wise to the fact that my contribution to the firm is negligible, that essentially I treat the office as a day centre, somewhere to keep out of the cold, get a cup of tea, check my emails, have a nice sit down. I try to remember which days the jobs pages are in the local paper, wonder how much I'll get for signing on at the job centre. What if he saw me in Comet? What if he noticed how quickly I left as soon as I noticed he was there. I have angered him. He pulls a crumpled piece of paper from his pocket.

'Do you want to sponsor me?' he asks. The piece of paper is full of scribbled names, and in the column next to them the amount they have pledged. 'It's to raise money for leukaemia research,' he tells me, clicking a ballpoint and handing it to me. The word at the top in bold, capital letters is MARATHON. Admittedly the word in front of it is HALF, but I am still impressed. I scan-read the names to ascertain how much I should sponsor him. I see Poppy's signature. £10. I offer the same.

'Thanks,' he says, flashing a warm smile. He pats my shoulder. I watch as he walks back round to his desk and imagine him wearing shorts and a vest, a sweatband around his forehead, his ventricles pulsating like hip hop. He goes back to his desk, ploughs himself into the folder he's been looking at all day.

Scott Mills opens his show by talking about what happened in last night's *EastEnders*. The BBC's first ever Director General, Lord Reith, declared that all programmes had the duty to educate, inform and entertain. I'm not sure he had Scott Mills in mind when he drew up the radio's charter in 1927. I can't help but think that teenagers deserve something better to listen to while they are doing their homework. Mills talks about a clip from YouTube, a video of a baby that stops crying as soon as

'Never Gonna Give You Up' by Rick Astley is played. A lady phones in and suggests to Mills they play the clip to see if it works with her crying baby.

It doesn't. When she is off the phone, Scott Mills and his co-host Chappers make fun of her, calling her Forrest Gump. It seems a bit harsh on someone trying to inject a bit of life into a show that so far has just talked about *EastEnders*. Perhaps if Scott and Chappers want to broadcast to the intelligentsia they should see if they can succeed Eddie Mair presenting Radio 4's *PM*.

Walking home from work I still have the image of Alan Medlicott running in a group of people, waving at a face he recognizes in the crowd. A girl offers him water, he smiles and nods thank you. I think of him with an oversized cheque, shaking hands with a man wearing a stethoscope. I've seen Alan Medlicott in his battered Volvo, I've seen him over-analysing spreadsheets, making panic phone calls to head office, saying in a breathless voice: 'I need to speak to Stephen Hughes.' It's good that he is doing something for people. What can I tell my grandchildren? That I once met Stuart Maconie? I'd like to do something that involves more than eating ham sandwiches and sitting at my desk. I decide to fill in the *People's Playlist* selection of songs on the Future Radio website. I think about my favourite songs, the way I would introduce them. Which Blur song would I choose? Which song by the Smiths? This is the hardest I have worked since I started here.

At seven o'clock Zane Lowe presents *In New Music We Trust*.

'Johnny in Whitehaven is with us, Carmel is with us, Sarah in Alabama is with us, Ally at Newcastle Uni is with us.' These people are all logged on to Zane's page on the Radio 1 website. His show is interactive, he sometimes lets people online choose which song to play next, his enthusiasm means that everyone listening feels part of the show. His passion is exhausting; there is no time to catch up on sleep while he's on air, he doesn't give you the opportunity to read any of the day's papers, even to go to the toilet. He is captivating, his sentences sound like remixes, his excitement is relentless, a vital injection of passion into Radio 1's day. As he is presenting the show I imagine him to be fighting crocodiles, abseiling, running across a desert with bricks in his rucksack.

'This is a brand-new tune from Kings of Leon. Put the volume up!' Lowe encourages. 'Unless you're scared. You're not scared, are you?' My radio is already at full blast, this is the only way to listen to Zane, to get involved. I remember listening to his first show on Radio 1; he replaced the much-loved Steve Lamacq and arrived with a strong fan base from his days at XFM. Within minutes of hearing his show I was won over, it was the most exciting radio I'd heard for a long time, nothing like anything I'd ever heard.

'Tori in Scotland has texted in to say me and my mum are rocking out to this,' Zane tells us. 'Stay connected, girls, here's Crystal Castles, also going out to Wayne, at footie training in the rain.' I listen in the kitchen while making stir-fry. I chop veg at a frantic pace, throw bean sprouts into the wok to the rhythm of Zane's voice. I add tomatoes, water chestnuts, Szechuan sauce to the sound of drum and bass. I make stir-fry in the same way as Morecambe and Wise prepare their breakfast.

'That was off the grid,' Zane tells us at the end of the track.

'We hadn't planned on playing it, just stuck it in at the last minute. Let's get it going! Turn the volume up! Here's Foals!'

Zane's show finishes and my food is ready as Westwood is back on air. The politest man in hip hop speaks to fashion correspondent Miss Info in New York as I twist noodles around my fork. She brings him Hot Ghetto Gossip, tells him about P Diddy's fashion show last night: Missy Elliott, Nelly and Snoop Dog all preview their own clothing lines.

'Check out my blog,' she tells him, and then Westwood plays his Top Five Heavy Hits – tracks by Timbaland, Snoop Dog, Fat Joe, Rick Ross and Usher. After doing the washing-up I make tomorrow's sandwiches – tuna, mayo, sweetcorn, chunky slices of granary. Radio 1 has been transformed since Scott Mills went home, evening draws in and the playlist is forgotten, specialist presenters play tunes they are passionate about, and the late shows are so good that you can't help but wonder why the output earlier in the day isn't better. Radio works when you have either excellent output, or an engaging presenter. If both happen, that's when radio can be special and is a more immediate art form than any other. When neither happens, that's when you have Edith Bowman.

'They'd be a good tug-of-war team,' Belfast's Colin Murray says after playing 'I'm a Realist' by the Cribs. It is slightly more tranquil listening to Murray after Westwood and Zane Lowe, at least he seems to be sitting down while he is presenting his show, taking breaths occasionally. After playing songs by MGMT, and Vincent Vincent and the Villains, he introduces *The Black Hole*, forty-five minutes of undiluted Internet downloads.

'If you have heard something good online, send it to us and

we'll play it. First is Harry Hill,' Murray says and plays a clip from a recent episode of Hill's *TV Burp*. After that is a mash-up of the Killers and Muse, then a clip from Family Guy, Hot Chip performing Marvin Gaye's 'Sexual Healing' and Murray Lachlan Young's 'Go Keith Go' poem, a tribute to Keith Richards falling out of a coconut tree.

'If you see something that makes you laugh, send it in,' Murray says. 'Simple as that.' He closes with a clip of Bob by 'Weird' Al Yankovic, to the tune of Bob Dylan's 'Subterranean Homesick Blues', with the words changed so that every line is a palindrome. I feel the clip needs to be seen as well as heard, and so switch on my computer. This is when radio and the Internet work well together. I head to the BBC website and watch the video for the song, mesmerized by the palindromes.

'If I had a hi fi.'

'Nurse, I spy gypsies run.'

'Ma is as selfless as I am.'

'Oozy rat in a sanitary zoo.'

Murray plays Vampire Weekend, Seasick Steve, Hot Club de Paris, dedicating each song to a listener who has texted in during the song.

'This is by Death Cab for Cutie. It's for Willie in Kent. If ever there's a name you don't want to mispronounce, that must be it.'

Also on air with Murray is Natasha, the show's producer, who has the most heartbreakingly beautiful voice, like Mariella Frostrup gargling fudge, with a Welsh lilt that melts the hearts of everyone who listens.

'David has texted in to say he's hungry but doesn't know what kind of sandwich to make.'

'Mozzarella, tomato and basil,' Tasha suggests.

'You can't give him advice, you're a vegetarian! Stick some salami in there. Or maybe do a toastie.'

'Ooh.'

'Cheese toastie, Worcester Sauce.'

'Beans!'

'What?'

'Beans.'

'He wants a sandwich, Tasha. Not a meal. Don't push him over the top or he'll never listen again. This is the new single by Sons and Daughters.'

'We shouldn't have talked about food on air,' Murray says after the record. 'We've got a load of texts and emails from people who have had to go and make themselves something to eat. I've got a theory about food. Are you one of those people that always take ages to decide what they want when they're in a restaurant?'

'Not really,' Tasha says. 'Vegetarians don't normally have much to choose from.'

'You should eat meat then. My mate was vegetarian for thirty years, and finally caved in and ate a whole Domino's Meat Feast pizza. But if your partner always takes ages to decide what they want, which is one of those things that on a first date is quite sweet but pretty soon gets really annoying, then you shouldn't even open the menu. You should close your eyes, sniff, get a sense of the atmosphere, sniff again, work out what it is you want to eat. And then find the thing on the menu that is closest to what you want.'

'Maybe not on a first date though,' Tasha suggests. 'You'd look pretty weird.'

I listen to the rest of Murray's show in bed, lamenting the decline of Radio 1. But also aware that perhaps I am too old to appreciate it now. I'm not a teenager, I'm not a student. I'm getting older – it hurts when I play football and I rarely know which song is at number 1. Maybe people younger than me want to hear about Edith Bowman's baked potatoes, and love the contributions of sidekicks like Chappers and Comedy Dave. Radio 1 doesn't excite me, it's the radio equivalent of the multiplexes you get on the edges of towns, with cinema, bowling, Pizza Hut, Nando's. Young people go there and have a good time, but it all seems soulless, it could be so much better. As I start to fall asleep I know that in the morning millions will be going through the same cycle again, switching their beeping alarm clocks off, turning Chris Moyles on, going to school, university, work, then coming home, listening to Scott Mills in traffic jams. Not me though. I'll be appreciating radio's rich tapestry.

22

ONLINE RADIO

'Bringing radio hurtling into the digital age'

Nathalie Schwarz

'We're at the beginning of a journey,' Nathalie Schwarz explained as her assistant brought in our coffees. 'We're experimenting with on-demand broadcasting and our listeners are giving really positive feedback.'

I had contacted Schwarz because her name appeared in practically every article I'd read about the future of radio. At that time, as well as being Director of Channel 4 Radio, Schwarz was also a key figure in the 4 Digital Consortium, a second radio multiplex which had been set up to rival the BBC in which Channel 4 would play a central role along with networks such as Sky News Radio and Sunrise UK.

'Listeners tend to be loyal to their radio station, which puts stations in a very powerful position,' she told me, resting her spoon beside her coffee cup. 'People want to engage with their favourite radio stations, which has always been part of radio's

DNA, we just need to bring it into the digital age. Technology plays to radio's strengths and we want to use that here at Channel 4, be a bit bolder, get the oomph back again.'

Nathalie and I spent an hour talking enthusiastically about our shared love of radio, specifically Channel 4's online presence, where you could download podcasts relating to *Big Brother*, *Richard and Judy* and *Hollyoaks*, as well as *SlashMusic* with Tom Ravenscroft, which had been essential listening for me ever since it was recommended by Jan from Bearsuit.

In the weeks that passed after that meeting however it became apparent that outside the plush offices of Channel 4 the same optimism for the launch was not shared. In October 2008 it was finally confirmed that Channel 4 Radio was to be no more; it was permanently de-tuned before its first words had been spoken. Its demise was greeted with a sense of inevitability: the launch date had been postponed, press coverage had become increasingly negative, and away from the core BBC stations digital radio was not in a healthy state. There seemed little likelihood of the second multiplex succeeding when the first was doing so badly; stations were being closed down with worrying regularity – even my own beloved The Jazz had been closed down by its owners GCap Media after little more than a year on air, with poor advertising revenues blamed. The Jazz was part of a mass exodus of digital stations, including Core, Planet Disney and Oneword, the latter being replaced by a station called Birdsong, and consisting of a looped recording of birds singing in chorus twenty-four hours a day, which proved an unlikely ratings winner, with rumours it was attracting more listeners than the spoken-word station it had replaced.

While sitting with Nathalie Schwarz, two bronze Sony Awards hanging on the office walls, the possibility of failure had not seemed remotely possible. As a result I had been telling anyone who would listen how Channel 4 Radio was going to blow our minds, revolutionize the way radio was made. Most people had no idea there were any plans afoot; those more well informed shrugged and said 'Are you sure?' Perhaps Schwarz had been preaching to the converted when talking to me about radio. I had been speaking to so many people involved with radio that I couldn't bring myself to look at things objectively any more. Even going into Future Radio I had been like a little kid in an aeroplane's cockpit wearing the captain's hat. I had become too close to radio; at no stage had I paused to think about the financial side of things. I had been beguiled by Schwarz and the potential of building a radio station from scratch. Closing stations like The Jazz and Disney meant that it made little sense for a second digital radio multiplex to be created when the existing model could not even be sated, with gaping holes where radio stations used to be. When the abandonment of Channel 4 Radio was announced the key issue cited was money – the costs were great and the chances of them being recouped had become increasingly unlikely. The moneymen were fleeing from digital radio, advertisers weren't interested, bosses were writing words like *revenue* and *loss* on flipcharts and scratching their heads.

Outside of the scaremongering and the station closures, digital radio seems in safe hands. BBC 7 and 6 Music have been big success stories, and the luxury of listening without static and interference to stations previously only available on medium wave such as talkSPORT has been worth the price of the increasingly low cost of a radio set alone. Another station thriving while others suffer is the UK-based Internet station LastFM.com, which has over 21 million users. It is funded by selling online advertising space and is aimed at music fans. If you like a band – for example, Bearsuit – you type their name in and the online radio streams similar bands that should cater to your tastes. So after a Bearsuit song it plays Ballboy, another band once championed by John Peel. If I type in Pouya Mahmoodi, the Iranian guitarist I heard on Resonance FM, it recommends a band called Porcupine Tree. It's a really exciting website, and means that if I have heard a band on Mark Radcliffe's show, or on Zane Lowe, or F F Friction, I can find out more about them, listen to more of their music, meet other people who like them. There's even an option to buy music, but that's a little archaic for me.

Reading about the demise of Channel 4 Radio made me think of Jane Anderson at the *Radio Times*: that the joy of listening to Radio 4 was the beauty of not knowing what's coming on next. And that kind of radio will always exist – surely BBC Radio 4 will survive long after the earth has crumbled like an Oxo cube – but radio in the twenty-first century has to be different, it has to go hand-in-hand with the Internet. Perhaps a multiplex was the wrong idea for Channel 4. Richard Wheatley, Chief Executive of the Local Radio Company, which owns and operates twenty-one local radio stations, described DAB as 'the Betamax of radio', questioning the logic of buying a piece of equipment that offered services already available online. Everything Nathalie Schwarz had told me remained true but it seemed the format was wrong;

Channel 4 has an Internet-savvy audience – people who would cherry-pick their schedule, the Sky Plus generation who want to hear things which suit their own tastes and interests at their own convenience. Despite speaking passionately about radio and its potential I realized Schwarz glossed over the idea of the multi-plex; it seemed it was not the format she had been excited about as much as the output, the variety of programmes, engaging a new type of listener. Channel 4 Radio already had an online presence, and if there is anything that can inject radio with a shot of adrenalin it is the Internet.

Internet radio really can work – *This American Life* is a weekly hour-long programme on Chicago Public Radio whose podcasts have half a million downloads each week. Each episode focuses on a different subject, stories of real-life America, and is as enter-taining and informative as any radio show I have ever heard. I've spent hundreds of hours devouring its output through the tinny speakers of my laptop. At times the show can be extremely moving; the episode 'Separated at Birth' focused on two baby girls who were taken home by the wrong mothers, with reflec-tions from the girls as grown women on how it had impacted on their lives. At other times *This American Life* relishes in the ridicu-lous, like the episode 'Superpowers' featuring a girl who for years actively took all the training she believed necessary to become a superhero – including firing bazookas and learning Russian. Other episodes are just staggering: the episode 'Mistakes Were Made' focuses on Bob Nelson, a TV repairman who became involved with cryogenics and ended up storing dead bodies in capsules of dry ice, confident that one day they would wake up and live again.

I spend the evening listening to radio online. To say online radio options are limitless is not much of an exaggeration: in the time it takes to download one podcast three more will have been uploaded from bedrooms around the world. Anyone with a microphone and a basic grasp of where to plug it in can present their own show and have it available to anyone who is prepared to click on the right page. As well as podcasts you can listen to radio stations across the world; after a few seconds of buffering you can hear stations in Helsinki or Brazil, or the Caribbean gospel choirs and steel drums of Barbados radio. In the same way, even if you are thousands of miles from the UK, you can still tune in to Ken Bruce, *Test Match Special*, Scott Mills.

By the time I get to bed I have made myself a full schedule to listen to the next day at work and I look forward to sitting at my desk typing my customary data while being station controller for the day. On my playlist is a free podcast by Ricky Gervais and Stephen Merchant that was made for NME Radio, followed by a brand-new episode of *This American Life*, Simon Mayo's *Book Panel*, Radio 4's *News Quiz* and as the day draws on I'll be treated to the show I look forward to most of all – Tommy Boyd's latest podcast from Play Radio. Podcasting used to be something that would strike fear into the generations who grew up with lino floors and *Listen with Mother*, but the terminology is no longer terrifying or geeky. Things have moved on, anyone can download, the retired are as likely to podcast as students. Look at the BBC website for proof – this is a brave new world, one where you can download *The Archers*, *Farming Today* and *In Our Time* with Melvyn Bragg. Unless it is fourteen-year-olds downloading these shows, the way people listen to radio has changed. But the Internet has not taken anything away from radio's traditional values: there will always be radios in kitchens, beside beds. No matter what happens with the Internet, people will continue to wake up with Wogan, tune in to the *Shipping Forecast*, have a bath while listening to *Book at Bedtime*.

23

BBC RADIO FIVE LIVE

*'The small one from the Chuckle Brothers supping a pint of
bitter in Ealing.'*
(email to Richard Bacon responding to sightings of TV
presenters doing unusual things)

I couldn't listen to the radio at work today, there was a team
meeting, an oval table, at its epicentre a plate of biscuits nobody
could reach. Alan Medlicott had prepared a PowerPoint presen-
tation. Men in suits made notes and nodded their heads at
appropriate places, while I sat at the end thinking about football.
We discussed the absence of Craig, the possibilities of new manage
ment, the lack of an annual pay rise. I fall asleep as soon as I get
home, snooze through *The Simpsons* and *The News* and when I
wake it's dark outside. As people across the country are settling
down to *Book at Bedtime* and *Night Waves*, I am more awake than
at any other part of the day, so decide to listen to Five Live
throughout the night. It's the station of choice for the insomniacs
of Britain, with many local BBC stations switching to Five Live's

coverage in the early hours. I listen to Richard Bacon's show. 'Do you think that companies have an obligation to behave ethically?' asks the former *Blue Peter* presenter, in response to a *Panorama* programme on BBC 1 profiling high-street stores' use of sweatshops.

'The power lies with the consumer,' argues David Middleton, chairman of the Institute of Economic Affairs. 'If consumers don't care about ethics and just want to be able to buy things for as little as possible, then companies must provide cheap goods. If the consumers aren't worried then businesses don't need to be worried. There shouldn't be this concern of being politically correct.'

'I don't know what to say to that,' the *Observer*'s Dan McDougall replies after a brief silence needed to digest the thoughts of his fellow guest. McDougall has spent years examining sweatshops, he helped to unearth the scale of child labour involved in manufacturing clothing for Gap. 'Maybe you should take a look at Indian sweatshops, maybe you should see the nine-year-olds who have to work fourteen-hour days. Consumers have a right to know where their clothes come from. People deserve to be made aware if something untoward is going on. And when people do find out that these kinds of conditions exist, they are appalled. It's deception.'

'David Middleton, are you genuinely suggesting that trading ethically is a synonym for being politically correct?' Bacon asks.

'Yes.'

'So what would you do if you found out that workers making clothes for your company were being beaten, sexually abused?'

'Nothing.'

'You'd do nothing about it?'

'Well, what can I do?'

'You could cut off the supplier.'

'Why should I?'

'David, I think you are a dinosaur,' McDougall tells him. 'Have you ever been to a sweatshop?'

'No.'

'Have you ever been to India, Pakistan, Bangladesh?'

'No.'

'Have you ever seen people being beaten and forced to work against their will? I'm shocked you are not ashamed of your views. Business ethics apply to Indian workers just as much as to Westerners.'

'I recognize that conditions in some countries are awful. But it was awful in this country two hundred years ago. We've moved on.'

'So why don't we help other countries move on?' Bacon asks.

'A company's job is to serve the consumer, not to impose political opinions. Many companies pretend to have a sincere social and corporate responsibility.'

'You are showing an appalling attitude to the rights of children,' McDougall tells him, his anger increasing. 'You're living in the wrong century. The reality is, you are saying that children should be forced to work to make money for Western countries. Nobody wants to wear a garment that has been made by children. I find your attitude inhumane. A child being made to work has no freedom. No future. And it's all to make millions of dollars of profit.'

'I like profit.'

The texts and emails Bacon reads out have little tolerance of Middleton's attitude towards sweatshops; he came out with some extraordinary comments that were incredible to hear live in a radio debate. After the eleven o'clock news the mood is lightened; Emma Jones, a freelance showbiz reporter, whatever one of those is, is in the studio to talk about whether or not celebrities have a duty to act as role models.

'Everything about Paris Hilton says shallow is okay,' she claims. 'It's a terrible example to give to twelve-year-olds.'

'Being vacuous isn't so bad,' argues Alex Bilmes, the features editor of GQ magazine. 'It's a bit sad, perhaps, but it doesn't harm anyone. Besides, Paris Hilton is a media construct, she is a brand, we don't know what she does when she gets home. She could read Dickens for all we know.'

'But she is a bad role model,' Jones maintains. 'Lily Allen is a bad role model. Amy Winehouse, Pete Doherty, they're all bad examples of society.'

'But surely it can be a good thing when celebrities mess up so spectacularly?' asks Bilmes. 'Britney Spears is a good deterrent. Who would want to be like Britney? Children don't aspire to be like someone who is clearly so troubled, so unhappy.'

Bacon asks people to phone in with their thoughts, and examples of good or bad role models.

Sally calls in. 'The Beatles started smoking weed and so everyone else did. People like to copy their heroes.'

Andrew calls in. 'The worst role models of all are politicians, they consistently fail to meet standards, are greedy, yet are seen as people who should represent society.'

Bacon closes the show by talking about his former *Blue Peter* colleague, Stuart Miles, who is reported to be doing a one-man show as a drag character at the Edinburgh Fringe Festival.

'Text in if you have ever seen kids' TV presenters in places you wouldn't expect to see them,' he urges.

Sightings trickle in: 'The small one from the Chuckle Brothers supping a pint of bitter in Ealing.'

'Timmy Mallett in a pub in Coventry.'

'Bodger from *Bodger and Badger* in the Lost Vagueness field at Glastonbury.'

One to five a.m. is *Up All Night* with Rhod Sharp, one of radio's most prolific journalists, who has presented groundbreaking programmes for the station, including broadcasts from Cuba's Buena Vista Social Club and from Ground Zero shortly after 9/11. He devised *Up All Night* when Five Live launched in 1994, winning four Sony Awards in its first ten years. Five Live was created because of public demand; at the start of the first Gulf War, Radio 4's FM frequency was taken over by a rolling news service to give listeners access to important events in the Middle East as they unfolded. Radio 4's regular output continued on its Long Wave frequency, and its FM slot became known as Scud FM, which was put together by BBC journalists and producers from programmes such as *Today*, giving up their days off to broadcast the latest news. When the troubles eased, Radio 4 reclaimed its FM frequency but there was still demand from listeners who had enjoyed being able to rely on a rolling news service, and this led to the creation of Five Live. Rhod Sharp's show captures the essence of the station, topical, intelligent but with a more informal tone than had previously been used when broadcasting news, both from the UK and worldwide.

'There are six hundred Starbucks stores closing down in the

US,' reveals Janet Adami from the *Wall Street Journal*. 'The chain tried to do too much, too soon. They conducted research that showed people would not cross the road to get a coffee, so they opened up stores on both sides of the street.'

Rhod Sharp talks to people on the phone about Barack Obama, drug-smuggling in Morocco, the Freedom Tower sky-scraper, a meeting between the Dalai Lama and the Chinese authorities, the poetry of Edward Morgan, all subjects about which he can speak intelligently and respond with articulate questions, and quote from people as diverse as John McCain and Lewis Hamilton. My brain starts to tire, and I start to wish I was as well informed on world politics as Sharp; he is engaging to listen to even in these early hours. I vow to read more newspapers, listen to more news-based radio. Next time I can't sleep instead of lying wide awake I'll switch on Five Live, nourish my brain after a day of data entry. Then there is a story I am more able to compre-hend – Rhod Sharp speaks to a spokesman from a zoo in America.

'So the chimp has disappeared?'

'Yes. Mo the chimp. He spent so much time with humans that he could use a knife and fork and open doors.'

'Is there a chance he could wander back to the zoo?'

'Every chance. I'm sure he is desperate to be back. He loves it here. He gets to watch TV.'

'Maybe you could lay a trail . . . of bananas?'

I imagine that presenter and producer are both looking at each other, shrugging their shoulders, wondering why airtime of one of the most popular radio stations in the UK is given to this zoo worker with his long pauses and gloomy tone as he pontificates on the whereabouts of Mo the chimp.

Once the best wishes of the UK have been sent across to the American zoo, Cashman Peters speaks to Sharp. Peters is the show's slightly camp US correspondent.

'Last week my cat fell down a nine-foot shaft,' he reveals. 'So I built a ladder out of pieces of wood I found lying around. I cooked some chicken and spread it across each rung of the ladder and the cat came running back up. I was so proud of myself!'

'Well done!' Sharp says dryly.

'Well, it's more interesting than a lost monkey!' Cash is immediately entertaining and has the energy needed to sustain the interest of listeners, whether they are driving through the night, unable to sleep or just can't be bothered to go to bed.

'What are you on to talk about tonight?' Sharp asks him. 'Not just rescuing your cat?'

'No, I'm talking about the decline of television, and how it won't be long before no one watches it. TV is run by disrespectful and arrogant fat cats, moronic weasels who only care about making money. They are ruining something we used to love so much! Text-crawl at the bottom of the screen during programmes, quarter-screen credits, announcers talking over theme tunes, schedules interfered with. So many programmes are available on the Internet, why would you watch it any other way?'

'You sound very passionate about this, Cash.'

'I just think I should be in charge of everything. Things would run much more smoothly.'

As the hours tick by the stories become more digestible; less economic, more humanitarian. As well as Cash in San Francisco there are correspondents in Jamaica and Russia and reviews of the morning's papers. I start to wonder whether I should go to sleep, but I'm enjoying *Up All Night* and it seems a shame to stop listening when there's less than an hour of the show remaining. The clock on my wall is now creeping towards five. My alarm will be blazing in two hours. The digits 07:00 will look at my tired face. They will remind me that I stayed up too late. Folding their arms, they will say: 'We are not angry. Just disappointed.' Peter Gibbs from the Weather Centre tells us today will be mild, 11 to 13 degrees. Rain in Scotland and Northern Ireland. Brighter spells in the West Midlands. A threat of rain later. I look out of my window, daylight is about to show its face. At the end of my road a man in a high-visibility jacket cycles to work.

24

BBC 7

'He was giving you coin, you were giving him bootie.'

(*The Mighty Boosh*)

I walk into work and there is a girl sat in Craig's seat. He has regenerated.

'This is Lisa,' Alan Medlicott says to me. 'It's her first day.'

'Hi, Lisa,' I say, stretching across to shake her hand. She has decorated her desk, already she has put up photo frames. One of the photographs is of her wearing a wedding dress, kissing the groom, confetti falling from the sky. Another picture is of a little girl in a high-chair with chocolate around her mouth. Lisa takes a pencil case from her bag. She has got her own felt tips. I look at my own workplace: a Sellotape dispenser I don't use and coffee-cup stains like the Olympic rings.

I feel the need to make a good impression with Lisa so decide not to put my headphones on this morning. I don't want her to think I'm rude. When she goes home tonight, once their little girl is asleep, her husband will pour her a glass of white wine and ask about her first day. Whether I want to be or not I am part of her daily routine; she will mention me, and I don't want her to have to explain that she sits opposite a misanthropic weirdo who doesn't even have his own stapler. It would be nice to have colleagues rather than people I work with. Maybe I should stop bringing my radio to work with me, to integrate myself back into society without the need of little pieces of sponge in my ears to help me through the day.

During my lunch break of Brie and cranberry sandwiches (oh yes) Alan Medlicott takes Lisa into the meeting room and tells me they will be in there for the rest of the day, so I put my headphones on. I hear the familiar theme tune to *Dad's Army* on BBC 7. Sixty-seven of the original television scripts were specially adapted for radio and broadcast between 1973 and 1975. The jokes work just as well on radio as on TV, the timing of Corporal Jones standing to attention a split second after the rest of the troop is as consistently funny as any recurring joke in sitcom and radio takes nothing away from it.

In today's episode 'The Day the Balloon Went Up', a stray barrage balloon has to be grounded and ends up taking off with Captain Mainwaring still holding on to it, crashing through washing lines, flying past couples canoodling. He has Jones for company, a slight change to the original television version, where he was on the balloon alone.

Even when I watched *Dad's Army* when I was little I was aware of how funny it was. There has never been a stronger cast for a sitcom, never such a variety of central characters. In this episode Godfrey is wearing his slippers because he's got gout. Pike is wearing a muffler because his mum's worried about him getting croup. Corporal Jones has brought in kidneys from his butcher's shop for Mrs Mainwaring.

Half-past twelve is a repeated episode of the general knowledge music quiz *Counterpoint*, hosted by the late Ned Sherrin, the much-loved presenter of culture show *Loose Ends* until his death in 2007. The contestants, rather than being celebrities, are Mr Whittaker, Mrs McConby and Mr Turnball. I look forward to joining in with the answers but as the first question is identifying the closing moments of an overture, and the next about the Metropolitan Opera House in New York, I realize I am a bit out of my depth. I like Blur.

After a tense tie-break Mrs McConby beats Mr Whittaker, her victory due to the fact that she knows that the correct name for a lute player is a 'lutenist'.

I check my emails and Terry Lee has asked if I want to come to Future Radio tomorrow to do my *People's Playlist*. He asks me to make a CD of my twelve songs, and says that I'll be shown how to use all the equipment.

At one o'clock I listen to 'On Guard', the first half of a short story by Evelyn Waugh about Hector and Millicent, a married couple who have to live apart while Hector looks after a planta-tion abroad. He thinks about making his wife wear a girdle of chastity while he is away. Waugh's prose is well suited to radio, two minutes of airtime is taken by a single description of Millicent's nose. Disappointingly, it is the first of two parts, so we have to wait until next week to find out what happens to the puppy Hector buys his wife as a gift.

Claire Rayner reads from her autobiography *How Did I Get There from Here?* It is the last of the five episodes following the life of the agony aunt. She tells how when *Hers* magazine needed a gritty columnist, she was asked to contribute real-life scenarios she had encountered working in a hospital. As she was writing the column she realized that instead of trying to recall cases, it would be more interesting to use real-life problems that the readers had. It became incredibly popular, Rayner ran the page like an outpatients' clinic, referring contributors to professionals when necessary. She replied to every letter privately, even the ones that were published in the magazine. Six weeks before she started writing her autobiography, she was diagnosed with breast cancer.

'I said "Oh bugger" and had a weep,' Rayner recalls. 'I coped because I was phlegmatic.' One breast needed to be removed, and she agreed when her doctor suggested that they both came off.

'I married my best friend,' she says when assessing how she had survived the ordeal, and in the thousands of snippets of advice and words of wisdom she has administered in her career there can be nothing as straightforward as that.

Two o'clock is *CBeebies*, songs, rhymes and stories in one of the few slots on radio especially for children. Radio 4 have *Go for It*, but other than that there is not much entertainment for toddlers with chocolate around their mouths. Perhaps the most notable is Fun Radio, available online and on digital, which has programmes with titles such as *Nap Time* and *Animal Hour*. Its website has competitions, a gallery where you can send in pictures, and a bouncing ball game, where I could only score 4, but I blame my mouse. It sticks sometimes. Guiding *Bob the Builder* characters around a maze is a long way from *Listen with Mother*, on the BBC Light Programme from 1950, where for fifteen minutes every day the children of

Britain would be asked if they were sitting comfortably until the programme controversially ended in 1982.

BBC 7's schedule gives genres their own hour-long segments: classic comedy, modern comedy, fantasy, and 5 p.m. is time for science fiction. It kicks off with *The Voice of God*, set on a ship called *Hurricane Balse*. I don't like sci-fi; it is a genre I have largely avoided, with the exception of having read *The Hitchhiker's Guide to the Galaxy* when I was fourteen and owning a *Red Dwarf* video. The only thing I know for certain is that every science-fiction film, story or novel contains a man confronted with certain death saying to a woman, 'You go, I'll stay.' The woman always replies with something like 'I wouldn't miss this for the world.' Which is what happens in *The Voice of God*. Just once I'd like the woman to say 'Okay then' and go home and watch *Wife Swap*.

A short story follows, 'Thanasphere', one of a collection that Kurt Vonnegut wrote for magazines in the 1950s, and features Lieutenant Dave, who is head of Operation Cyclops. A man is in a spaceship orbiting Earth, and discovers that space is filled with the voices of the dead. He hears the crying of a dead child, an old woman shouting in German.

I think about leaving work early, Alan Medlicott won't find out, but I struggle with breaking the rules, so stay in my chair until 5.29, claiming a minor victory. The signal on my personal DAB player is too shaky to listen to as I walk home, so I give my ears a rest for a while, knowing that I am just missing repeats of *Dad's Army* and *Counterpoint* from earlier on, although I am intrigued as to whether I would get any more questions right on the music quiz this time. I would definitely get one. Lutenist.

*

Back at home after cooking enough chilli to last the rest of the week I listen to *Robin and Wendy's Wet Weekends*, which is described by the announcer as 'a light, gentle comedy', which sounds like a euphemism for being crap. The opening joke is about women drivers, and I resign myself to spending half an hour listening to light and gentle clichés.

'You break up one happy family and you are never allowed to forget it,' Derek moans. Derek and Maureen are the next-door neighbours of Robin and Wendy. Each episode follows the four characters doing light and gentle things. Robin is a manic depressive building a model village in his garage. Wendy goes on an assertiveness-training course, which ends up with the light and gentle character outing her trainer as a racist homophobe.

Some of BBC 7 today has been really good, but a lot of it left me underwhelmed, I couldn't understand why most of these programmes were being aired. Which is the same feeling as I had when I was listening to 6 Music. I'd be happier if they combined the two stations, creating a BBC Archive station, *Hancock's Half Hour* followed by *Peel Sessions*, a profile of the Rolling Stones, and then repeats of *The League of Gentlemen* and *Little Britain*. As well as giving opportunities for new bands and comedians it would be the only station people (well me) would ever want to listen to. The reason that I am still listening to BBC 7 tonight and not watching TV, dining in a restaurant, attending the theatre or slamming tequila down my throat in one of Norwich's trendy bars is because of the show on at ten o'clock, a comedy that the words light and gentle cannot be applied to. *Boosh*.

Acerbic, mystical BBC 3 comedy *The Mighty Boosh*, like Alan Partridge and *Dead Ringers* before it, started on radio. Originally, one series was recorded for London Live, and was later broadcast on Radio 4 in 2001. This episode, 'Mutants', is also featured in the first television series, but the script is vastly changed. The plot involves the two main characters, Vince and Howard, breaking into a zoo's secret laboratory after Vince has a conversation with a python called Mr Rogers who tells him that the zoo worker Bob Fossil has been turning animals into mutants: a moth with the legs of a hawk, an owl with antlers, an ostrich with the legs of a priest, a swan with the eyes of Boris Becker, postman's shins with a buffalo's anus. Vince and Howard's secret mission to free the mutant race is slightly spoiled after Vince invited the residents of an old people's home to join them. Vince isn't allowed to go on the mission, he has to stay behind making mochas for the elderly.

'Have you got a torch?'

'No, but I've got a latte.'

The evolution of comedy is perhaps radio's finest achievement. Its first sitcom was *Band Waggon*, starring Richard Murdoch and Arthur Askey, who created the illusion for their listeners of living on the roof of Broadcasting House. Radio comedy truly began when *The Goons* came along in 1951, and the DNA of Spike Milligan, Harry Secombe and Peter Sellers can be traced in *Monty Python*, Peter Cook and as a result every comedy to be made since. The sixties was the Golden Age of comedy, those not pitching their tents at Woodstock or chasing the Beatles' limousines down Carnaby Street were listening to *Round the Horne*, *I'm Sorry I Haven't a Clue* and *The Goodies*. The 1980s were less productive, audiences and programme makers alike were distracted by colour television, but by 1987 people were able to stop watching Carol Vorderman on *Countdown* for long enough to make shows such as *Hey Rrradio* and *The Mary Whitehouse Experience* on Radio 1, which briefly housed the country's biggest comedy talent – David Baddiel, Rob Newman, Jack Dee and later Armando Iannucci, Lee & Herring and Chris Morris. While at Radio Bristol, Morris allegedly filled the newsroom with helium, and the newsreaders only realized that their voices were octaves higher when they were going out live on air. Years later, at Radio 1, Morris told his listeners that if there was any news of the death of Michael Heseltine he would let them know, prompting MPs to prematurely eulogize him live on air.

While this was happening on Radio 1, Radio 4, for many the true home of comedy, was nurturing the next twenty years of comedy talent. Its labs were full of test tubes and Petri dishes that would later cultivate the starts of television and film: *Little Britain*, *The League of Gentlemen*, *Mitchell and Webb*, *Dead Ringers*. By then – unlike when *Steptoe and Son* and *Hancock's Half Hour* aired to mass radio audiences – *Round the Horne* had 15 million listeners. There was only a small, if devoted, fan base, listening figures look bleak if you compare them with television viewers and DVD sales the stars would later achieve. It takes a loyal listener to plough through Radio 4's comedy output, when you listen to some programmes you wonder how they got 'comedy' into their description and how they were ever made. Some of these even resurface on BBC 7, such as *Robin and Wendy's Wet Weekends*. But in most instances programmes deserve repeated listens, such as the next programme on tonight.

For One Horrible Moment, written and narrated by the *Guardian* film critic Peter Bradshaw, focuses on the sexual fascination the main character has for a girl called Susan 'who looks a bit like me'.

When he tries to give his father a hug, his dad puts down a plastic Next Customer Please separator bar to keep the two apart. He has a bed-wetting problem, something that the whole town knows about due to his dad making, photocopying, stapling and distributing a publication about it, featuring news, views, cartoons and a crossword.

Crème de la Crime stars Punt and Dennis and is a 'light and gentle' comedy about the murder of Christopher Marlowe. They use reconstructed scenes and character witnesses. They suggest that Shakespeare killed Marlowe, that he was a serial murderer. I would say that the show was *Much Ado About Nothing* but that is a pun so bad that it is the one Punt and Dennis end the programme on.

25

FUTURE RADIO (2)

'Tea, John?'

(Alan Medlicott)

I wake long before my alarm beeps, but despite it being 5 a.m. and having my curtains drawn, the sun is so hot it renders sleep impossible. I get dressed and spend time I would still normally be asleep listening to the songs I have chosen for *People's Playlist*, my own *Desert Island Discs*, one that you don't even have to be famous to be invited on. I pick out the CDs: Blur, Be Your Own Pet, Status Quo. It is very early in the morning to be so eclectic. I leave the house earlier than normal and for the first time this year don't need a coat. I listen to Future as I walk to work.

'I went to Brighton at the weekend,' Terry Lee says, 'but my clutch went so I had to be towed. I was only covered to travel a short distance, so had to find a safe place to leave it and get the train back via London. If you've had similar adventures with broken-down cars please text in and share them with us.'

With a lot of breakfast show DJs I would be delighted to hear they'd suffered mild misfortune over the weekend, but I feel genuinely sorry for Terry Lee and his clutch. After playing 'True Confessions' by the Undertones he reads emails and texts sent in from listeners about their cars.

'Kate's exhaust fell off on the M11. Mark had to be towed from Scotland last summer. But the most worrying text of all is from Stewie,' Terry laughs, 'who was on the M3 and his brakes failed as he was driving at 80 miles per hour. Please get back in touch with us Stewie, we need to know more.'

You get a slightly altered perception of people's lives by leaving home at a slightly earlier time. The lady in the red coat is just locking up her house, putting her keys in her handbag. The three schoolboys are yet to be joined by their friend on the bicycle, I still haven't seen the man walking his Alsatian. I arrive at work early and sit on a bench by a patch of grass behind the main building, enjoying listening to the radio.

'This is for everyone about to start work,' Terry Lee says at five to nine. It's 'Bohemian Like You' by the Dandy Warhols and as the song fades out I take off my headphones and go inside. I say hello to Alan Medlicott and Lisa and start my day. Work has been much better since Lisa arrived, I feel comfortable in her presence, something I never felt when Craig worked there, but that is more my fault than his.

'Cup of tea?' Alan Medlicott asks. Lisa nods. He looks over at me. 'Tea, John?'

'Yes please,' I say, slightly startled. Alan Medlicott has never offered me a cup of tea before. I pass him my mug and he walks to the kitchen.

'He's nice, isn't he?' Lisa says. I nod. 'He works too hard though. Last night he was here until eight o'clock. Is he married?'

'I don't know,' I say, although I have always imagined him to have a wife. She would be a teacher, they always go to the same part of France for their holidays, they have a daughter at university who comes back every Christmas. Mrs Medlicott makes jam. They wear matching pyjamas and spend weekends in the garden.

'What about you?' she asks. 'Girlfriend?'

'No.'

'Aah,' she says, like she's just seen newborn kittens. 'There's some pretty girls here,' she points out to me, and Alan Medlicott returns with a tray of mugs before Lisa can lead me by the hand and rearrange my social life. She unwraps a bar of Dairy Milk from her desk drawer, snaps a piece off for each of us. Go Team.

'Do you want a lift to Future Radio?' Lisa asks at 5.30 as we tuck our chairs underneath our desks and say goodbye to Alan Medlicott. I told her about *People's Playlist* this afternoon as we worked, she went through the twelve songs she'd choose, I explained each of my choices to her, and we walk out together.

She bleep bleeps her car unlocked and I head to the passenger seat. Lisa is parked next to Poppy's Toyota Yaris and as my fingers unfurl beneath the handle of the Punto I sense the sun glistening on the blonde ponytail of my favourite accountant walking towards us.

'See you tomorrow, Poppy,' I say as she gets into her car.

'See you tomorrow,' she replies. I shut the door behind me, adjust the seat and wind down the window, the fabric of the chair scorched by the sun. Poppy does the same, there are no trees to shadow the car park from the glare of this sun. Lisa puts her keys in the ignition but I beckon her to stop before she revs; I can hear a familiar noise coming from Poppy's car.

'Are you listening to Scott Mills?' I ask, my head leaning out of the window.

Poppy nods. 'Don't you like him?' she asks.

I shake my head. She smiles and turns the volume up to max, reverses, and as Punto follows Yaris out of the car park the whole of the industrial estate is forced to listen to the chatter of Scott Mills and Chappers. At the end of the road Lisa indicates left, Poppy indicates right, waves into her rear-view mirror and disappears to continue with her secret life, not to be seen again until tomorrow morning, 9 a.m., bobble in her hair, sensible shoes.

'That's Poppy,' I say to Lisa, and she nods. She understands. As we drive I put on the CD I have made for my *People's Playlist*, she *aahs* at Sandra's story and laughs uncontrollably about Mark Radcliffe reading my notebook. It feels good to get to know her, she tells me her daughter's name is Sophie, her husband is called Daniel, he works for a property management company.

'Good luck,' she says, pulling up on a grass verge by the tall green gates. I get out, thank her for the lift and as she drives away I walk up the mud track towards the Future offices. I pass a man in a duffel coat tuning an acoustic guitar, and two little boys who add the final touches to their skate ramp, consisting of bits of wood balancing on bricks.

'I'm here to see Terry Lee,' I tell the man on the front desk. By now I am familiar with doing this, and I realize how far I have come since that day spent listening to Virgin Radio all day. Since then I have introduced myself at the BBC and Channel 4, but this is a very different prospect to talking to the *Radio Times* or Nathalie Schwarz.

As I wait for Terry I sit with Simone and we talk about my love of John Peel, and the show based on the record collection I won, about how much music there is in my record box that deserves to be heard, if not by millions then at least by the select few who tune in to Future Radio in Norwich. She encourages me to write out a proposal for the show and send it to her as soon as I can with a detailed description of how the show would work. She tells me she has mentioned it to the station manager who really likes the idea.

Terry comes through and takes me to the studio, where we sit at the desk and he talks me through all the controls. Soon I am moving faders up and down with ease, and it takes less than an hour to record all of my links for the *People's Playlist*. I talk about my secret fondness of Status Quo, my love of Morrissey, how I'm never happier than when I'm listening to the Super Furry Animals or Bearsuit. I lean towards the microphone with much more confidence than I expected, and manage to speak fluently without any need for notes. Terry tells me I do well, that he likes my choice of music and that an editor will put the finishing touches to the tape before it goes to air. After saying goodbye to Terry and Simone I walk home in high spirits, listening to Future on my headphones, singing along to every song they play, Kate Nash, the Ting Tings, Squeeze. I spend the evening listening to my favourite songs, then before I go to bed reach across to my radio and flick from station to station.

'If a bhangra album ever comes out on the day it's supposed to I will eat an item of my own clothing,' says F F Friction, and dedicates a song to Dali, working in his dad's chip shop. Graham Torrington asks: 'With a click of your finger can you reel in an ex, whenever, wherever?' Colin Murray plays 'House of Cards' by Radiohead, and says that last night he had a dream he was married to Natasha.

'I hope tonight you have a dream we're divorced,' Tasha tells him.

'If parents were taken to court and fined it might make them more responsible for their children's behaviour,' a lady tells Max on talkSPORT. 'I hate it when people say that kids are scum. But when they are out on the streets, running riot, where are the parents? Where are the guardians?'

'I know very little about construction management,' says Gideon Coe, 'but I'm willing to learn. Here's Grandaddy live at Glastonbury 2003.' On Five Live Richard Bacon is talking to the royal photographer Ian Lloyd about whether or not *Hello!* magazine is still relevant. Lloyd recalls being at Uri Geller's wedding, where Michael Jackson was the best man, and a lot of guests were complete strangers to both bride and groom. 'Love Cats' by the Cure is on Radio 2, Classic FM plays something relaxing. On Future Kev O'Connor's *Boogie Bureau* plays the Soul Vigilantes.

'The way you learn accents,' Geoff says on Virgin, 'is to think of one key phrase, then work your way outwards. That's not just me saying that. It's my friend who was once taught by the lady who played Raquel in *Coronation Street.*' Geoff chuckles, plays the Hoosiers, and I realize that at some stage over the last few months I have learned to stop worrying and manage to enjoy the

Hoosiers. I know that wherever I am in the world I will have access to the radio. I'm now able to pinpoint the best possible station to listen to at any time of the day or night. Over the last couple of months I've barely switched my television on. Radio has given me everything I have needed, whether it is being entertained by Johnny and Denise, educated by Five Live or angered by Jon Gaunt, I've never wanted to stop listening, I've felt I've learnt much more about myself and the world just by playing with the dial on my radio.

I settle on *The Geoff Show* for the rest of the night, and as I listen I think about the songs I would play if I had my own show on Future. I look through my box of records, move the best ones towards the front. Maybe I will never become more involved in radio than just being a listener, but at least I've realized my ambition now, have made some contacts, and it's something exciting I can think about when I'm at home at night, making tomorrow's sandwiches.

ACKNOWLEDGEMENTS

For their continued help, support and friendship I would like to thank Tim Clare, Joe Dunthorne, Chris Gomm, Patrick Lappin, Molly Naylor, Joel Stickley, Dan Walker, Hannah Walker and Luke Wright.

Thanks to all at Simon & Schuster, particularly Andrew Gordon and Angela Herlihy. Special thanks to my agent, Rebecca Winfield, for the invaluable guidance and advice she has given me.

There are many people who have generously helped contribute to the book and I would like to express my sincere gratitude to Jane Anderson, Tom Bell, Tommy Boyd, Simone Hayes, Lisa Horton, Gill Hudson, Terry Lee, Stuart Maconie, Nicholas Parsons, Mark Radcliffe, Jan Robertson, Iain Ross, Terry Saunders, Nathalie Schwarz and Arlo White.

NOTE ON THE AUTHOR

John Osborne graduated from the University of East Anglia in 2004. He has taught English in Austria and Germany, and had poetry published in the *Guardian*. *Radio Head* is his first book.